HERITAGE GALLERIES & A[...]

Presents

JULES REIVER SIGNATURE AUCTION #390, VOLUME II
JANUARY 24-28, 2006 — DALLAS, TEXAS

MAIN EXHIBITION OF LOTS

Heritage Galleries & Auctioneers
3500 Maple Avenue
Dallas, TX 75219

Saturday, January 21 ....10 AM-6 PM CT
Sunday, January 22.......................................10 AM-6 PM CT
Monday, January 23 ....9 AM-8 PM CT
Tuesday, January 24...9 AM-6 PM CT
Wednesday, January 25 ....9 AM-6 PM CT
Thursday, January 26.......................................9 AM-6 PM CT
Friday, January 27..9 AM-6 PM CT
Saturday, January 28 ....10 AM-1 PM CT

PUBLIC, INTERNET AND MAIL BID AUCTION #390

Heritage Galleries & Auctioneers
3500 Maple Avenue
Dallas, TX 75219

Session 5........Thurs., Jan. 26 ......NOON CT...Lots 20,666-21,295
Session 6........Thurs., Jan. 26 ......6 PM CT ......Lots 21,296-21,909
OnLine Session............. Closes Mon., Jan. 30 .... 6-10 PM CT
Lots 28,698-29,366

See Volumes I and III for additional sessions.

LOT SETTLEMENT AND PICK UP

Wednesday-Saturday • 10 AM – 1 PM CT

Lots are generally sold at the approximate rate of 200 per hour, but it is not uncommon to sell 150 lots or 300 lots in any given hour. Please plan accordingly so that you don't miss the items you are bidding on.

America's #1 Numismatic Auctioneer
HERITAGE
Galleries & Auctioneers

3500 Maple Avenue, 17th Floor, Dallas, Texas 75219-3941 • 214-528-3500 • 800-US COINS (872-6467)

e-mail: Bid@HeritageGalleries.com • View full-color images at HeritageGalleries.com/Coins

THIS SALE IS CATALOGED BY HERITAGE GALLERIES & AUCTIONEERS
AND PRESENTED BY HERITAGE NUMISMATIC AUCTIONS, INC.,
LICENSED BY THE STATE OF TEXAS

Auctioneer Samuel Foose: Texas 00011727

Cataloged by Mark Van Winkle, Chief Cataloger; Brian Koller, Catalog Production Manager; Mark Borckardt, Senior Cataloger; Jon Amato, Jim Jones, Jim Matthews, Tom Reynolds and John Salyer

Photography by Jody Garver, Chief Photographer; Byron Carroll, Piper Crawley, Lucas Garritson, Deign Rook, Colette Warren, Tony Webb, Jason Young, and Shaun Zokaie

Production and design by Cathy Hadd, VP of Marketing; Carl Watson, Creative Director; Mandy Bottoms, Cindy Brenner, Janet Brown, Keith Craker, Mary Hermann, Matt Pegues, Michael Puttonen, Debbie Rexing, and Marsha Taylor

Dear Bidder,

I was impressed by Jules Reiver the first time that I met him over 20 years ago at a coin show in his beloved hometown of Wilmington, Delaware – and I later discovered that this was not an uncommon reaction. It is rare to meet a true numismatist whose depth of knowledge is matched by his willingness to share that information. Jules wasn't just willing – sometimes I think that he had to share his fascination with the minutiae of minting to really enjoy his hobby.

It is certainly true that his collection – notable for it completeness in variety and die state – is likely never to be duplicated, and that the Reiver pedigree will stand as a tribute to his scholarship for generations and generations of numismatists to come. That is as it should be. What has made his efforts truly memorable was his willingness to share. Thankfully, those future generations will have his writings to consider as well as his coins, but they cannot help but miss some of the essence of this collector's collector.

While Jules could never contain his energy, you immediately knew that he was a stalwart father and family man. Later I would come to discover that his dedication to his wife Iona and his family was more than matched by his dedication to his country, and his heroism during WWII reflected this quality. Like his coin varieties, the more you learned about Jules, the more you wanted to know. Considering the energy and zeal that Jules brought to numismatics, one can only imagine this dynamo as a young man!

After his heart attack, Jules began to focus on United States copper and silver coinage issued from 1793 though 1839 – emphasizing the die varieties and die states. For more than four decades, he pursued varieties in seven different denominations – and his collections ranked with those of the most intense specialists pursuing only one series. Before his final purchases, he had amassed more than 5,000 significant issues. Such was his level of dedication and enthusiasm. I shall most remember his willingness to share his knowledge with his fellow numismatists, and I treasure our encounters.

Greg

Greg Rohan
President

Dear Bidder,

Heritage is thrilled to present the incomparable Jules Reiver Collection – a collection of such depth and diversity that it is likely never to be duplicated, a collection whose pedigree will stand all tests of numismatic time. Just as Jules was a man to be remembered, so too will be his coins. Mr. Reiver – Jules to his thousands of friends – was a collector's collector, a specialist who shared his knowledge and collections with anyone willing to learn, knowing that through sharing numismatic knowledge was more than doubled.

A mechanical engineer by training, Jules was an expert in methodology and organization. His parents had owned a window and flooring store in Wilmington, Delaware, so Jules became adept at measuring, estimating, and installation at a young age. He met his future wife Iona while attending the University of Delaware, and they were married in 1943. In his early career with DuPont, his mechanical engineering skills were used to supervise construction of new buildings. The outbreak of World War II interrupted his career with DuPont, and Jules was called to Army duty in July 1942. He rose through the ranks, and commanded the first anti-aircraft battery to land on Omaha Beach in Normandy in June 1944. During the *Battle of the Bulge* later that year, his battery heroically turned back the German offensive aimed at a major gasoline depot (featured in the movie The Battle of the Bulge). Jules received the Bronze Star and was promoted to major by the end of WWII. While in Germany, Jules obtained a few Leica cameras – the quality of these lenses and optical equipment advanced his photography hobby.

Jules returned to Delaware and the family flooring and window covering business after the War. Jules and Iona settled in Wilmington where they purchased their home and raised four children. Jules had many hobbies and collections, and the stability of his family life and career allowed him to focus his dynamic energy on his favorites: photography, convertible cars, and coins. He became an expert photographer of coins, a talent that would greatly assist him in teaching others about his growing specialty. [He collected automobiles by the number of cylinders, ultimately obtaining 4, 6, 8, 12 and 16 cylinder convertibles; his 12 cylinder 1949 Lincoln coupe won Best of Show at the Indianapolis Antique Auto Show].

A heart attack in the 1960s – along with the pleading of his doctors – convinced Jules to slow down the hectic pace of his life. Jules heeded their advice and slowly turned over some of his business responsibilities to his son Ted. Jules already had a number of coins, and had been studying dies and die pairings for years; now he dove headlong into numismatics, widening his interests beyond the *Guide Book* to include foreign, ancient, tokens, medals and even a scattering of paper money. Attending the September 1968 Merkin Sale, Jules purchased a number of rare die varieties for his growing collections. Jules became a regular feature at New York City auctions – and elsewhere.

Jules' collection evolved to focus on die varieties and die states of all United States copper and silver coinage, from 1793 through 1839. Over the ensuing forty years, he assembled what experts conclude to be the most complete collection of its kind. While a few specialists may have finer or slightly more complete collections of individual series, Jules' holdings were typically in the top five of every denomination and series – thus standing as one of the most significant collections ever formed. Virtually every die pairing is included, as well as any and all die states that he could obtain. Grades were irrelevant to Jules if the coin available was a different die state than something he already owned.

In sum, the vastness of this research collection is hard to understate. A specialist may work for decades to complete a single denomination, yet through his boundless energy, Jules accomplished this in seven different denominations. Perhaps most significantly, his collections and experiences were shared with the collecting community through his many books and pamphlets on die varieties, and countless speeches at national and local club meetings. Jules even hosted a weekly radio show about coins in Wilmington, where he answered the questions of anyone who called in. The numismatic world will long remember Jules Reiver for his kindness and his willingness to share his knowledge with so many collectors. We will always miss him – he was a friend to the community, and he was a true friend to me.

Mark R Borckardt

Mark Borckardt
Senior Cataloger

Mail Bidding at Auction

Mail bidding at auction is fun and easy and only requires a few simple steps.

1. Look through the catalog, and determine the lots of interest.
2. Research their market value by checking price lists and other price guidelines.
3. Fill out your bid sheet, entering your maximum bid on each lot using your price research and your desire to own the lot.
4. Verify your bids!
5. Mail Early. Preference is given to the first bids received in case of a tie. When bidding by mail, you frequently purchase items at less than your maximum bid.

Bidding is opened at the published increment above the second highest mail or Internet bid; we act on your behalf as the highest mail bidder. If bidding proceeds, we act as your agent, bidding in increments over the previous bid. This process is continued until you are awarded the lot or you are outbid.

An example of this procedure: You submit a bid of $100, and the second highest mail bid is at $50. Bidding starts at $51 on your behalf. If no other bids are placed, you purchase the lot for $51. If other bids are placed, we bid for you in the posted increments until we reach your maximum bid of $100. If bidding passes your maximum: if you are bidding through the Internet, we will contact you by e-mail; if you bid by mail, we take no other action. Bidding continues until the final bidder wins.

Mail Bidding Instructions

1. **Name, Address, City, State, Zip**
   Your address is needed to mail your purchases. We need your telephone number to communicate any problems or changes that may affect your bids.
2. **References**
   If you have not established credit with us from previous auctions, you must send a 25% deposit, or list dealers with whom you have credit established.
3. **Lot Numbers and Bids**
   List all lots you desire to purchase. On the reverse are additional columns; you may also use another sheet. Under "Amount" enter the maximum you would pay for that lot (whole dollar amounts only). We will purchase the lot(s) for you as much below your bids as possible.
4. **Total Bid Sheet**
   Add up all bids and list that total in the appropriate box.
5. **Sign Your Bid Sheet**
   By signing the bid sheet, you have agreed to abide by the Terms of Auction listed in the auction catalog.

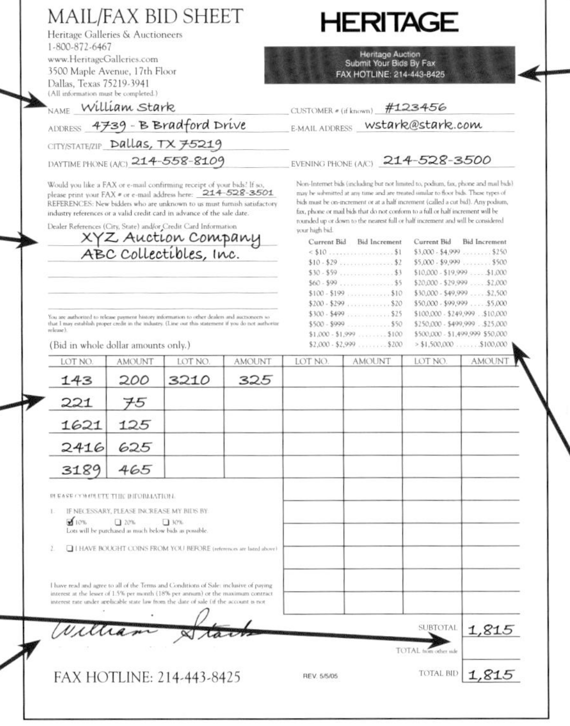

MAIL/FAX BID SHEET

HERITAGE

Heritage Galleries & Auctioneers
1-800-872-6467
www.HeritageGalleries.com
3500 Maple Avenue, 17th Floor
Dallas, Texas 75219-3941
(All information must be completed.)

Heritage Auction
Submit Your Bids By Fax
FAX HOTLINE: 214-443-8425

NAME William Stark
CUSTOMER # (if known) #123456
ADDRESS 4739 - B Bradford Drive
E-MAIL ADDRESS wstark@stark.com
CITY/STATE/ZIP Dallas, TX 75219
DAYTIME PHONE (A/C) 214-558-8109
EVENING PHONE (A/C) 214-528-3500

Would you like a FAX or e-mail confirming receipt of your bids? If so, please print your FAX # or e-mail address here: 214-528-3501
REFERENCES: New bidders who are unknown to us must furnish satisfactory industry references or a valid credit card in advance of the sale date.

Dealer References (City, State) and/or Credit Card Information
XYZ Auction Company
ABC Collectibles, Inc.

You are authorized to release payment history information to other dealers and auctioneers so that I may establish proper credit in the industry. (Line out this statement if you do not authorize release).

Non-Internet bids (including but not limited to, podium, fax, phone and mail bids) may be submitted at any time and are treated similar to floor bids. These types of bids must be on-increment or at a half increment (called a cut bid). Any podium, fax, phone or mail bids that do not conform to a full or half increment will be rounded up or down to the nearest full or half increment and will be considered your high bid.

Current Bid	Bid Increment	Current Bid	Bid Increment
< $10	$1	$3,000 - $4,999	$250
$10 - $29	$2	$5,000 - $9,999	$500
$30 - $59	$3	$10,000 - $19,999	$1,000
$60 - $99	$5	$20,000 - $29,999	$2,000
$100 - $199	$10	$30,000 - $49,999	$2,500
$200 - $299	$20	$50,000 - $99,999	$5,000
$300 - $499	$25	$100,000 - $249,999	$10,000
$500 - $999	$50	$250,000 - $499,999	$25,000
$1,000 - $1,999	$100	$500,000 - $1,499,999	$50,000
$2,000 - $2,999	$200	> $1,500,000	$100,000

(Bid in whole dollar amounts only.)

LOT NO.	AMOUNT	LOT NO.	AMOUNT	LOT NO.	AMOUNT	LOT NO.	AMOUNT
143	200	3210	325				
221	75						
1621	125						
2416	625						
3189	465						

PLEASE COMPLETE THIS INFORMATION:

1. IF NECESSARY, PLEASE INCREASE MY BIDS BY:
   ☑ 10% ☐ 20% ☐ 30%
   Lots will be purchased as much below bids as possible.
2. ☐ I HAVE BOUGHT COINS FROM YOU BEFORE (references are listed above)

I have read and agree to all of the Terms and Conditions of Sale: inclusive of paying interest at the lesser of 1.5% per month (18% per annum) or the maximum contract interest rate under applicable state law from the date of sale (if the account is not

William Stark

SUBTOTAL 1,815
TOTAL from other side
TOTAL BID 1,815

FAX HOTLINE: 214-443-8425

REV. 5/5/05

The official prices realized list that accompanies our auction catalogs is reserved for bidders and consignors only. We are happy to mail one to others upon receipt of $1.00. Written requests should be directed to Customer Service.

6. **Fax Your Bid Sheet**
   When time is short submit a Mail Bid Sheet on our exclusive Fax Hotline. There's no faster method to get your bids to us *instantly*. Simply use the **Heritage Fax Hotline number: 214-443-8425**.

When you send us your original after faxing, mark it "Confirmation of Fax" (preferably in red!)

7. **Bidding Increments**
   To facilitate bidding, please consult the following chart. Bids will be accepted on the increments or on the half increments.

Interactive Internet™ Bidding

You can now bid with Heritage's exclusive *Interactive Internet*™ program, available only at our web site: HeritageGalleries.com. It's fun, and it's easy!

1. Register online at: **HeritageGalleries.com**
2. View the full-color photography of every single lot in the online catalog!
3. Construct your own personal catalog for preview.
4. View the current opening bids on lots you want; review the prices realized archive.
5. Bid and receive immediate notification if you are the top bidder; later, if someone else bids higher, you will be notified automatically by e-mail.
6. The *Interactive Internet*™ program opens the lot on the floor at one increment over the second highest bid. As the high bidder, your secret maximum bid will compete for you during the floor auction, and it is possible that you may be outbid on the floor after Internet bidding closes. Bid early, as the earliest bird wins in the event of a tie bid.
7. After the sale, you will be notified of your success. It's that easy!

Interactive Internet™ Bidding Instructions

1. **Log Onto Website**
   Log onto **HeritageGalleries.com** and chose the portal you're interested in (i.e., coins, comics, movie posters, fine arts, etc.).

2. **Search for Lots**
   Search or browse for the lot you are interested in. You can do this from the home page, from the Auctions home page, or from the home page for the particular auction in which you wish to participate.

3. **Select Lots**
   Click on the link or the photo icon for the lot you want to bid on.

4. **Enter Bid**
   At the top of the page, next to a small picture of the item, is a box outlining the current bid. Enter the amount of your secret maximum bid in the textbox next to "Secret Maximum Bid." The secret maximum bid is the maximum amount you are willing to pay for the item you are bidding on (for more information about bidding and bid increments, please see the section labeled "Bidding Increments" elsewhere in this catalog). Click on the button marked "Place Absentee Bid." A new area on the same page will open up for you to enter your username (or e-mail address) and password. Enter these, then click "Place Absentee Bid" again.

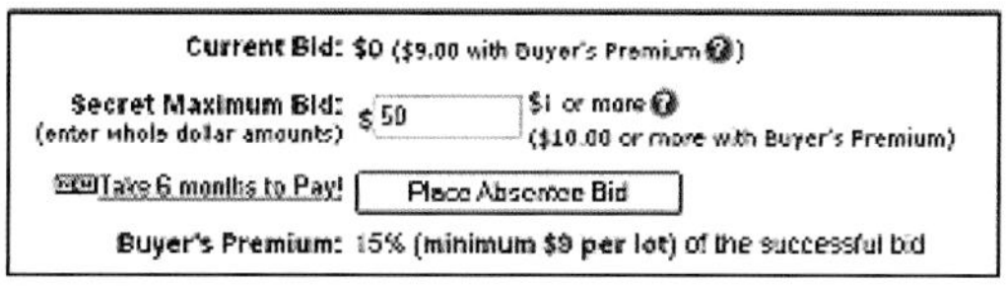

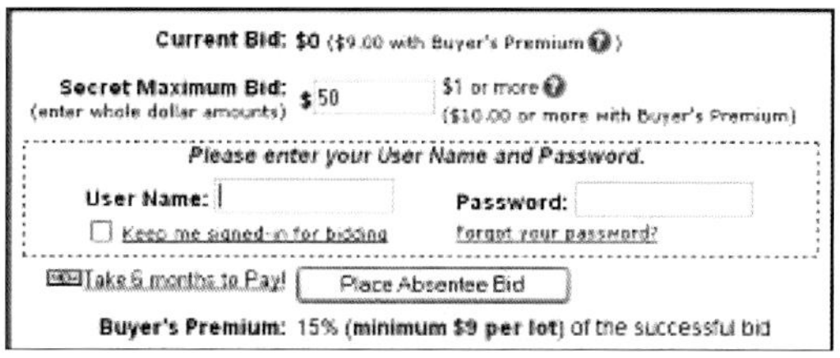

5. **Confirm Absentee Bid**
   You are taken to a page labeled, "Please Confirm Your Bid." This page shows you the name of the item you're bidding on, the current bid, and the maximum bid. When you are satisfied that all the information shown is correct, click on the button labeled, "Confirm Bid."

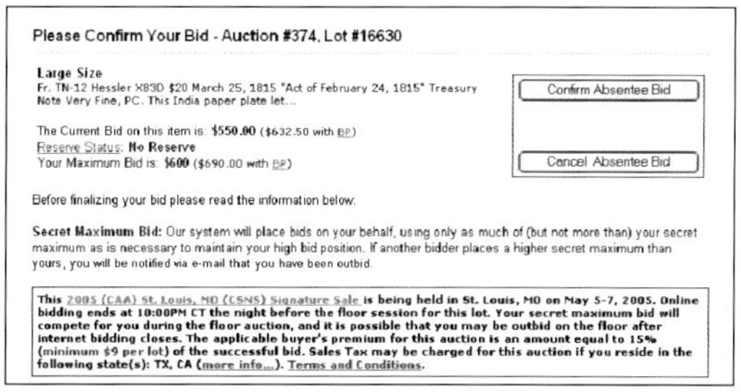

6. **Bidding Status Notification**
   One of two pages is now displayed.
   a. If your bid is the current high bid, you will be notified and given additional information as to what might happen to affect your high bidder status over the course of the remainder of the auction. You will also receive a Bid Confirmation notice via email. 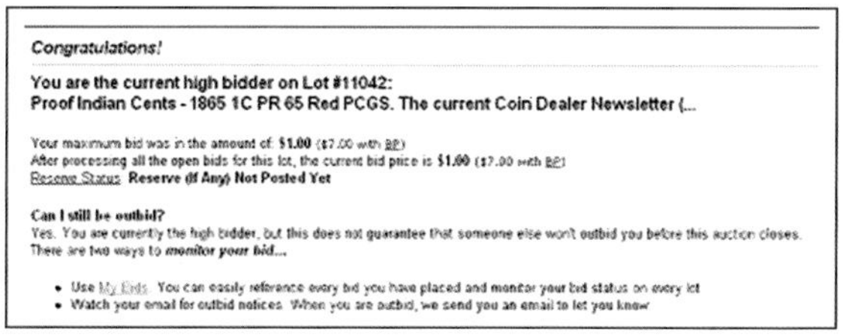
   b. If your bid is not the current high bid, you will be notified of that fact and given the opportunity to increase your bid.

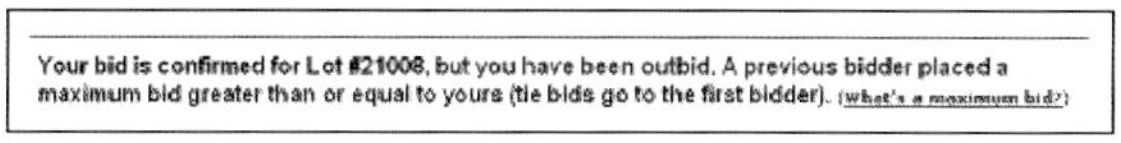

TERMS AND CONDITIONS OF SALE

AUCTIONEER AND AUCTION:

1. This Auction is presented by Heritage Numismatic Auctions. Inc.; or its subsidiary Currency Auctions of America, Inc.; or their affiliate, Heritage Auctions, Inc. d/b/a Heritage Galleries & Auctioneers, Heritage Art Auctions, Heritage Fine & Decorative Arts Auctions, Heritage Comics Auctions, Heritage-Slater Americana, Heritage Vintage Movie Posters, or Heritage Sports Collectibles Auctions, as identified with the applicable licensing information on the title page of the catalog or on the Internet site (the "Auctioneer"). The Auction is conducted under these Terms and Conditions of Auction and applicable state and local law.

BUYER'S PREMIUM:

2. On bids placed through Heritage, a Buyer's Premium of fifteen percent (15%) for Heritage Numismatic Auctions Inc, Heritage-CAA, and Heritage Comics Auctions and Heritage Movie Posters or nineteen and one-half percent (19.5%) for Heritage Sports Collectibles, Heritage Music & Entertainment Memorabilia, Heritage Art Auctions, Heritage Americana and Heritage Galleries & Auctioneers of the hammer price will be added to the successful bid. If the bid is placed through eBay Live a Buyer's Premium equal to the normal Buyer's Premium plus an additional five percent (5%) of the hammer price will be added to the successful bid up to a maximum Buyer's Premium of Twenty Two and one-half percent (22.5%). There is a minimum Buyer's Premium of $9.00 per lot.

AUCTION VENUES:

3. Exclusively Internet, Continuous Internet, Internet Currency, Amazing Comics Auctions, Amazing Sports Auctions, and Online Session are Auctions conducted on the Internet. Signature Auctions accept bids on the Internet first, followed by a floor bidding session; bids may be placed prior to the floor bidding session by Internet, telephone, fax, or mail.

BIDDERS:

4. Any person participating or registering for the Auction agrees to be bound by and accepts these Terms and Conditions of Auction ("Bidder(s)").
5. All Bidders must meet Auctioneer's qualifications to bid. Any Bidder who is not a customer in good standing of the Auctioneer may be disqualified at Auctioneer's sole option and will not be awarded lots. Such a determination may be made by Auctioneer in its sole and unlimited discretion, at any time prior to, during, or even after the close of the Auction.
6. If an entity places a bid, then the person executing the bid on behalf of the entity agrees to personally guarantee payment for any successful bid.
7. Auctioneer reserves the right to exclude any person it deems in its sole opinion is disruptive to the Auction or is otherwise commercially unsuitable.
8. CREDIT REFERENCES: Bidders who do not have established credit with the Auctioneer must either furnish satisfactory credit information (including two collectibles-related business references) well in advance of the Auction or supply valid credit card information. Bids placed through our Interactive Internet program will only be accepted from pre-registered Bidders; Bidders who are not members of HeritageGalleries.com or affiliates should pre-register at least two business days before the first session to allow adequate time to contact references.

BIDDING OPTIONS:

9. Bids may be placed for a Signature Auction as set forth in the printed catalog section entitled "Choose your bidding method." For Exclusively Internet, Continuous Internet, Internet Currency, Amazing Comics Auctions, Amazing Sports Auctions, and Online Session auctions, see the alternatives shown on each website. Review at HeritageCoins.com/Common/howtobid.php.
10. Presentment of Bids: Non-Internet bids (including but not limited to podium, fax, phone and mail bids) are treated similar to floor bids in that they must be on-increment or at a half increment (called a cut bid). Any podium, fax, phone, or mail bids that do not conform to a full or half increment will be rounded up or down to the nearest full or half increment and will be considered your high bid.
11. Auctioneer's Execution of Certain Bids. Auctioneer cannot be responsible for your errors in bidding, so carefully check that each bid is entered correctly. When identical mail or FAX bids are submitted, preference is given to the first received. To ensure the greatest accuracy, your written bids should be entered on the standard printed bid sheet and be received at Auctioneer's place of business at least two business days before the Auction start. Auctioneer is not responsible for executing mail bids or FAX bids received on or after the day the first lot is sold, nor Internet bids submitted after the published closing time; nor is Auctioneer responsible for proper execution of bids submitted by telephone, mail, FAX, e-mail, Internet, or in person once the Auction begins. Internet bids may not be withdrawn until your written request is received and acknowledged by Auctioneer (FAX: 214-443-8425); such requests must state the reason, and may constitute grounds for withdrawal of bidding privileges. Lots won by mail Bidders will not be delivered at the Auction unless prearranged in advance. The decision of the Auctioneer and declaration of the winning Bidder is final.
12. Caveat as to Bids. Bid increments (over the current bid level) determine the lowest amount you may bid on a particular lot. Bids greater than one increment over the current bid can be any whole dollar amount. It is possible under several circumstances for winning bids to be between increments, sometimes only $1 above the previous increment. Please see: *"How can I lose by less than an increment?"* on our website.
13. Bidding Increments: The following chart governs current bidding increments.

Current Bid	Bid Increment	Current Bid	Bid Increment
< $10	$1	$3,000 - $4,999	$250
$10 - $29	$2	$5,000 - $9,999	$500
$30 - $59	$3	$10,000 - $19,999	$1,000
$60 - $99	$5	$20,000 - $29,999	$2,000
$100 - $199	$10	$30,000 - $49,999	$2,500
$200 - $299	$20	$50,000 - $99,999	$5,000
$300 - $499	$25	$100,000 - $249,999	$10,000
$500 - $999	$50	$250,000 - $499,999	$25,000
$1,000 - $1,999	$100	$500,000 - $1,499,999	$50,000
$2,000 - $2,999	$200	> $1,500,000	$100,000

CONDUCTING THE AUCTION:

14. Notice of the consignor's liberty to place reserve bids on his lots in the Auction is hereby made in accordance with Article 2 of the Texas Uniform Commercial Code. A reserve is an amount below which the lot will not sell. THE CONSIGNOR OF PROPERTY MAY PLACE WRITTEN RESERVE BIDS ON HIS LOTS IN ADVANCE OF THE AUCTION; ON SUCH LOTS, IF THE HAMMER PRICE DOES NOT MEET THE RESERVE, THE CONSIGNOR MAY PAY A REDUCED COMMISSION ON THOSE LOTS. Reserves are generally posted online about 3 days prior to the Auction closing on Internet-Only Auctions, and 7 days prior to the Auction on Signature Auctions. Any successful bid placed by a consignor on his consigned lot on the Auction floor or by telephone during the live session, or after the reserves for an Auction have been posted, will be considered an unqualified bid, and in such instances the consignor agrees to pay full Buyer's Premium and Seller's Commissions on any lot so repurchased.
15. The highest qualified Bidder shall be the buyer. In the event of any dispute between floor Bidders at a Signature Auction, Auctioneer may at his sole discretion reoffer the lot. Auctioneer's decision shall be final and binding upon all Bidders.
16. Auctioneer reserves the right to refuse to honor any bid or to limit the amount of any bid which, in his sole discretion, is not submitted in "Good Faith," or is not supported by satisfactory credit, numismatic references, or otherwise. A bid is considered not made in "Good Faith" when an insolvent or irresponsible person, or a person under the age of eighteen makes it. Regardless of the disclosure of his identity, any bid by a consignor or his agent on a lot consigned by him is deemed to be made in "Good Faith".
17. All items are to be purchased per lot as numerically indicated and no lots will be broken. Auctioneer reserves the right to withdraw, prior to the close, any lots from the Auction.
18. Bids will be accepted in whole dollar amounts only. No "buy" or "unlimited" bids will be accepted. Bidders will be awarded lots at approximately the increment of the next highest bid. No additional commission is charged for executing bids. Off-increment bids may be accepted by the Auctioneer at Signature Auctions.
19. Auctioneer reserves the right to rescind the sale in the event of nonpayment, breach of a warranty, disputed ownership, auctioneer's clerical error or omission in exercising bids and reserves, or otherwise.
20. Outage Policy: Auctioneer occasionally experiences Internet and/or Server outages during which Bidders cannot participate or place bids. If such outage occurs, we may at our discretion extend bidding for the auction up to 24 hours. At our discretion, Auctioneer may consider two outages that occur very closely to one another to be one outage when extending such Auction. This policy applies only to widespread outages and not to isolated problems that occur in various parts of the country from time to time.
21. Scheduled Downtime: Auctioneer periodically schedules system downtime for maintenance and other purposes; this scheduled downtime is not covered by the Outage Policy.
22. The Auctioneer or its affiliates may consign items to be sold in the Auction, and may bid on those lots or any other lots. Auctioneer or affiliates expressly reserve the right to modify any such reserve bids on these items or any others at any time prior to the live auction or the online closing based upon data made known to the Auctioneer or its affiliates. The Auctioneer may extend advances, guarantees, or loans to certain consignors, and may extend financing or other credits at varying rates to certain Bidders in the auction.
23. The Auctioneer has the right to sell certain items after the close of the sale. Items sold by Auctioneer post sale shall be considered sold during the auction and all these Terms and Conditions shall apply to such sales including but not limited to the payment of the buyer's fee, return rights and disclaimers.

PAYMENT:

24. All sales are strictly for cash in United States dollars. Cash includes: U.S. currency, bank wire, cashier checks, travelers checks, and bank money orders, all subject to reporting requirements. Credit Card (Visa or Master Card only) and PayPal payments may be accepted up to $10,000 from non-dealers at the sole discretion of the auctioneer, subject to the following limitations: a) sales are only to the cardholder, b) purchases are shipped to the cardholder's registered and verified address, c) Auctioneer may pre-approve the cardholder's credit line, d) a credit card transaction may not be used in conjunction with any other financing or extended terms offered by the Auctioneer, and must transact immediately upon invoice presentation, e) rights of return are governed by these Terms and Conditions, which supersede those conditions promulgated by the card issuer, f) floor Bidders must present their card. Personal or corporate checks may be subject to clearing before delivery of the purchases.
25. Payment is due upon closing of the Auction session, or upon presentment of an invoice. Auctioneer reserves the right to void an invoice if payment in full of the invoice is not received within 7 days after the close of the Auction.
26. Lots delivered in the States of Texas, California, or other states where the Auction may be held, are subject to all applicable state and local taxes, unless appropriate permits are on file with us. Bidder agrees to pay Auctioneer the actual amount of tax due in the event that sales tax is not properly collected due to: 1) an expired, inaccurate, inappropriate tax certificate or declaration, 2) an incorrect interpretation of the applicable statute, 3) or any other reason.. Lots from different Auctions may not be aggregated for sales tax purposes.
27. In the event that a Bidder's payment is dishonored upon presentment(s), Bidder shall pay the maximum statutory processing fee set by applicable state law.
28. If the Auction invoice(s) submitted by Auctioneer is not paid in full when due, the unpaid balance will bear interest at the highest rate permitted by law from the date of invoice until paid. If the Auctioneer refers the invoice(s) to an attorney for collection, the buyer agrees to pay attorney's fees, court costs, and other collection costs incurred by Auctioneer. If Auctioneer assigns collection to its in-house legal staff, such attorney's time expended on the matter shall be compensated at a rate comparable to the hourly rate of independent attorneys.
29. In the event a successful Bidder fails to pay all amounts due, Auctioneer reserves the right to resell the merchandise, and such Bidder agrees to pay for the reasonable costs of resale, including a 10% seller's commission, and also to pay any difference between the resale price and the price of the previously successful bid.
30. Auctioneer reserves the right to require payment in full in good funds before delivery of the merchandise to the buyer.
31. Auctioneer shall have a lien against the merchandise purchased by the buyer to secure payment of the Auction invoice. Auctioneer is further granted a lien and the right to retain possession of any other property of the buyer then held by the Auctioneer or its affiliates to secure payment of any Auction invoice or any other amounts due the Auctioneer from the buyer. With respect to these lien rights, Auctioneer shall have all the rights of a secured creditor under Article 9 of the Texas Uniform Commercial Code. In addition, with respect to payment of the Auction invoice(s), the buyer waives any and all rights of offset he might otherwise have against the Auctioneer and the consignor of the merchandise included on the invoice.
32. If a Bidder owes Auctioneer or its affiliates on any account, Auctioneer and its affiliates shall have the right to offset such unpaid account by any credit balance due Bidder, and it may secure by possessory lien any unpaid amount by any of the Bidder's property in their possession.
33. Title shall not pass to the successful Bidder until all invoices are paid in full. It is the responsibility of the buyer to provide adequate insurance coverage for the items once they have been delivered.

RETURN POLICIES:

34. A MEMORABILIA lot (Autographs, Sports Collectibles, or Music, Entertainment, Political, Americana and/or Pop Culture memorabilia): The Auction is not on approval. When the lot is accompanied by a Certificate of Authenticity (or its equivalent) from an independent third party authentication provider, buyer has no right of return. Under extremely limited circumstances not including authenticity (e.g. gross cataloging error), a purchaser who did not bid from the floor may request Auctioneer to evaluate voiding a sale; such request must be made in writing detailing the alleged gross error, and submission of the lot to Auctioneer must be pre-approved by Auctioneer. A bidder must notify the appropriate department head (check the inside front cover of the catalog or our website for a listing of department heads) in writing of the purchaser's request and such

notice must be mailed within three (3) days of the mail bidder's receipt of the lot. Any lot that is to be evaluated for return must be received in our offices within 30 days after Auction. AFTER THAT 30 DAY PERIOD, NO LOT MAY BE RETURNED FOR ANY REASONS. Lots returned must be in the same condition as when sold and must include the Certificate of Authenticity, if any. No lots purchased by floor bidders may be returned (including those bidders acting as agents for others). Late remittance for purchases may be considered just cause to revoke all return privileges.

35. COINS, CURRENCY, COMICS AND SPORTSCARDS Signature Auctions: The Auction is not on approval. No certified material may be returned because of possible differences of opinion with respect to the grade offered by any third-party organization, dealer, or service. No guarantee of grade is offered for uncertified Property sold and subsequently submitted to a third-party grading service. There are absolutely no exceptions to this policy. Under extremely limited circumstances, (e.g. gross cataloging error) a purchaser, who did not bid from the floor, may request Auctioneer to evaluate voiding a sale; such request must be made in writing detailing the alleged gross error, and submission of the lot to the Auctioneer must be pre-approved by the Auctioneer; bidder must notify Ron Brackemyre, (ext. 312) in writing of the such request and such notice must be mailed within three (3) days of the mail bidder's receipt of the lot. Any lot that is to be evaluated must be in our offices within 30 days after Auction. Grading or method of manufacture do not qualify for this evaluation process nor do such complaints constitute a basis to challenge the authenticity of a lot. AFTER THAT 30-DAY PERIOD, NO LOTS MAY BE RETURNED FOR REASONS OTHER THAN AUTHENTICITY. Lots returned must be housed intact in the original holder. No lots purchased by floor Bidders may be returned (including those Bidders acting as agents for others). Late remittance for purchases may be considered just cause to revoke all return privileges.

36. Exclusively Internet, Internet Currency, Amazing Comics Auctions, Amazing Sports Auctions, Continuous Internet and Online Session auctions: THREE (3) DAY RETURN POLICY. All lots (Exception: Third party graded notes are not returnable for any reason whatsoever) paid for within seven days of the Auction closing are sold with a three (3) day return privilege. You may return lots under the following conditions: Within three days of receipt of the lot, you must first notify Auctioneer by contacting Customer Service by phone (1-800-872-6467) or e-mail (Bid@HeritageGalleries.com), and immediately mail the lot(s) fully insured to the attention of Returns, Heritage, 3500 Maple Avenue, 17th Floor, Dallas TX 75219-3941. Lots must be housed intact in their original holder and condition. You are responsible for the insured, safe delivery of any lots. A non-negotiable return fee of 5% of the purchase price ($10 per lot minimum) will be deducted from the refund for each returned lot or billed directly. Postage and handling fees are not refunded. After the three-day period (from receipt), no items may be returned for any reason. Late remittance for purchases revokes all Return-Restock privileges.

37. All Bidders who have inspected the lots prior to the auction will not be granted any return privileges, except for reasons of authenticity.

DELIVERY; SHIPPING AND HANDLING CHARGES:

38. Postage, handling and insurance charges will be added to invoices. Please either refer to Auctioneer's website HeritageGalleries.com for the latest charges or call Auctioneer.

39. Auctioneer is unable to combine purchases from other auctions or Heritage Rare Coin Galleries into one package for shipping purposes. Successful overseas Bidders shall provide written shipping instructions, including specified customs declarations, to the Auctioneer for any lots to be delivered outside of the United States. NOTE: Declaration value shall be the item(s) hammer price together with its buyer's premium.

40. All shipping charges will be borne by the successful Bidder. Due to the nature of some items sold, it shall be the responsibility for the successful bidder to arrange pick-up and shipping through third parties, as to such items Auctioneer shall have no liability. Any risk of loss during shipment will be borne by the buyer following Auctioneer's delivery to the designated common carrier, regardless of domestic or foreign shipment. Any request for shipping verification for undelivered packages must be made within 30 days of shipment by Auctioneer.

41. In the event an item is damaged either through handling or in transit, Auctioneer's maximum liability shall be the amount of the successful bid including the Buyer's Premium. On the fall of Auctioneer's hammer, Buyers of Fine Arts and Decorative Arts lots assumes full risk and responsibility for lot, including shipment by common carrier, and must provide their own insurance coverage for shipments.

CATALOGING, WARRANTIES AND DISCLAIMERS:

42. NO WARRANTY, WHETHER EXPRESSED OR IMPLIED, IS MADE WITH RESPECT TO ANY DESCRIPTION CONTAINED IN THIS AUCTION OR ANY SECOND OPINE. Any description of the items or second opine contained in this auction is for the sole purpose of identifying the items for those Bidders who do not have the opportunity to view the lots prior to bidding, and no description of items has been made part of the basis of the bargain or has created any express warranty that the goods would conform to any description made by Auctioneer.

43. Auctioneer is selling only such right or title to the items being sold as Auctioneer may have by virtue of consignment agreements on the date of auction and disclaims any warranty of title to the Property.

44. Translations of foreign language documents are provided as a convenience to interested parties. Heritage makes no representation as to the accuracy of those translations and will not be held responsible for errors in bidding arising from inaccuracies in translation.

45. In the event of an attribution error, Auctioneer may at its sole discretion, correct the error on the Internet, or, if discovered at a later date, to refund the buyer's money without further obligation. Under no circumstances shall the obligation of the Auctioneer to any Bidder be in excess of the purchase price for any lot in dispute.

46. Auctioneer disclaims any warranty of merchantability or fitness for any particular purposes.

47. Auctioneer disclaims all liability for damages, consequential or otherwise, arising out of or in connection with the sale of any property by Auctioneer to Bidder. No third party may rely on any benefit of these Terms and Conditions and any rights, if any, established hereunder are personal to the Bidder and may not be assigned. Any statement made by the Auctioneer is an opinion and does not constitute a warranty or representation. No employee of Auctioneer may alter these Terms and Conditions, and, unless signed by a principal of Auctioneer, any such alteration is null and void.

48A. COINS – Coins sold referencing a third-party grading service are sold "as is" without any express or implied warranty, except for a guarantee by Auctioneer that they are genuine. Certain warranties may be available from the grading services and the Bidder is referred to them for further details: ANACS, P.O. Box 182141, Columbus, Ohio 43218-2141; Numismatic Guaranty Corporation (NGC), P.O. Box 4776, Sarasota, FL 34230; Professional Coin Grading Service (PCGS), PO Box 9458, Newport Beach, CA 92658; and ICG, 7901 East Belleview Ave., Suite 50, Englewood, CO 80111.

49. All non-certified coins, currency, and comics are guaranteed genuine, but are not guaranteed as to grade, since grading is a matter of opinion, an art and not a science, and therefore the opinion rendered by the Auctioneer or any third party grading service may not agree with the opinion of others (including trained experts), and the same expert may not grade the same item with the same grade at two different times. Auctioneer has graded the non-certified numismatic items, in the Auctioneer's opinion, to their current interpretation of the American Numismatic Association's standards as of the date the catalog was prepared. There is no guarantee or warranty implied or expressed that the grading standards utilized by the Auctioneer will meet the standards of ANACS, NGC, PCGS, ICG, CGC, CGA or any other grading service at any time in the future.

50. Since we cannot examine encapsulated notes or comics, they are sold "as is" without our grading opinion, and may not be returned for any reason. Auctioneer shall not be liable for any patent or latent defect or controversy pertaining to or arising from any encapsulated collectible. In any such instance, purchaser's remedy, if any, shall be solely against the service certifying the collectible.

51. Due to changing grading standards over time, differing interpretations, and to possible mishandling of items by subsequent owners, Auctioneer reserves the right to grade items differently than shown on certificates from any grading service that accompany the items. Auctioneer also reserves the right to grade items differently than the grades shown in the catalog should such items be reconsigned to any future auction.

52. Although consensus grading is employed by most grading services, it should be noted as aforesaid that grading is not an exact science. In fact, it is entirely possible that if a lot is broken out of a plastic holder and resubmitted to another grading service or even to the same service, the lot could come back with a different grade assigned.

53. Certification does not guarantee protection against the normal risks associated with potentially volatile markets. The degree of liquidity for certified coins and collectibles will vary according to general market conditions and the particular lot involved. For some lots there may be no active market at all at certain points in time.

RELEASE:

54. In consideration of participation in the auction and the placing of a bid, a Bidder expressly releases Auctioneer, its officers, directors and employees, its affiliates, and its outside experts that provide second opines from any and all claims, cause of action, chose of action, whether at law or equity or any arbitration or mediation rights existing under the rules of any professional society or affiliation based upon the assigned grade or a derivative theory, breach of warranty express or implied, representation or other matter set forth within these Terms and Conditions of Auction or otherwise, except as specifically declared herein; e.g., authenticity, typographical error, etc., and as to those matters, the rights and privileges conferred therein are strictly construed and is the exclusive remedy. Purchaser, by non-compliance to its express terms of a granted remedy, shall waive any claim against Auctioneer.

DISPUTE RESOLUTION AND ARBITRATION PROVISION:

55. By placing a bid or otherwise participating in the auction, such person or entity accepts these Terms and Conditions of Auction, and specifically agrees to the alternative dispute resolution provided herein. Arbitration replaces the right to go to court, including the right to a jury trial.

56. Auctioneer in no event shall be responsible for consequential damages, incidental damages, compensatory damages, or other damages arising from the auction of any lot. Auctioneer's maximum liability shall not exceed the high bid on that lot, which bid shall be deemed for all purposes the value of the lot. In the event that Auctioneer cannot deliver the lot or subsequently it is established that the lot lacks title, provenance, authenticity, or other transfer or condition issue is claimed, Auctioneer's liability shall be limited to recission of sale and refund of purchase price. After one year has elapsed, Auctioneer's maximum liability shall be limited to any commissions and fees Auctioneer earned on that lot.

57. Any claim as to provenance or authenticity must be first transmitted to Auctioneer by credible and definitive evidence and there is no assurance after such presentment that Auctioneer will validate the claim. Authentication is not an exact science and contrary opinions may not be recognized by Auctioneer. Even if Auctioneer agrees with the contrary opinion of such authentication, our liability for reimbursement for such service shall not exceed $500.

58. Provenance and authenticity are not guaranteed by the Auctioneer, but rather are guaranteed by the consignor. Any action or claim shall include the consignor with Auctioneer acting as interpleador or nominal party. While every effort is made to determine provenance and authenticity, it is up to the Bidder to arrive at that conclusion prior to bidding.

59. If any dispute arises regarding payment, authenticity, grading, description, provenance, or any other matter pertaining to the Auction, the Bidder or a participant in the Auction and/or the Auctioneer agree that the dispute shall be submitted, if otherwise mutually unresolved, to binding arbitration in accordance with the commercial rules of the American Arbitration Association (A.A.A.). A.A.A. arbitration shall be conducted under the provisions of the Federal Arbitration Act with locale in Dallas, Texas. Any claim made by a Bidder has to be presented within one (1) year or it is barred. The prevailing party may be awarded his reasonable attorney's fees and costs. An award granted in arbitration is enforceable in any court of competent jurisdiction. No claims of any kind (except for reasons of authenticity) can be considered after the settlements have been made with the consignors. Any dispute after the settlement date is strictly between the Bidder and consignor without involvement or responsibility of the Auctioneer. NOTE: Purchasers of rare coins or currency through Heritage have available the option of arbitration by the Professional Numismatists Guild (PNG); if an election is not made within ten (10) days of an unresolved dispute, Auctioneer may elect either PNG or A.A.A. Arbitration.

60. In consideration of his participation in or application for the auction, a person or entity (whether the successful Bidder, a Bidder, a purchaser and/or other Auction participant or registrant) agrees that all disputes in any way relating to, arising under, connected with, or incidental to these Terms and Conditions and purchases or default in payment thereof shall be arbitrated pursuant to the arbitration provision. In the event that any matter including actions to compel arbitration, construe the agreement, actions in aid or arbitration or otherwise needs to be litigated, such litigation shall be exclusively in the Courts of the State of Texas, in Dallas County, Texas, and if necessary the corresponding appellate courts. The successful Bidder, purchaser, or Auction participant also expressly submits himself to the personal jurisdiction of the State of Texas.

MISCELLANEOUS:

61. Agreements between Bidders and consignors to effectuate a non-sale of an item at Auction, inhibit bidding on a consigned item to enter into a private sale agreement for said item, or to utilize the Auctioneer's Auction to obtain sales for non-selling consigned items subsequent to the auction, are strictly prohibited. If a subsequent sale of a previously consigned item occurs in violation of this provision, Auctioneer reserves the right to charge Bidder the applicable Buyer's Premium and consignor a Seller's Commission as determined for each auction venue and by the terms of the seller's agreement.

62. Acceptance of these terms and conditions qualifies Bidder as a Heritage customer who has consented to be contacted by Heritage in the future. In conformity with "do-not-call" regulations promulgated by the Federal or State regulatory agencies, participation by the Bidder is affirmative consent to being contacted at the phone number shown in his application and this consent shall remain in effect until it is revoked in writing. Heritage may from time to time contact Bidder concerning sale, purchase and auction opportunities available through Heritage and its affiliates and subsidiaries.

63. Storage of purchased coins and currency: Purchasers are advised that certain types of plastic may react with a coin's metal or transfer plasticizer to notes and may cause damage. Caution should be used to avoid storage in materials that are not inert.

STATE NOTICES:

64. Notice as to an Auction Sale in California. Auctioneer has in compliance with Title 2.95 of the California Civil Code as amended October 11, 1993 Sec. 1812.600, posted with the California Secretary of State its bonds for it and its employees and the auction is being conducted in compliance with Sec. 2338 of the Commercial Code and Sec. 535 of the Penal Code.

Non-dealer bidders are granted 90 days to pay their invoice provided a 20% down payment is received within 7 days of the auction. Bidders taking advantage of these special terms will receive their lots when their invoice is paid in full, regardless of an existing Heritage line of credit.

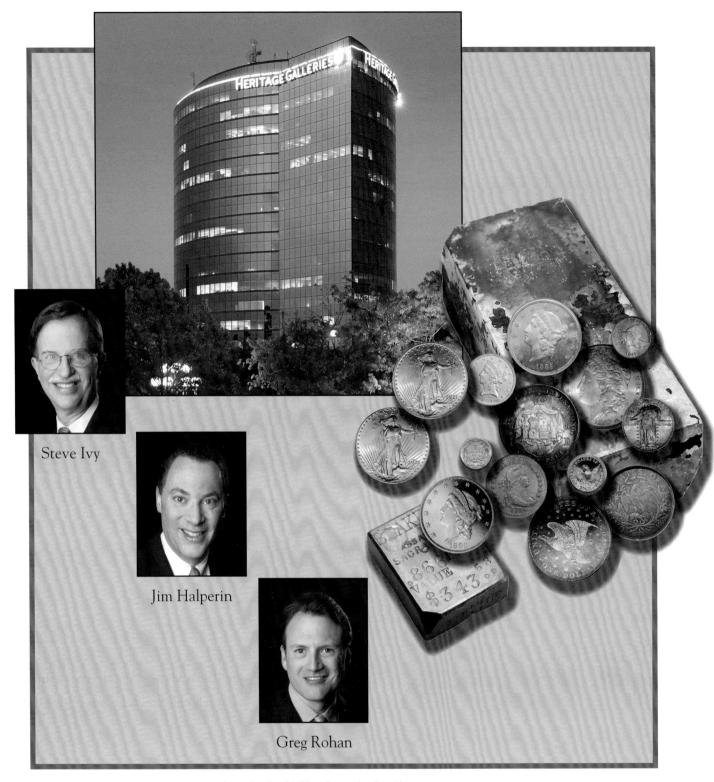

SESSION FIVE

Public-Internet Auction #390
Thursday, January 26, 2006, Noon CT, Lots 20666-21295

A 15% Buyer's Premium ($9 minimum) Will Be Added To All Lots.

Visit HeritageGalleries.com/Coins to view full-color images and bid.

FLYING EAGLE CENTS

Gem Snow-3 Proof 1856 Flying Eagle Cent

20666 **1856 PR65 NGC.** Snow-3. This lovely Gem has the recut 5 in the date associated with Snow's Obverse 1, but the die scratch beneath the right ribbon end is not evident. However, it is not either of the other known die pairings for Obverse 1 (Snow-1, tilted ONE CENT; and Snow-10, Low Leaves) and repunching on the E in CENT is present on its upper right edge. Snow-3 is the second most common die marriage of 1856 Flying Eagle Cents, but carries a premium over Snow-9 because it is scarcer, and because Snow-9 is considered a proof-only variety, while most examples of Snow-3 are considered business strikes by specialists. NGC and PCGS no longer certify any 1856 Flying Eagle Cents as business strikes, but encapsulate them as proofs regardless of surfaces and Snow variety. The bold strike, the absence of strike doubling, and the moderately reflective fields suggest that the present piece is a proof example of Snow-3, rather than a business strike. An intricately struck Gem, the fields display light honey-gold color while the luminous devices are tan in hue. The fields are lightly mirrored, and are void of contact. A faint and fully retained lamination, as made, is near 1 o'clock and is accompanied by slightly deeper gray color. Envelope Included. (#2037)

Legendary Gem 1856 Flying Eagle Cent

20667 **1856 PR65 NGC.** Snow-9. Considered a Proof-only variety without any known business strikes from these dies. The obverse has a short die line from the border to the upper right serif of I in UNITED. The reverse center dot is attached to the left side of N in CENT, just below the serif. A pinpoint-sharp Gem of this perennially popular key date Small Cent. Although technically a pattern, the 1856 is typically collected as part of the Flying Eagle Cent series. Its historical importance is unquestioned, not only because it introduced the Small Cent denomination, but because demand for examples fueled the growth of the coin collecting hobby throughout the second half of the nineteenth century. This attractive piece has dominant dusky peach-gold color. Well preserved, only the faintest hairlines are noted on the central reverse, and a few tiny flyspecks are found beneath a glass. Only the fleck above the E in ONE can be seen with the unaided eye.

Two past collectors were responsible for the availability of this issue, even today. Detroit resident George W. Rice "collected" 1856 Flying Eagle cents, to the tune of 756 coins. These coins were acquired in the 1890s and early 1900s, and most were sold when the Rice collection was dispersed in 1911. Many coins from the Rice hoard were immediately acquired by Pennsylvanian John A. Beck who was assembling his own accumulation. By the time of his death in 1924, Beck had acquired 531 examples of this popular date. The Beck Collection was held for another 50 years, finally be sold in the mid 1970s. Today, chances are good that any 1856 Flying Eagle cent was once owned by either or both of these two famous collectors. Envelope Included. (#2037)

1857 Small Cent With Uncirculated Details

20668 **1857—Obverse Spot Removed—NCS. Unc. Details.** The removed spots appear to be above the eagle's tail and east of the date; the measure was so skillfully performed, that it probably would have all but escaped notice by most collectors. The eagle's plumage details are boldly and deeply defined. Envelope Included. (#2016)

Affordable 1858 Large Letters Cent

20669 **1858 Large Letters—Improperly Cleaned—NCS. Unc. Details.** High Leaves, Closed E in ONE. Lightly polished at one time, the fields are faintly hairlined but have retoned to an attractive tan shade. Close examination reveals a scattering of shallow strike-throughs within the wreath on the reverse. Envelope Included. (#2019)

20670 **1858 Large Letters MS61 NGC.** Low Leaves, Open E in ONE. A crisply struck if slightly subdued golden-brown example with smooth, glossy surfaces. The dies are moderately rotated. Small Letters and Large Letter obverse subtypes were paired with three different reverse subtypes (High Leaves, Low Leaves Closed E, and Low Leaves Open E) to create six different subtype combinations. (#2019)

See the Online Session listings in the back of this volume for additional Reiver selections.

Select Uncirculated 1858 Cent With Small Letters

20671 **1858 Small Letters MS63 NGC.** Low Leaves, Closed E in ONE. Tan surfaces with frosty luster. The die states are advanced with some rim cuds noted. Close examination shows that several design features lack sharpness because of die erosion; something that happens when dies continue to be used after they're essentially worn out. The 1858 with Small Letters really constitutes a one-year design type, although probably not regarded as such by most type collectors; all the Flying Eagle cents coined in 1857 were the Large Letters type. Envelope Included. (#2020)

Collectible 1858/7 Small Cent

20672 **1858/7 AU53 NGC.** Olive tan surfaces. A typical strike with softness noted at the eagle's tail and at the highpoints of the wreath. Only a tiny vestige of the 7 in still visible in the date, but the variety can be readily identified by the presence of a die chip in the field midway between the date and the eagle's abdomen. Another tall-tale sign is that the tip of the eagle's right wing is detached. Envelope Included. (#2022)

Beautifully Preserved Near-Gem 1859 Indian Cent

20673 **1859 MS64 NGC.** Golden brown surfaces. A few tiny flecks were probably all that prevented NGC from assigning the MS65 designation. Interestingly, the dies were slightly skewed at the time this piece was struck. Although the reverse centering is close to perfect, the obverse rim is very broad at 4 o'clock and very narrow at 10 o'clock. Perhaps we can infer from this that the reverse was the anvil die on at least some of the cents coined in 1859. (#2052)

Gem Uncirculated 1859 Cent

20674 **1859 MS65 NGC.** A lovely Gem that exhibits frosty devices and satiny fields. Most design features are sharp, save for the tips of a few feathers in the Indian's headdress. The surfaces are about 30% brilliant, with tan and lilac iridescence in the remaining areas. Outstanding eye appeal. Envelope Included. (#2052)

1859 Indian Cent PR63 NGC

20675 **1859 PR63 NGC.** Sharply struck. The devices are frosty and the fields are nicely reflective. Mostly brilliant surfaces with blushes of tan and violet. A spot beneath the 8 in the date is mentioned more for purposes of identification than for any other reason. The 1859 is especially popular with Indian cent enthusiasts because of its status as a one-year design type. Beginning in 1860 the reverse design featured an oak wreath and shield motif. Only 800 Proof cents are thought to have been minted during the year. Envelope Included. (#2247)

1860 Cent, Uncirculated Details

20676 **1860—Improperly Cleaned—NCS. Unc. Details.** Wispy hairlines create a slightly cloudy appearance. A decent strike with some softness noted at the tops of the feathers in the Indian's headdress. The die state of the obverse is advanced with several tiny rim cuds noted. A small planchet flaw, as made, can be seen on the reverse rim near the base of the wreath. Envelope Included. (#2058)

Uncirculated 1862 Cent

20679 **1862 MS62 NGC.** Tan surfaces. The devices are frosty and the fields are nicely reflective. The strike is about average with softness noted at the tops of the Indian's headdress feathers. A few tiny flecks probably account for the assigned grade. Envelope Included. (#2064)

Affordable 1861 Cent

20677 **1861—Edge Corrosion—NCS. Unc. Details.** Tan surfaces. Sharply struck and attractive, with the fields exhibiting considerable prooflike character. Close examination reveals a few tiny flecks. The edge corrosion mentioned on the NCS label is obscured by the NCS holder. Envelope Included. (#2256)

1863 Cent With Uncirculated Details

20680 **1863—Improperly Cleaned—NCS. Unc. Details.** A typical strike with softness noted at the tips of the feathers in the Indian's headdress. The luster is subdued. Both surfaces exhibit golden-brown toning with blushes of blue and pink. (#2067)

Gem Uncirculated 1861 Indian Cent

20678 **1861 MS65 NGC.** Fully lustrous and warmly toned in intermingled hues of tan, blue, and pink. The strike is about average with softness noted at the tips of the Indian's headdress feathers. Only a small portion of the Uncirculated 1861 cent population is this nicely preserved. Envelope Included. (#2061)

Near-Gem 1864 Copper-Nickel Cent

20681 **1864 Copper-Nickel MS64 NGC.** Partially brilliant with blushes of tan. The strike is average with softness noted at the tips of the feathers in the headdress. A few tiny flecks can be seen under magnification. Envelope Included. (#2070)

See the Online Session listings in the back of this volume for additional Reiver selections.

Conditionally Scarce 1864 Copper Nickel Cent PR64 NGC

20682 **1864 Copper Nickel PR64 NGC.** Sharply struck with virtually all design features defined to full advantage. Both surfaces are essentially brilliant, with just a hint of tan. A few tiny flecks on the reverse are probably all that prevented NGC from assigning the PR65 grade designation. Although the number of proofs issued for the variety isn't known with certainty, the figure usually reported is 370 pieces, which would make it the lowest production figure for any date in the Copper Nickel Indian cent series. Population: 8 in 64, 12 finer (8/05). Envelope Included. (#2265)

Select Uncirculated 1864-L Cent, Snow-10a

20683 **1864 L On Ribbon MS63 Red and Brown NGC.** Snow-10a, FS-006.73. Lustrous and attractive. Struck from lightly clashed dies. Virtually all obverse design features are sharp including engraver Longacre's initial "L" on the ribbon of the Indian's headdress. Both surfaces are about 30% mint red with blushes of violet-brown in the remaining areas. Close examination reveals a few scattered flecks on both the obverse and reverse. The date is widely recut within the loops of the 86. Envelope Included. (#2080)

1865 Plain 5 Cent, Uncirculated Details

20684 **1865 Plain 5—Altered Color—NCS. Unc. Details.** Sharply struck and lustrous. Lightly clashed dies; an impression from the letter C in CENT is visible in the field in front of Liberty's eye. Streaky toning is noted on the obverse. (#92084)

1866 Cent, Uncirculated Details

20685 **1866—Altered Color—NCS. Unc. Details.** Frosty luster. The surfaces are partially brilliant with blushes of pale tan and lilac. Most design features are sharp. A few tiny flecks are noted. Envelope Included. (#2087)

1867 Cent, MS62 Red and Brown NGC

20686 **1867 MS62 Red and Brown NGC.** The obverse is satiny and about 20% red, with blushes of navy blue and pink in the remaining area. The reverse exhibits mottled blue and tan toning with subdued luster. (#2089)

Well Detailed 1867 Cent

20687 **1867—Altered Color—NCS. Unc. Details.** Snow-5b. Most design features are sharp, and the surfaces are predominantly brilliant with wisps and blushes of pink and blue. Struck from lightly clashed dies. The 18 in the date is nicely repunched south. Envelope Included. (#2090)

Sharp Proof 1868 Small Cent

20688 **1868—Altered Color—NCS. Proof.** The devices are sharp and frosty and the fields are nicely reflective. The surfaces are mostly brilliant with blushes of pink and violet. Close examination reveals a few scattered flecks. The dies are rotated nearly 180 degrees from coin turn, unusual for the series. Envelope Included. (#2293)

Well Defined 1869 Indian Cent

20689 **1869—Altered Color—Unc. Details.** Snow-3, FS-008.3. Subdued luster. Warmly toned in hues of tan, navy blue, and lilac, with some hints of coppery brilliance. A faint retained lamination, as made, is noted east of the N in ONE. Envelope Included. (#2094)

Choice Uncirculated 1869 Cent

20690 **1869 MS64 Red and Brown NGC.** Sharply struck and attractive. The surfaces are about 40 to 50% faded mint red with blushes of tan, blue, and pink. An inconspicuous mark on the upper left obverse field and a few tiny flecks are noted. Boldly die clashed on the right inside wreath. Envelope Included. (#2095)

Important 1869/69 Cent, MS64 Red and Brown

20691 **1869/69 MS64 Red and Brown NGC.** Snow-3e, FS-008.3. A high-grade example of this popular variety which exhibits bold recutting at the 69 in the date. The scarce Snow-3e subvariety is the reverse with the interesting mint-made flaws on the shield and the lower interior of the O in ONE. The surfaces are perhaps 50% red on the obverse and 20% red on the reverse. This example has two heavy die cracks or die scratches on the reverse: one within the azure portion of the shield and another within the O of ONE. Some spots on the obverse (visible without magnification) prompt us to suggest in-person examination prior to bidding. (#2096)

1870 One Cent With Uncirculated Details

20692 **1870—Improperly Cleaned—NCS. Unc. Details.** Satiny luster. Tan surfaces with blushes and wisps of navy blue. Most design features are sharp. Rick Snow's Type Two Doubled Die Reverse, caused by dual use of Type Three (bold N in ONE) and Type One (Shallow N in ONE) working hubs while creating the working reverse die. (#2098)

Sharply Struck Near-Gem 1870 Indian Cent

20693 **1870 MS64 Red and Brown NGC.** Perhaps 40% mint red with pleasing violet-blown in the remaining areas. Most design features are sharp including the feathers in the Indian's headdress. All four diamonds on the ribbon are visible. A touch of striking softness can be seen on some of the horizontal bars of the reverse shield. Envelope Included. (#2098)

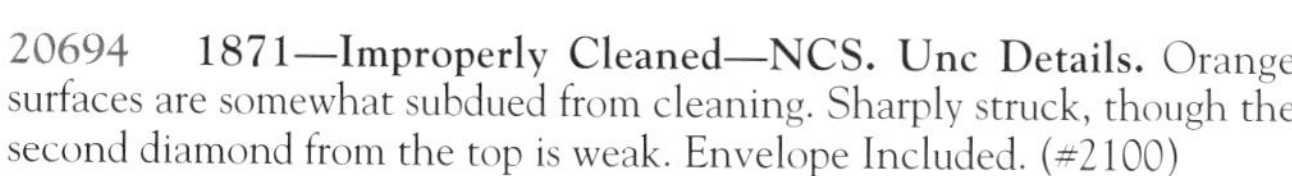
20694 **1871—Improperly Cleaned—NCS. Unc Details.** Orange surfaces are somewhat subdued from cleaning. Sharply struck, though the second diamond from the top is weak. Envelope Included. (#2100)

Well Defined Proof 1872 Cent

20695 **1872—Altered Color—NCS. Proof.** Sharply struck with most design features defined to full advantage. The satiny devices contrast nicely with the mirror fields. The surfaces are essentially brilliant with blushes of pale lilac. A low mintage date. (#2305)

Lovely Gem 1872 Indian Cent

20696 **1872 PR66 Red and Brown NGC.** A lovely Gem example having sharp frosty devices and glittering mirror fields. The surfaces are mostly blazing red with blushes of pink and blue. Here's a prize for the numismatist who demands outstanding quality. The reported mintage figure for proof cents of 1872 is 950 pieces. Envelope Included. (#2304)

20697 **1873 Open 3—Improperly Cleaned—NCS. AU Details.** Coppery-gold surfaces are lightly hairlined and semi-bright from cleaning. The design elements are well impressed. Envelope Included. (#2107)

Nearly Red Gem 1873 Closed 3 Indian Cent

20698 **1873 Closed 3 MS66 Red and Brown NGC.** The two types of 1873, having either an "Open 3" or "Closed 3" in the date, were made popular by the numismatic collector and writer Harry X Boosel. Boosel, who was popularly referred to as "Mr. 1873," made frequent appearances at national coin shows over a period of several decades. Curiously, X was his entire middle name, not an initial, thus is properly not punctuated. The Closed 3 coins were struck early in the year, in both proof and business strike quality. Later, business strikes of the Open 3 Indian Cents were produced.

Sharply struck with satiny luster. The surfaces are essentially faded red. In fact, it is difficult not to call this fully red in color. It is truly a remarkable Premium Gem example, and is equal to the finest of its type to be certified as MS66RB by NGC. According to their own on-line census, this grading services has certified five examples at this grade level with none finer. Envelope Included. (#2111)

1874 Cent, Uncirculated Details

20699 **1874—Altered Color—NCS. Unc. Details.** Frosty luster. Mostly red surfaces with some blushes of lilac-brown. The left borders and the feather tips are indifferently struck, while the remainder of the designs are bold. A faint fingerprint is noted on the portrait. Envelope Included. (#2120)

Affordable 1875 Cent With Unc. Details

20700 **1875—Altered Color—NCS. Unc. Details.** Lustrous surfaces. Predominantly tan with blushes and wisps of blue. Most design features are sharp. An attractive example and worthy of a generous bid as such. Envelope Included. (#2121)

Collectible Gem 1876 Indian Cent

20701 **1876 MS65 Red and Brown NGC.** A lovely, sharply-struck Gem example having frosty devices and satiny fields. The surfaces are perhaps 50% mint red with tan in the remaining areas. Outstanding both technically and aesthetically. Envelope Included. (#2125)

Scarce, Key Date 1877 Cent With Uncirculated Details

20702 **1877—Improperly Cleaned—NCS. Unc. Details.** Shallow N in ONE. Both surfaces exhibit nearly uniform light golden brown toning. The left obverse field is faintly hairlined, and a small spot is noted at 9 o'clock on the reverse. Here's a scarce and desirable item certain to find a home in the cabinet of an appreciative specialist. Envelope Included. (#2127)

Handsome 1877 Choice Proof Indian Cent

20703 **1877 PR64 Red and Brown NGC.** A handsome example of this important key issue. Virtually all design features are sharp, and each of the four diamonds on the Indian's ribbon is visible. The frosty design elements contrast nicely with the mirror fields. The obverse is about 50% red, while the reverse is about 30% red. Envelope Included. (#2319)

20704 **1878—Altered Color—NCS. Unc Details.** Yellow-gold surfaces display streaks of lime-green. Nicely struck, including relatively strong definition on all four diamonds. Envelope Included. (#2130)

Lovely Proof 1879 Indian Cent

20705 **1879 PR64 Red and Brown NGC.** Slight evidence of a repunched date is visible, especially at the bottom of the 1. Sharply struck and almost fully brilliant with some faint hints of pink and blue at the centers. The fields are glittering mirrors and the devices exhibit a texture intermediate between satiny and frosty. A few tiny flecks on the obverse are probably all that prevented NGC from assigning the PR65 designation. A slight haze and even slighter mellowing of the color prevented a full Red designation. Only 3,200 proof cents were coined during the year, struck from two different obverse dies. Envelope Included. (#2326)

20706 **1880 PR64 Brown NGC.** Luminous orange-tan surfaces display what may be the remnants of a fingerprint in the left obverse field. The design elements are sharp, including clarity in the four diamonds. Envelope Included. (#2327)

Near Red Gem 1881 Proof Indian Cent

20707 **1881 PR66 Red and Brown NGC.** Take a look at the placement of the digits in the date, with the 18 higher than the following 81. Walter Breen suggested that this was "an attempt to make a curved date out of a straight logotype." A superlative Gem example having sharp devices and blazing mirrored fields. Both surfaces are very nearly full red despite the Red and Brown designation by NGC. The reverse in particular shows pronounced cameo contrast. Here's one of the finest survivors from a mintage of just 3,575 pieces. Envelope Included. (#2331)

1882 Cent With Uncirculated Details

20708 **1882—Altered Color—NCS. Unc Details.** Sharply struck and lustrous. Both surfaces are about 90% red with wisps and tinges of golden brown and blue. Lightly dipped, thus the NCS designation, yet this is an attractive and desirable example. Envelope Included. (#2144)

20709 **1882 PR63 Red and Brown NGC.** Bright orange surfaces display a mild cameo-like effect. Sharply struck, including the four diamonds and the feathers. A carbon spot is visible in the upper right obverse field. Envelope Included. (#2334)

20710 **1883 PR64 Brown NGC.** Coppery-tan patina bathes reflective surfaces that display sharply struck design elements. A few tiny flecks are noted in the reverse field. Envelope Included. (#2336)

Appealing Gem 1884 Proof Indian Cent

20711 **1884 PR66 Red and Brown NGC.** Rick Snow described a Proof variety with light repunching on the second 8. This example has miniscule die defects in the loops of both 8s, but there is no actual evidence of recutting. Sharply struck and attractive. The surfaces are essential faded red with pink and violet highlights. Both the obverse and reverse show slight cameo contrast. Magnification reveals a few tiny flecks, but these do not detract from the superlative eye appeal of this beauty. Only 3,942 proofs were struck, and few of them could match the quality offered here. Envelope Included. (#2339)

20712 **1885—Altered Color—NCS. Proof.** An intricately struck and satiny specimen. Recolored in rich orange shades, with hints of lilac color on the highpoints near the bust truncation. Near the end of the line for the Type One obverse hub, identified by the location of the lowest headdress feather, which points between the IC in AMERICA. Envelope Included. (#2342)

Lustrous Mint State 1886 Type One Cent

20713 **1886 Type One MS64 Red and Brown NGC.** A major hub change took place in 1886, and examples are known as either Type One or Type Two. The former have the lowest headdress feather pointing between IC in AMERICA, while the latter have the lowest feather pointing between CA. In all grades and formats, business strike and proof, Type One examples are more plentiful than Type Two. Collecting interest for these two major design types is extremely high. Discovery of the two different types is attributed to collector James Reynolds of Flint, Michigan, whose article about them appeared in the *Numismatic Scrapbook Magazine* issue of June 1949 (per Dave Bowers) or August 1954 (per Walter Breen). Rick Snow suggested that this collector was from Tucson, Arizona. The surfaces are about 25% mint red with golden-brown toning in the remaining area. Pale blue, violet, and sea green iridescent highlights can be seen on both the obverse and reverse. Envelope Included. (#2154)

20714 **1886 Type Two—Improperly Cleaned—NCS. Unc. Details.** The bright orange-gold color is quite deceptive, although an occasional tiny spot is seen on the obverse. Faint marks on the cheek will be missed by many observers. A sharply struck, late dies example of this scarce subtype. For the Type Two, the final headdress feather points between the CA in AMERICA. Envelope Included. (#92154)

20715 **1887 PR64 Brown NGC.** A fully struck proof with even brown-purple patina over each side. Envelope Included. (#2348)

1888 Indian Cent

20716 **1888—Reverse Corroded—NCS. UNC Details.** Mostly mint red with substantial prooflike character. A spot near the reverse border at 8 o'clock accounts for NCS label designation. A personal examination is recommended to prospective bidders. Envelope Included. (#2353)

20717 **1889 PR64 Red and Brown NGC.** Even brown patina with a significant underlying presence of mint red. An attractive coin with a well-balanced appearance. Envelope Included. (#2355)

1890 Cent With Unc. Details

20718 **1890—Altered Color—NCS. Unc Details.** Subdued frosty luster. Mostly red surfaces with pale tan and violet iridescent highlights. Envelope Included. (#2177)

Choice Proof 1890 Cent

20719 **1890 PR64 Red and Brown NGC.** Boldly struck and essentially blazing red despite the NGC "RB" label designation. Both surfaces show pleasing contrast between the sharp devices and glittering mirror fields. Outstanding eye appeal for the grade. Only 2,740 proofs were coined in 1890; this being a decline in production compared to most years of the 1880s. Envelope Included. (#82359)

Gem Cameo Proof 1891 Indian Cent

20720 **1891 PR65 Red and Brown Cameo NGC.** A delightful Gem having sharp frosty devices and glittering mirror fields. The obverse is almost fully brilliant. The reverse exhibits just a hint of pink iridescence. Here's a prize certain to highlight virtually any cabinet of Indian cents. The mintage of 2,350 pieces represents the smallest production figure up till that time since 1878, but in subsequent years, because of a decline in demand, mintage statistics dropped off even further. Envelope Included. (#92362)

Gem Proof 1892 One Cent

20721 **1892 PR65 Red and Brown NGC.** Mostly faded red surfaces with wisps and blushes of pink, blue, and violet. Nearly all design features are about as sharp as one could desire. From a proof mintage of just 2,745 pieces. Envelope Included. (#2364)

20722 **1893—Obverse Corroded—NCS. Proof.** A dark spot is southeast of the 3 in the date, and is accounted for the NCS label. A couple of less relevant spots are seen on the I and D in UNITED. Lightly hairlined, but sharply struck and flashy with luminous orange-red color. Glimpses of forest-green patina emerge on the obverse margin. Envelope Included. (#2366)

20723 **1894 PR64 Brown NGC.** Deep cherry-red over each side with a presence of olive over the reverse. A grease stain (as struck) is present on the face of the Indian. Envelope Included. (#2369)

20724 **1895—Altered Color—NCS. Unc. Details.** This lustrous and nicely struck chestnut-gold piece has minimal carbon, and only a couple of small marks on the obverse. The color is quite deceptive, and would fool many veteran copper collectors. Envelope Included. (#2190)

20725 **1896—Improperly Cleaned—NCS. Unc. Details.** Luminous apricot color cedes to lilac-red tints on the portrait highpoints. A smooth and affordable piece that comes with the Jules Reiver pedigree. Envelope Included. (#2193)

Well Detailed 1897 Indian Cent

20726 **1897—Altered Color—NCS. Unc Details.** Lustrous and mostly brilliant with blushes and hints of pink and violet. Most design features are sharp. Close examination reveals a few scattered spots and flecks. Envelope Included. (#2198)

20727 **1897 MS64 Red NGC.** Even, blazing orange-red mint luster is seen over each side. Only kept from the Gem category by a few marks on the cheek. Envelope Included. (#2198)

See the Online Session listings in the back of this volume for additional Reiver selections.

1898 Indian Cent, Unc. Details

20728 **1898—Altered Color—NCS. Unc Details.** Brilliant, lustrous, and sharply struck. A few scattered spots and flecks are noted, most prominently above the M in AMERICA. Envelope Included. (#2201)

Lovely Gem 1899 One Cent

20729 **1899 MS65 Red NGC.** A lovely frosty Gem example having faded red surfaces. Most design features are sharp save for the tips of the first three feathers in the Indian's headdress. Envelope Included. (#2204)

20730 **1900—Altered Color—NCS. Unc. Details.** Crisply struck with good luster and mellowed tan-gold color. The Indian's neck has a small gray spot. The peak of the 1 in the date appears recut, and the obverse rim has a slender die break between 8 and 10 o'clock. Envelope Included. (#2205)

20731 **1902 MS64 Brown NGC.** The reverse is mostly brown but there is quite a bit of original red present on the obverse. A bit softly struck. Envelope Included. (#2211)

Choice Uncirculated 1903 Indian Cent

20732 **1903 MS64 Red and Brown NGC.** Frosty luster. The obverse is about 50 percent mint red with tan in the remaining area. The reverse is about 30 percent red with blushes of violet-brown. Most design features are crisp including each of the four diamonds on the obverse ribbon. Envelope Included. (#2216)

Gem Type 1904 Indian Cent

20733 **1904 MS65 Red and Brown NGC.** Lustrous surfaces. Both the obverse and reverse are predominantly red with blushes of tan and lilac. Most design features are sharp. Envelope Included. (#2219)

20734 **1905 MS64 Red and Brown NGC.** Coppery-orange surfaces display splashes of light brown and cobalt-blue on the obverse. The design features are well impressed, including clarity in all four diamonds. A few minute marks occur on the Indian's cheek, and some light flecks are scattered over each side. (#2221)

Choice Uncirculated 1906 Indian Cent

20735 **1906 MS64 Red and Brown NGC.** Lustrous and attractive. Both surfaces are about 50 percent red with pale tan in the remaining areas. Most design features are sharp save for the tips of two or three feathers in the Indian's headdress. Envelope Included. (#2225)

Near-Gem 1906 Cent

20736 **1906 MS64 Red and Brown NGC.** Perhaps 50 percent mint red with blushes of pale tan, pink, and blue. A few scattered flecks and spots are noted which were probably all that prevented NGC from assigning the MS65 grade designation. Envelope Included. (#2225)

20737 **1907—Altered Color—NCS. Unc. Details.** Boldly struck with soft cartwheel luster and smooth straw-gold surfaces. Slight striking softness at 10 o'clock on the obverse, and opposite and 8 o'clock on the reverse, suggests the flan was defective (as made) at that location just prior to the strike. The base of the 7 in the date may be lightly repunched. Envelope Included. (#2226)

Glittering Choice Proof 1908 Indian Cent

20738 **1908 PR64 Red and Brown Cameo NGC.** The sharp frosty devices contrast beautifully with the glittering mirror fields. Both surfaces are very nearly full red despite the "RB" designation on the NGC label. Close examination reveals some scattered obverse flecks. Only 1,620 proofs were minted, an infinitesimal figure in comparison with today's production levels, and low even by the standards of the 1880s when proof mintages were often more than twice as large. Envelope Included. (#82413)

Semi-Key 1908-S Indian Cent

20739 **1908-S—Altered Color—NCS. Unc Details.** Faded red surfaces. Most design features are sharp. There are some indications that a small spot may have been removed from the field in front of Liberty's neck. A few scattered flecks can be seen under magnification. Envelope Included. (#2234)

Sharp, Branch Mint 1908-S One Cent

20740 **1908-S—Altered Color—NCS. Unc Details.** Lustrous with faded red surfaces. The majority of design features are boldly defined. Attractive despite the stigma implied by the NCS label designation. Envelope Included. (#2234)

20741 **1909—Altered Color—NCS. Unc. Details.** Bright pale-gold color is deceptive. The wood-grain surfaces are unblemished, and luster is prominent throughout this assertively struck piece. Envelope Included. (#2235)

Scarce Near-Gem 1909-S Indian Cent

20742 **1909-S MS64 Red and Brown NGC.** Lustrous surfaces. Both the obverse and reverse have at least 50% mint red with blushes of violet-brown. The reverse is sharp. A few of the obverse design details are "mushy," a feature probably caused by die wear (resulting from the extended use of the obverse die) rather than inadequate striking pressure. A scant 309,000 examples were minted; by far the lowest production figure of any date in the Indian cent series. Moreover, the 1909-S Indian cent holds the honor of having the lowest mintage of any cent issue coined during the 20th-century; even the celebrated 1909-S VDB Lincoln cent has a production figure more than 50% higher, coming in at 484,000 pieces.

Two examples of this date are included in the present sale, and they appear to have different mintmark sizes or shapes. This specimen has an open mintmark, especially at the bottom with the lower left serif distant from the curve above. The specimen in the next lot has a mintmark that appears to be closed, with both the upper and lower serif touching or nearly touching the nearby curves. We are not aware that these differences, which were first recorded by Jules, have ever been published to date. Envelope Included. (#2238)

Highly Collectible 1909-S Cent MS64 Red and Brown

20743 **1909-S MS64 Red and Brown NGC.** Intermingled faded red and tan complements the satiny surfaces. The tips of the first three feathers in the Indian's headdress are soft, but most other design features are sharp. A scattering of tiny spots and flecks are noted, thus accounting for the assigned grade. This example has nearly full red color on both sides. Envelope Included. (#2239)

LINCOLN CENTS

Choice Uncirculated 1909-S VDB Cent

20744 **1909-S VDB MS64 Red and Brown NGC.** A handsome example of this scarce and celebrated variety, which perhaps rates as the single most popular and eagerly sought issue of the 20th-century. The surfaces are fully lustrous and about 50% red with pale tan and violet iridescence in the remaining areas. There's scarcely a collector who has never heard of the 1909-S VDB, and millions of Lincoln cent enthusiasts of yesteryear dreamed of the possibility that they might be able to find an example in pocket change. Likewise, advanced Lincoln cent specialists or old would celebrate the day that they had saved sufficient funds for a lovely Uncirculated example to highlight their cabinets. Although nearly a century has passed since the 1909-S VDB first came to the attention of the numismatic community, its allure and desirability have never diminished. Here's your chance to join in a long and distinguished tradition of pride that comes from the ownership of one of America's favorite numismatic delicacies. (#2428)

1909-S Over Horizontal S Cent MS64 Red and Brown

20745 **1909-S S Over Horizontal S MS64 Red and Brown NGC.** Referred to by Walter Breen in his *Complete Encyclopedia* as "S over lazy S." A close-up photo of the repunched mintmark feature is provided in Walter's book. The surfaces are lustrous and perhaps 30% mint red with blushes of tan and blue. This variety is popular, but evidently not rare, as the premium commanded by examples in various grades is typically only slightly higher than the price for an ordinary 1909-S. (#92434)

20746 **1910-S MS63 Red and Brown NGC.** Sharply struck with a woodgrain texture and heavily spotted on the reverse. (#2439)

20747 **1911 MS65 Red and Brown NGC.** A sharply struck, pleasing coin with most of the mint luster remaining. (#2442)

Choice Uncirculated 1911-S Lincoln Cent

20748 **1911-S MS64 Red and Brown NGC.** Delicate tan, blue, and violet iridescence complements the lustrous surfaces. Traces of fiery mint red can be seen around the letters, numerals, and central motifs. A scarce issue that's eagerly sought in all grades. Demand can be attributed in large measure to the small mintage (by Lincoln cent standards) of just 4,026,000 pieces. (#2448)

Lustrous Gem 1912 Lincoln Cent

20749 **1912 MS65 Red NGC.** Fully lustrous and sharply struck. The obverse is a blazing red. The reverse is nearly full red with blushes of delicate pink and violet. (#2452)

20750 **1913-D MS64 Brown NGC.** As with many of the Lincoln cents Jules owned, this piece also shows a significant amount of original mint red in addition to the brown one would expect from the NGC designation. Fully struck. (#2462)

20751 **1913-S MS63 Red and Brown NGC.** Fully struck, with rich satin luster and attractive reddish-brown coloration, accented by red-gold highlights on each side. Scattered carbon flecks are noted on the obverse, and a pair of small contact blemishes are seen on the reverse, below N in ONE and C in CENT. A pleasing Mint State example of this early Lincoln cent issue. Envelope Included. (#2466)

Gem Mint State 1914-D Lincoln Cent

20752 **1914-D MS65 Red and Brown NGC.** The 1914-D is scarce in all grades, and is one of the most elusive issues in the Lincoln series at the Uncirculated level; something that almost guarantees the issue will remain a favorite with collectors for decades to come. Pleasing satiny luster. The surfaces are essentially full faded red with blushes of pleasing pale blue and violet. Nearly all design features are boldly and deeply defined including Lincoln's hair and the details of the wheat ears. Walter Breen wrote in his *Encyclopedia* that a hoard of 700 examples remained together until the early 1950s. Today, we have no further information regarding this lost hoard. (#2472)

Choice Uncirculated 1914-S Lincoln Cent

20753 **1914-S MS64 Red and Brown NGC.** Subdued satiny luster. Mostly tan and violet iridescence with some traces of fiery mint red surviving, especially on the reverse. The strike is about average for the issue with softness noted at the top of ONE in the denomination, and at the bottoms of LURI in PLURIBUS. (#2475)

Pleasing 1915 Lincoln Cent

20754 **1915—Altered Color—NCS. Unc Details.** Pleasing satiny luster. The obverse is perhaps 20 percent mint red with violet-tan iridescence in the remaining area. The reverse is a full blazing red, virtually as bright as the day it came from the dies. This is the type of toning that's sometimes seen on coins that come from the end or the roll. Very attractive overall despite the NCS label designation. (#2479)

Choice Uncirculated 1915-S Cent

20755 **1915-S MS64 Red and Brown NGC.** About 50 percent mint red with blushes of tan and violet. The luster is satiny and attractive. Lincoln's hair and the wheat ear details all show bold definition. (#2484)

Well Defined 1916-S Cent

20756 **1916-S MS64 Red and Brown NGC.** Satiny luster. The obverse is about 50 percent mint red with tan in the remaining area. The reverse is essentially pale violet-brown with some hints of faded red. The majority of design features show bold definition. (#2493)

Near-Gem 1917 Cent

20757 **1917 MS64 Red NGC.** Fully lustrous and sharply struck. The obverse is bright red. The reverse shows wisps and blushes of pink iridescence. A scattering of tiny flecks is noted within the wreath on the reverse, a feature which explains why NGC didn't assign the MS65 grade designation. (#2497)

20758 **1917-D MS63 Red NGC.** Blazing red surfaces with a few hints of violet. The strike is probably about average, with softness noted on Lincoln's hair and at the wheat ears; this is probably caused by die wear rather than a lack of striking pressure. Die wear becomes a noticeable characteristic when dies continue to be used after they've essentially worn out. A scattering of tiny flecks on both surfaces probably accounts for the modest MS63 grade designation, but these are scarcely noticeable without magnification. (#2500)

Choice Uncirculated 1917-S Cent

20759 **1917-S MS64 Red and Brown NGC.** Satiny luster. Both surfaces are about 40 percent red with delicate tan and violet. The majority of design features are boldly defined. A few tiny flecks are noted under magnification, but don't measurably impact the overall aesthetic quality. (#2503)

Collectible 1919-D Cent

20760 **1919-D MS64 Red and Brown NGC.** Satiny luster. The obverse is almost fully red. The reverse is about 50 percent red with blushes of tan and violet. Most design features are sharp save for the letters of E PLURIBUS UNUM which are softly defined. (#2518)

20761 **1920-D MS63 Red NGC.** Lustrous and vibrant, the surfaces are drenched in rich copper-gold and lemon coloration that is disturbed only by light carbon flecks. Nicely struck for a branch mint issue, although slightly soft over the highest points of the design. The carefully preserved surfaces only show a few wispy blemishes, on the lower reverse, and a small dark-green spot is noted between S and U of PLURIBUS UNUM. A partial fingerprint fragment is observed in the left obverse field. (#2527)

Pleasing 1920-S Lincoln Cent

20762 **1920-S MS64 Red and Brown NGC.** Pleasing satiny luster. The surfaces are about 50 percent red with delicate tan and violet iridescence in the remaining areas. On the obverse a touch of softness is noted above Lincoln's ear. On the reverse the upper half of O in ONE is softly struck as are the letters PLU in PLURIBUS. (#2529)

20763 **1921-S MS62 Brown NGC.** Medium brown surfaces display hints of faded orange-red. A mint-green tint is noted in the left obverse field. Softly struck on the reverse, but well detailed on the obverse, with no significant contact marks. Scattered flyspecks limit the grade. (#2534)

20764 **1922-D MS63 Red and Brown NGC.** Slightly soft on the obverse, as usual, but fully and crisply detailed on the reverse. A small clash mark (as struck) is noted just behind Lincoln's head, but the lustrous, well preserved surfaces seem almost entirely free of blemishes or contact marks. (#2538)

Elusive Gem 1924-D Cent

20765 **1924-D MS65 Red and Brown NGC.** Frosty luster. The surfaces are about 30 percent mint red with blushes of tan and violet. Lincoln's hair and beard shows striking softness as does the upper half of the O in ONE, but most of the other features are sharp. (#2553)

20766 **1924-S MS64 Brown NGC.** Well struck with full satiny luster and layers of purple-red and red-gold coloration over both sides. A couple of tiny nicks are detected on ON of ONE, under magnification. The obverse seems blemish-free. The coin is essentially carbon-free, save for a handful of scattered flyspecks on each side. An attractive near-Gem Lincoln cent. (#2555)

20767 **1925-S MS63 Brown NGC.** A significant amount of original mint red remains for a coin that is labeled as Brown. (#2564)

Near Full Red 1926-D Cent, MS64

20768 **1926-D MS64 Red and Brown NGC.** An attractive example that's almost fully red despite the "RB" designation on the NGC label. Magnification reveals a few tiny flecks, which were probably all that prevented NGC from assigning the MS65 designation to this beauty. (#2571)

20769 **1926-S MS62 Brown NGC.** Streaky brown patina on the obverse with strong, bright underlying mint red. The reverse is deep brown. (#2573)

20770 **1927-D MS64 Red and Brown NGC.** Well struck with a dusky overlay of brown patina and significant underlying mint red. (#2580)

Gem Uncirculated 1927-S Cent

20771 **1927-S MS65 Red and Brown NGC.** A satiny Gem example. Both surfaces are 50 percent mint red with blushes of vivid pink and blue. A scarce and desirable issue this nicely preserved. Census: 10 in 65, 1 finer (12/05). (#2583)

20772 **1931-S MS64 Red and Brown NGC.** Quite a bit of original mint red is still evident on each side of this important, low mintage semi-key issue. (#2619)

TWO CENT PIECES

Important 1864 Small Motto Two Cent Piece, Uncirculated Details

20773 **1864 Small Motto—Improperly Cleaned—NCS. Unc Details.** FS-000.5 Cleaned long ago and now retoned in a delicate lilac-brown shade with some blushes of deeper toning. Magnification reveals faint hairlines on both surfaces. The 1864 Small Motto is fully deserving of its status as a one-year design type, and some numismatists may acquire examples for that reason, but at present the 1864 Small Motto commands attention primarily because it's as a scarce *Guide Book* listed variety. (#3579)

Gem Uncirculated 1864 Large Motto Two Cent Piece

20774 **1864 Large Motto MS65 Brown NGC.** Fully lustrous. Violet brown surfaces with hints of faded mint red around the motifs. Most design features are sharp, save for the highpoints of two or three leaf clusters to the left of the shield. (#3576)

1865 Proof Two Cent Piece

20775 **1865 PR61 Brown NGC.** Variety with Plain 5 in date. Sharply struck. The obverse has mottled violet-brown toning with substantial amounts of faded red visible. The reverse is mostly red, in our opinion, with blushes of pale blue and violet. Close examination reveals some obverse spots. The two cent pieces of 1865 come in two formats, either with a "Plain" or "Fancy" 5 in the date. The *Guide Book* refers to these varieties as having "the tip of the 5 either plain or curved," respectively. Although the distinctions between the varieties have not created enormous attention in the numismatic community, alert two cent specialists frequently desire to obtain attractive examples of both types. (#3627)

1866 Two Cent Piece With Unc Details

20776 **1866—Improperly Cleaned—NCS. Unc Details.** Muted luster. The surfaces are about 25 percent red with blushes and splashes of lilac iridescence and charcoal gray toning. A small spot is noted in the field beneath EN in CENTS. (#3588)

Outstanding 1867 Two Cent Piece MS64 Brown NGC

20777 **1867 MS64 Brown NGC.** Predominantly violet-brown surfaces with generous amounts of faded mint red still visible despite the "BN" designation on the NGC label. Most design features show bold definition. Outstanding eye appeal for the grade. (#3591)

1868 Two Cent Piece Unc Details NCS

20778 **1868—Altered Color—NCS. Unc Details.** Mostly red surfaces with blushes of pink-violet. The devices are frosty and the fields are satiny. The majority of design features are boldly and deeply defined. (#3597)

Pleasing 1869 Two Cent Piece MS64 Brown NGC

20779 **1869 MS64 Brown NGC.** Mostly brown surfaces with delicate blue and violet highlights. Substantial amounts of faded mint brilliance can be seen despite the "BN" designation on the NGC label. Most design features show bold definition, and both the obverse and reverse exhibit pleasing satiny luster. (#3603)

Proof 1870 Two Cent Piece PR64 Red and Brown NGC

20780 **1870 PR64 Red and Brown NGC.** Sharply struck and attractive. The obverse is almost fully mint red. The reverse is about 30% red, with sea-green and violet iridescence in the remaining areas. Although the proof mintage for 1870 is not known with certainty, 1,000 pieces is the production figure usually reported. (#3643)

1871 Two Cent Piece PR64 Red and Brown NGC

20781 **1871 PR64 Red and Brown NGC.** The obverse is essentially faded red. The reverse is about 50% red with blushes of blue and violet. Most design features are about as sharp as could be desired. Perhaps as few as 960 proof two cent pieces were produced during the year; this is the mintage figure for silver proof sets dated 1871, and presumably the vast majority of proof 1871 two cent pieces now known were included in these sets. (#3646)

Scarce 1872 Two Cent Piece PR64 Red and Brown NGC

20782 **1872 PR64 Red and Brown NGC.** Both surfaces are predominantly blazing red, and the frosty devices contrast beautifully with the reflective fields. Most design features are about as sharp as could be desired. The 1872 is a scarce and desirable date. Only 65,000 two cent pieces were minted during the year, and perhaps as few as 950 of these were proofs. These were made for inclusion in the silver proof sets of the year, together with cents, trimes, half dimes, dimes, quarters, half dollars, and dollars. (#3649)

Gem Proof 1873 Closed 3 Two Cent Piece

20783 **1873 Closed 3 PR65 Red and Brown NGC.** Two cent pieces dated 1873 were issued in two formats: either with a "Closed 3" in the date, which numeral resembles an "8," or with an "Open 3," which is not likely to be confused with any other numeral. Both types were produced in proof format only and have mintages estimated at a scant 600 pieces and 500 pieces, respectively. The 1873 is unquestionably the scarcest and most eagerly sought date in the two cent series, although the issues of 1864 are actually rarer in proof quality. Both surfaces are essentially faded mint red with blushes of delicate blue and green. Virtually all design features are boldly and deeply delineated. Here's a delightful Gem example coined during the final year of the two cent denomination. (#3652)

THREE CENT SILVER

Gem 1851 Three Cent Silver

20784 **1851 MS65 NGC.** Light chestnut-gray toning drapes this shimmering and attractively preserved Gem. Not fully struck in the center of the shield, as usual for business strikes of the series, but the rest of the design is intricately delivered by the dies. The Three Cent Silver was a billon denomination of necessity, since silver coins were absent from circulation in the early 1850s. An influx of California-mined gold made the yellow metal less valuable relative to silver, which became hoarded. (#3664)

Lustrous Gem 1851-O Silver Three-Cent Piece

20785 **1851-O MS65 NGC.** Both by size and by weight, these are the smallest coins produced by the United States Mint. The silver three-cent pieces are also the lowest denomination precious metal coinage produced in this country. Notable as the only trime issue coined at the New Orleans Mint, or for that matter, at any branch mint. Just 720,000 were struck. Frosty luster. Both surfaces exhibit delicate ivory-gray toning with wisps and tinges of golden brown. The strike is about average for the issue showing some areas of softness. The shield outline on the obverse as well as some of the ornamentation on the reverse are rather indistinct. (#3665)

Popular 1851-O Three Cent Silver MS65

20786 **1851-O MS65 NGC.** Gentle sky-blue and honey tints endow this lustrous and lovely Gem. Only a hint of softness on the center of the horizontal shield lines, and a few trivial grazes are near the denomination. The sole branch mint issue of the Three Cent denomination, which otherwise was struck solely at Philadelphia during its long run in silver (1851 to 1873) and copper-nickel (1865 to 1889). Census: 46 in 65, 14 finer (12/05). (#3665)

Attractive Near Gem 1852 Three Cents

20787 **1852 MS64 NGC.** The 1852 Three Cent Silver is the first issue of any denomination to have a mintage above 10 million pieces. In fact, the production exceeded 18.6 million pieces, all needed in commerce to replace hoarded silver. Not surprisingly, the 1852 is not rare in Mint State, but the present satiny pearl-gray and tan near-Gem would nonetheless improve most type sets. The strike is a bit soft in the centers, where it exhibits light mint-made roller marks. The preservation, however, is exemplary. Envelope Included. (#3666)

Dynamic Gem 1852 Three Cent Silver

20788 **1852 MS65 NGC.** Dazzling luster illuminates this gently toned cream-gray example. Better struck than usual for the type, but it is the impressively clean surfaces that ensure classification as a Gem. Struck from lightly clashed dies. The Three Cent Silver is similar to other obsolete denominations, such as the Three Cent Nickel and the Two Cent and Twenty Cent Pieces, in that mintages were high when the denomination was first introduced, but fell to minimal levels by the end of the series. (#3666)

Cherrypicker's Variety 1854 Three Cent Silver, FS-004, "85/85" Overdate

20789 **1854 85/85 MS62 NGC.** FS-004. Pewter gray toning complements the centers, while wisps and tinges of electric blue ornament the rims. Most design features are sharp, save for two or three of the reverse stars, which are flat. The most distinctive feature of the variety is a knob of an extra 5 in the space between the 8 and 5 in the date. The variety is illustrated in *Walter Breen's Complete Encyclopedia,* on page 273. (#3670)

Prooflike (Proof?) 1855 Silver Three Cent Piece

20790 **1855 Doubled Date. MS64 Prooflike NGC.** Breen-2920. The presently offered example constitutes a vexing conundrum for the numismatist: was it made as a proof or is it simply a prooflike business strike? There would probably be no consensus among experienced numismatists. Those supporting a proof attribution would emphasize the mirror fields and cameo contrast as mentioned above; those favoring a prooflike attribution would point to softness at the base of the date and the flatness of some of the peripheral reverse stars. Lamentably, this is just one of many numismatic questions that will probably never be resolved to everyone's satisfaction. A handsome example toned in intermingled hues of blue and gold. The fields are reflective and the devices show substantial cameo contrast. Despite the considerable peripheral weakness that flattens the lower part of the date, considerable doubling is visible, more than is seen on most business strike examples of this date. Jules Reiver included this as part of his collection of proof three-cent silver pieces. (#3671)

1856 Three Cent Silver MS63 NGC

20791 **1856 MS63 NGC.** Golden-gray toning complements the satiny surfaces. The obverse die was evidently lapped before the present piece was struck because some of the low-relief details of the central star motif have disappeared. Most of the central design features of the reverse are sharp; the peripheral stars, however, are flat. (#3672)

Scarce Proof Issue 1856 Three Cent Silver PR64 NGC

20792 **1856 PR64 NGC.** Slightly bent. The frosty devices complement the reflective fields. Most design features show bold definition. Warmly and attractively toned in vivid hues of blue, violet, and gold. Scarce and desirable as indeed are all U.S. proof issues minted prior to 1858. Probably no more than a few dozen proof 1856 trimes could be accounted for. (#3703)

1857 Three Cent Silver MS63 NGC

20793 **1857 MS63 NGC.** Lustrous surfaces. Pewter gray toning with hints of gold, blue, and violet. Some faint clash marks can be seen on the reverse. The strike is typical, with a few areas of softness noted. Envelope Included. (#3673)

See the Online Session listings in the back of this volume for additional Reiver selections.

Gem Proof 1857 Silver Three Cent Piece

20794 **1857 PR65 NGC.** If you are searching for trimes that combine the dual attributes of rarity and beauty, your search stops here. Although Proofs minted in 1857 and earlier years appear at auction occasionally, they are not offered anywhere near as frequently as those dated 1858 or later. Even including 1858-dated examples, few Proofs of the Type II design survive today. Numismatics was in its infancy prior to 1858, and surviving proofs of the era are well deserving of their status as the "caviar" of numismatics. A splendid Gem example that commands admiration on both technical and aesthetic grounds. The design elements are sharp and frosty, while the fields are glittering mirrors. The obverse has delightful golden-gray iridescence at the center with pink and electric blue peripherally. The reverse exhibits stunning azure toning. Prominent diagonal die striae covers the obverse fields. (#3704)

Proof Near-Gem 1858 Three Cent Silver

20795 **1858 PR64 NGC.** Smoky gray toning, with vivid blue, violet, and gold iridescent highlights. Most design features are boldly and deeply defined save for some of the tiny stars at the reverse periphery. Although the proof mintage is not known with certainty, it may have been as small as 300 pieces. (#3705)

Desirable Choice Proof 1858 Three Cent Silver

20796 **1858 PR64 NGC.** A fully struck and prominently mirrored near-Gem, lightly toned and of even nicer quality than the grade implies. The double outline to the star is attenuated and (in places) broken near its southwest corner, as made. 1858 was the first year that proofs were struck for collectors. By coincidence, it was also the final year of the Type Two design for the Three Cent Silver. Thus, proof type demand is very strong for the present piece, from a low estimated production of 300+ pieces. (#3705)

Proof 1860 Three Cent Silver Unc Details

20797 **1860—Scratched—NCS. Unc Details.** The central areas are brilliant, while golden-brown and electric blue iridescence complements the borders. Close examination reveals some fine scratches on the reverse. (#3709)

Proof 1861 Three Cent Silver

20798 **1861—Bent—NCS. Proof.** Sharply struck. Delicate golden-gray surfaces, with pale blue and violet iridescent highlights. Both the obverse and reverse exhibit substantial cameo contrast. Slightly bent, but in all other respects very attractive. (#3710)

Lovely Premium Gem 1862 Three Cent Silver MS66 NGC

20799 **1862 MS66 NGC.** Frosty and attractive. Appealing dusky gray toning with delicate pink, blue, and gold iridescent highlights. The strike is about average for the issue with some areas of softness noticed at the highpoints of the design. Here's a lovely example; certainly among the finest trimes that Jules Reiver ever acquired for his collection. (#3680)

1862 Three Cent Silver MS64 NGC

20800 **1862 MS64 NGC.** Frosty luster. Mottled blue, golden-brown, and pewter gray toning. Probably not as sharply struck as the majority of specimens seen. Envelope Included. (#3680)

1862 Three Cent Silver MS62 NGC

20801 **1862 MS62 NGC.** Struck from lightly clashed dies. Both the obverse and reverse exhibit pronounced prooflike character. The strike is about average showing boldness in some areas and softness in others. Vivid golden-brown, blue, and violet toning complements both surfaces. (#3680)

1862/1 Three Cent Silver MS63 NGC

20802 **1862/1 MS63 NGC.** The devices are frosty and the fields are satiny. Both the obverse and reverse have delicate pewter gray toning. Pale golden-brown iridescence complements the obverse border. The strike is about average showing softness at the base of the shield on the obverse and at the laurel branch on the reverse. (#3681)

1863 Three Cent Silver PR61 NGC

20803 **1863 PR61 NGC.** Sharply struck. Delicate pewter gray toning overall, with wisps of pale gold at the obverse border. Some faint hairlines in the fields account for the assigned grade. Only 460 trimes were issued in 1863. When one considers the fact that many were ultimately spent and melted, while others ended up in jewelry, the question that arises is: how many still survive today? (#3712)

Important Proof 1863/2 Three Cent Rarity

20804 **1863/2 PR64 NGC.** The 1863/2 Overdate is a scarce and desirable variety that comprises just a small portion of the 460 proof trimes issued during the year. This is more correctly described as 1863/1862. All four digits are sharply doubled below. Walter Breen suggested that these Proof overdates were actually struck in 1864, based on his observations of die states. Regardless of their time of production, today the 1863/2 Proof overdates are quite rare. Sharply struck with intermingled vivid blue and violet iridescence. The obverse (especially) and reverse exhibit bold cameo contrast underneath the toning. Envelope Included. (#3713)

Pleasing 1863/2 Three Cent Silver PR62 NGC

20805 **1863/2 PR62 NGC.** A bold strike with virtually all design features showing full definition. The devices are frosty and the fields are reflective. Warmly toned in intermingled hues of navy blue and charcoal gray. Faint golden overtones can be seen on the reverse. The overall aesthetic quality is high for the grade. (#3713)

Scarce Proof 1864 Three Cent Silver PR61 NGC

20806 **1864 PR61 NGC.** Sharply struck. The centers are brilliant with wisps of blue and violet at the rims. The 1864 ranks as a scarce and highly-esteemed date. (#3714)

Low Mintage Proof 1864 Three Cent Silver PR64 NGC

20807 **1864 PR64 NGC.** Sharply struck. The frosty devices contrast nicely with the mirror fields. The obverse has intermingled gold and violet toning at the center, changing to blue at the border. The reverse exhibits intermingled hues of blue, lilac, and gold. The 1864 is a desirable, scarce issue having a scant mintage of just 12,470 pieces, or which a mere 470 are proofs. Envelope included. (#3714)

1865 Three Cent Silver Unc Details

20808 **1865—Environmental Damage—NCS. Unc Details.** Struck from lightly clashed dies. Most design features are sharp and the fields are reflective, a combination that would lead many numismatists to classify the presently offered piece as a proof; indeed, the distinction between proofs and prooflike business strikes is frequently more of an art than a science, and numismatic experts can often disagree when it comes to borderline cases. Envelope included. (#3685)

1865 Three Cent Silver PR63 NGC

20809 **1865 PR63 NGC.** Sharply struck with brilliant surfaces. Magnification reveals some faint hairlines in the fields. A mere 8,500 trimes were issued during the year, a figure which includes a scant 500 proofs. By this point in history trimes had shown themselves to be unpopular with the public, and there was little demand for them in the channels of commerce. This factor, together with the shortage of specie in the years following the Civil War and the creation of the larger and more convenient nickel three cent denomination, eventually doomed the trime to oblivion. The silver three cent denomination continued to stagger along for a few more years until 1873, at which time it was finally abolished. (#3715)

Nicely Toned 1866 Three Cent Silver PR64 NGC

20810 **1866 PR64 NGC.** Blushes of vivid blue, lilac, and gold iridescence enhance both the obverse and reverse. The devices are sharp and the fields are nicely reflective. Envelope Included. (#3716)

Visually Enticing 1866 Three Cent Silver PR64 Cameo NGC

20811 **1866 PR64 Cameo NGC.** A delightful example that exhibits glittering mirror fields and sharp, frosty design elements. The obverse has pleasing golden toning at the center, with blue and violet peripherally. The reverse is mostly brilliant with tinges of electric blue at the rim. Although, it's possible that the patient numismatist would be able to find a technically finer specimen, it's doubtful that a more aesthetically pleasing example could be found. (#83716)

1867 Three Cent Silver MS62 NGC

20812 **1867 MS62 NGC.** Intermingled gold, lilac, and blue iridescence. Wisps of charcoal-gray toning can be seen at the borders. The devices are frosty and the fields are lightly reflective. Most design features are sharply defined. The 1867 has one of the lowest mintages in the silver three cent series, just 4,625 pieces, a figure which consists of 4,000 business strikes together with 625 proofs. Although the mintage figure for business strikes was greater than for proofs, most of the proofs were saved, while the majority of business strikes would have ended up being spent and subsequently redeemed and melted; accordingly, Uncirculated business strikes often command bids substantially higher than can be obtained for proofs of a corresponding grade. Envelope Included. (#3687)

Proof 1867 Three Cent Silver

20813 **1867—Stained—NCS. Proof.** The obverse exhibits delicate champagne iridescence and bold cameo contrast. The reverse sports deep golden-gray toning, a feature which has caused the mirror quality of the field to be subdued. Perhaps this is an example that could benefit from being carefully "dipped" in order to restore the coin to its original appearance. (#3717)

Toned Proof 1868 Silver Three Cent Piece

20814 **1868 PR63 NGC.** Vivid blue, pink, and gold iridescence. Virtually all design features are fully and deeply defined, save for one or two leaves on the reverse olive sprig. (#3718)

Choice Proof 1868 Silver Three Cent Piece

20815 **1868 PR64 NGC.** This issue ranks as a scarce date with a scant mintage of just 4,100 pieces, of which only 600 were proofs. Sharply struck and essentially brilliant with just a hint of pale gold color on the obverse and golden-gray toning on the reverse. The obverse, in particular, shows bold cameo contrast. (#83718)

1869 Three Cent Silver Unc Details

20816 **1869—Bent—NCS. Unc Details.** Sharply struck. Virtually all design features show bold definition. Both surfaces exhibit warm blue, golden-gray, and lilac toning. A desirable issue with a scant mintage of just 5,100 pieces. Envelope Included. (#3719)

Important Proof 1869 Silver Three Cent Variation

20817 **1869 PR64 NGC.** Extra metal within both the 6 and the 9 suggests either a doubled date, or an overdate, listed as either Breen-2958 or 2960, depending on which variety this is. The shape of this extra metal leads us to believe that this is the doubled 69 variety, and not the elusive overdate, however, others may disagree. A bold strike with virtually all design features defined to full advantage. The obverse is mostly brilliant with a faint halo of champagne iridescence at the border. The reverse displays pale golden-gray toning. The obverse star and shield motif show delightful cameo contrast against the mirrored field. The 1869 ranks as a scarce issue, as indeed are all dates in the silver three-cent series between 1863 and 1873 inclusive. A mere 5,100 trimes were minted in 1869 of which only 600 were proofs. (#83719)

1870 Three Cent Silver Proof

20818 **1870—Bent—NCS. Proof.** Essentially brilliant in the central area with wisps and tinges of golden-brown and electric blue at the borders. Virtually all design features are as sharp as could be desired. A mere 4,000 examples were coined, including 1,000 proofs; one of the lowest production figures of the silver three cent denomination. (#83721)

Lovely Toned Proof 1870 Three Cent Silver

20819 **1870 PR63 NGC.** Deeply and attractively toned in hues of electric blue, orange-gold, pink, and violet. Virtually all design features are boldly and wonderfully defined. Only 4,000 trimes were coined in 1870, a figure which includes a mere 1,000 proofs. (#3721)

Mint State 1871 Three Cent Silver

20820 **1871 MS63 NGC.** Warmly and attractively toned in intermingled hues of blue, pink, and orange gold. Although some numismatists may view the presently offered piece as a proof, the evidence that it's a prooflike business strike is compelling; there are certain areas of softness that would routinely be sharply defined on proofs: the horizontal lines of the azure portion of the shield are not fully struck, the bow binding the bundle of arrows is soft, and there's flatness on the "I" elements in the denomination. We cheerfully concede that this piece is a borderline case, and we acknowledge that there will often be room for disagreement when it comes to making distinctions between proofs and prooflike business strikes. This example and the MS64 graded piece offered herein are both from the same pair of dies, exhibiting identical die polishing lines within the vertical spaces of the shield on the obverse. (#3722)

Proof 1872 Three Cent Silver

20822 **1872—Reverse Stained—NCS. Proof.** The obverse is essentially brilliant with pale gold at the border. The reverse exhibits warm golden-gray toning with the result that the mirror brilliance of the reverse field is subdued. Presumably, this is the basis for the NCS designation that the reverse is stained. Perhaps this piece would benefit from further conservation in order to restore the original blazing appearance. (#3723)

Prooflike Mint State 1871 Three Cent Piece

20821 **1871 MS64 NGC.** The central areas are brilliant with wisps and blushes of gold and blue at the borders. Here we have another example of a borderline case: are we looking at a proof or a prooflike business strike? The presence of frosty devices and mirrorlike fields suggests a proof designation, while certain strike characteristics, i.e. softness in the horizontal lines in the azure portion of the obverse shield and softness at the bow binding the bundle of arrows on the reverse, suggests that this is actually a prooflike business strike. Another factor that suggests this piece's business strike status is that the reverse shows a texture in some areas that is actually intermediate between mirrorlike and satiny. A mere 4,360 trimes were minted in 1871, and high-grade business strikes often command bids that are higher than those for proofs of a corresponding grade. Regarding the mintage, the Guidebook lists a total of 4,360 coins while Walter Breen's *Complete Encyclopedia* places the quantity at 100 less pieces. (#3722)

1872 Three Cent Silver PR63 NGC

20823 **1872 PR63 NGC.** The frosty design elements contrast nicely with the mirror fields. Warmly and attractively toned in intermingled hues of blue, gold, and violet. Most design features are sharp with the exception of a few of the tiny star elements at the reverse border, which show flatness at their centers. A mere 1,950 trimes were minted during the year, the second lowest production figure for any date in the denomination after the proof-only 1873. Envelope Included. (#3723)

Final Year Proof 1873 Three Cent Silver Closed 3

20824 **1873 Closed 3—Stained—NCS. Proof.** Pale golden-gray toning with attractive cameo contrast. Most design features are sharp. Beauty is in the eye of the beholder, and what one numismatist would regard as a "stain," another would simply regard as attractive "toning." There have been innumerable articles in the numismatic press over the years as to whether or not toning is a desirable feature on silver coins. Although there will probably never be a consensus on the issue, many collectors have come to regard toning as an aesthetic quality that contributes to pride of ownership. Only 600 trimes were minted in 1873, all of them proofs. Coined during the final year of the design type. (#83724)

Low Mintage Proof 1873 Three Cent Silver Closed 3

20825 **1873 Closed 3—Bent—NCS. Proof.** Sharply struck with pronounced cameo contrast. The central areas exhibit electric blue iridescence changing to gold and violet at the borders. A scarce and desirable proof-only issue. Only 600 examples were minted, by far the smallest output for any date in the entire silver three-cent series. Envelope Included. (#3724)

THREE CENT NICKELS

1866 Three Cent Nickel PR64 NGC

20826 **1866 PR64 NGC.** Pale golden-gray toning. The devices are sharp and frosty and the fields are nicely reflective. Magnification reveals a few tiny flecks which have virtually no impact on the overall aesthetic appeal of this beauty. Envelope Included. (#3762)

1866 Three Cent Nickel PR63 NGC

20827 **1866 PR63 NGC.** The devices are frosty and the fields are nicely reflective. Both surfaces exhibit delicate honey gold toning. Close examination reveals a few tiny flecks, which are probably all that prevented NGC from assigning a substantially higher grade. (#3762)

Pleasing 1867 Near-Gem Proof Three Cent Nickel

20828 **1867 PR64 NGC.** A melange of tan-gold and lime-green toning bathes luminous surfaces. The lines in all three pillars of the III are weakly struck, but the remaining design elements are well brought up. The surfaces of this Near-Gem Proof have been well preserved. An overall pleasing specimen. (#3763)

Near-Gem Proof 1868 Three Cent Nickel

20829 **1868 PR64 NGC.** Golden-gray surfaces exhibit sharply struck design elements, and reveal just a few minute ticks on the pillars of the III. A few minute spots are scattered over each side. (#3764)

Lovely Cameo Near-Gem Proof 1869 Three Cent Nickel

20830 **1869 PR64 Cameo NGC.** Essentially brilliant surfaces with just a hint or champagne and lilac iridescence. As indicated by the "cameo" designation on the NGC label, the sharp frosty design elements contrast boldly with the glittering mirror fields. (#83765)

Crisply Struck Proof 1870 Three Cent Nickel

20831 **1870 PR62 NGC.** Bright, milky-gray surfaces display sharply struck design elements. A light pinscratch-like mark (possibly from a staple) travels horizontally across the first two uprights of the III, and some inoffensive wispy hairlines are noted on Liberty's cheek and neck. (#3766)

1871 Three Cent Nickel PR64 NGC

20832 **1871 PR64 NGC.** Sharply struck with attractive golden-gray toning. The devices are frosty and the fields, although reflective, are somewhat subdued, as is frequently the case for many proof nickel three-cent and five-cent pieces of the era. (#3767)

20833 **1872 PR63 NGC.** Reflective pale gray surfaces with hints of champagne toning. (#3768)

1873 Three Cent Nickel Closed 3 PR63 NGC

20834 **1873 Closed 3 PR63 NGC.** The obverse is brilliant with bold cameo contrast. The reverse exhibits pale golden-gray toning. A tiny fleck beneath the 8 in the date is mentioned more for purposes of identification than for any other reason. Although both "Closed 3" and "Open 3" varieties are known for the date, all proofs seen are of the "Closed 3" type. (#3769)

Pleasing 1873 Closed 3 Three Cent Nickel, PR64 NGC

20835 **1873 Closed 3 PR64 NGC.** Semi-bright light gray, frosty surfaces display well struck design features reveal just a few minor, grade-defining handling marks. A minute fleck in the hair at Liberty's temple is mentioned for accuracy. A pleasing Near-Gem Proof. Envelope Included. (#3769)

See the Online Session listings in the back of this volume for additional Reiver selections.

1874 Proof Three Cent Nickel

20836 **1874—Environmental Damage—NCS. Proof.** Gunmetal gray toning with pleasing gold and lilac iridescent highlights. Close examination reveals evidence of a uniform micro-porosity on both surfaces, something which may have resulted if the piece had been dipped in a cyanide solution many years ago. During parts of the 19th and 20th centuries, cyanide was used by some collectors to remove toning and oxidation from their numismatic treasures. In addition to damaging the coins, at least one celebrated numismatist of yesteryear, J. Sanford Saltus, is said to have died when he accidentally took a sip of cyanide instead of ginger ale, while he was cleaning some of his coins. Envelope Included. (#3770)

1874 Three Cent Nickel PR65 NGC

20837 **1874 PR65 NGC.** Essentially brilliant surfaces with just a whisper of pewter gray iridescence. Although the word LIBERTY on Liberty's coronet is softly defined, most other design features are about as sharp as could be desired. (#3770)

1875 Three Cent Nickel PR64 NGC

20838 **1875 PR64 NGC.** Delicate golden-gray iridescence complements both surfaces. A small die chip on Liberty's cheek has an appearance of an imperfectly shaped "1." The obverse shows bold cameo contrast, while on the reverse, the mirror-quality of the field is partially subdued. This is a feature that is typical of many nickel three cent pieces seen. Evidently the minters were often eager to maintain the blazing mirror-quality of the obverse, but tended to ignore the subdued mirror-quality of the reverse. Since nickel is a very hard metal, it is likely that the dies would have required polishing after just a few hundred impressions in order to insure that the fields maintained their deep reflectivity. This is a step that the Mint evidently didn't always have the time or inclination to take. (#3771)

Elusive Uncirculated 1876 Three Cent Nickel

20839 **1876 MS62 NGC.** Well struck, with light gray surfaces that reveal a few obverse specks. Envelope Included. (#3744)

Outstanding 1876 Gem Proof Three Cent Nickel

20840 **1876 PR65 NGC.** The devices are sharp and frosty. The obverse is brilliant with pronounced cameo contrast. The reverse exhibits pale golden toning. Magnification reveals a fine lintmark on Liberty's cheek. Here's an outstanding example both technically and aesthetically, and worthy of a generous bid as such. (#3772)

Proof-Only 1877 Three Cent Nickel PR64 NGC

20841 **1877 PR64 NGC.** Essentially brilliant surfaces with just a hint of pewter gray. The devices are sharp and frosty, and the fields are glittering mirrors. Although there is no "cameo" designation on the NGC label, we feel that this coin well deserves to be regarded as such. The 1877 ranks as a celebrated proof-only issue. Although the mintage is not known with certainty, the usually reported figure is 510 pieces. Envelope Included. (#83773)

1877 Three Cent Nickel PR64 NGC

20842 **1877 PR64 NGC.** Sharply struck with frosty devices. The fields are nicely-reflective mirrors. Both surfaces are essentially brilliant with just a whisper of pale gold on the reverse. Here's a lovely example that we regard as worthy of a "cameo" designation, although not certified as such by NGC. (#3773)

1878 Three Cent Nickel PR35 NGC

20843 **1878 PR35 NGC.** Lilac-gray toning with pale champagne iridescent highlights. This piece presumably commenced its existence as a component in an 1878 proof set, but because of financial difficulties, or some other reason, the coin ended up being spent; alternatively, it may have served someone as a lucky pocket piece. Eventually, after many years, it acquired the appearance of a heavily-circulated business strike. The fact that 1878 is a proof-only issue, is the only clue that indicates that the piece offered here was ever anything other than a coin intended for circulation. Envelope Included. (#3774)

Scarce 1878 Three Cent Nickel PR64 NGC

20844 **1878 PR64 NGC.** Delicate golden gray toning. The devices are sharp and frosty and the fields are nicely reflective. Distinguished by the presence of a tiny toning spot beneath the 8 in the date. Here's a proof-only issue with a mintage of just 2,350 pieces, one of the two lowest production figures in the nickel three-cent series; only the 1877 is rarer. (#3774)

1879 Three Cent Nickel PR65 NGC

20845 **1879 PR65 NGC.** The devices are frosty and the fields are nicely reflective. Most design features are sharp, save for some of the high-relief foliage details on the right side of the reverse wreath. Both surfaces exhibit delicate golden-gray iridescence. (#3775)

20846 **1879 PR62 NGC.** Semi-reflective fields offer a mild contrast with the frosty devices that exhibit excellent definition throughout. A thin layer of light gray patina bathes unabraded surfaces. A small carbon spot is noted at 2 o'clock on the obverse rim. Envelope Included. (#3775)

Appealing Proof 1880 Three Cent Nickel PR63 NGC

20847 **1880 PR63 NGC.** Appealing pewter gray iridescence. Die polishing on the reverse has caused the ribbon tips and bow to become detached from the wreath. The design elements are frosty and the fields have a texture intermediate between satiny and mirrorlike, a characteristic frequently encountered on nickel proofs of the era. A small spot between the 2nd and 3rd "I" elements in the denomination is mentioned for accuracy's sake. Envelope Included. (#3776)

Gem Proof 1880 Three Cent Nickel

20848 **1880 PR65 NGC.** Attractive golden-gray toning. Die polishing on the reverse has caused the ribbon tips to become separated from the wreath, and some of the other low-relief design features are vestigial. The devices are frosty and the fields are reflective. (#3776)

Attractive 1881 Three Cent Nickel, PR64 NGC

20849 **1881 PR64 NGC.** All of the design elements are well brought up on this grayish-tan near-Gem Proof. Luminous surfaces are devoid of significant contact marks or numerous unsightly spots. This piece possesses decent technical and aesthetic quality. (#3777)

20850 **1882—Improperly Cleaned—NGC. XF Details.** Light gray surfaces reveal fine hairlines. The design elements are well detailed throughout. Envelope Included. (#3750)

Near-Gem Proof 1882 Three Cent Nickel

20851 **1882 PR64 NGC.** Pale golden toning with delicate champagne iridescent highlights. The frosty design elements contrast nicely with the reflective fields. Very pleasing from the aesthetic perspective. (#3778)

1883 Three Cent Nickel PR64 NGC

20852 **1883 PR64 NGC.** Appealing golden-gray toning. The devices are frosty. The fields are reflective, but not deeply so. Magnification reveals a scattering of tiny flecks on the obverse, which probably accounts for why NGC didn't assign the PR65 designation. Proof nickel three cent pieces reached an apex in popularity this year; 6,609 proofs were minted, an enormous figure compared with most of the other dates in the series. Envelope Included. (#3779)

Gem Proof 1883 Three Cent Nickel

20853 **1883 PR65 NGC.** Brilliant surfaces. The devices are sharp and frosty and the fields are reflective, but aren't deep mirrors. A few tiny flecks can be seen under low magnification. (#3779)

Premium Gem Proof 1884 Three Cent Nickel

20854 **1884 PR66 NGC.** Proof examples of this date, like many during the 1880s, are much more common than business strikes. Look at the mintages for example. The Philadelphia Mint struck 1,700 business strikes and 3,942 Proofs. While very few of the former survived, most of the latter still exist today. The typical Proof example has somewhat dull surfaces, even less vivid than this coin. Many of those dull Proof examples have been confused with business strikes in the past. This example, like most Proof survivors, has subdued nickel-gray surfaces, but the strike is essentially full. The devices are lustrous, and the fields are slightly mirrored. Wispy gold toning complements both sides, and the surfaces are pristine and unblemished. (#3780)

1884 Three Cent Nickel PR63 NGC

20855 **1884 PR63 NGC.** Essentially brilliant. The devices are frosty and the fields are glittering mirrors. Scattered spots and flecks on both surfaces account for the assigned grade and prompt us to suggest in-person examination to prospective bidders. Envelope Included. (#3780)

1885 Three Cent Nickel PR64 NGC

20856 **1885 PR64 NGC.** Warm golden-gray toning. The devices are frosty, while the mirror-quality of the fields is partially subdued, possibly because of the toning. Envelope Included. (#3781)

1885 Three Cent Nickel PR64 NGC

20857 **1885 PR64 NGC.** Delicate champagne iridescence. The devices are sharp with a texture intermediate between frosty and satiny. The fields are glittering mirrors. A tiny planchet flaw can be seen between the 2nd 8 and the 5 in the date, as made. A few trivial flecks are noted. (#3781)

1886 Three Cent Nickel PR64 NGC

20858 **1886 PR64 NGC.** Mostly brilliant surfaces with blushes of pale gold on the highpoints of the designs. The devices are frosty and the fields are reflective. The 1886 is a proof-only issue having a mintage of just 4,290 pieces. (#3782)

20859 **1886 PR62 NGC.** Light gray surfaces are imbued with whispers of powder-blue on the reverse, and dappled and streaky olive-green on the obverse. A moderate-sized carbon spot is visible at the point of Liberty's bust. Envelope Included. (#3782)

1887 Three Cent Nickel MS62 NGC

20860 **1887 MS62 NGC.** Medium gray toning complements subdued luster. The dentils are flatly struck between 10 o'clock and 2 o'clock at the obverse rim. A mere 7,961 nickel three cent pieces were coined in 1887. Survivors are eagerly sought in all grades and Uncirculated specimens are esteemed by specialists. Envelope Included. (#3755)

Gem Proof 1887/6 Three Cent Nickel

20863 **1887/6 PR65 NGC.** Pleasing delicate champagne iridescence. Vestiges of the 6 beneath the 7 are clear and prominent. The devices are frosty and the fields are nicely reflective. Faint clash marks can be seen on the reverse, an unusual feature for a proof impression. (#3784)

Gem Proof 1887 Three Cent Nickel

20861 **1887 PR65 NGC.** Appealing pewter-gray iridescence. The devices are frosty, and the fields are mostly reflective, although the mirror-quality of the reverse is subdued. Most design features are sharp, save for softness at the obverse rim between 10 o'clock and 1 o'clock, where the dentils are predominantly flat. (#3783)

1888 Three Cent Nickel PR64 NGC

20864 **1888 PR64 NGC.** Warm pewter gray toning with delicate champagne highlights. The devices are frosty, while the mirror-quality of the fields is subdued. A tiny fleck is noted to the left of the date. Envelope Included. (#3785)

1887/6 Three Cent Nickel PR63 NGC

20862 **1887/6 PR63 NGC.** Pale golden-gray iridescence. The overdate feature is clear with prominent vestiges of the 6 visible beneath the 7 in the date. The sharp frosty devices complement the reflective fields. Close examination reveals a scattering of flecks on the obverse which are probably all that prevented NGC from assigning the PR64 grade designation. Envelope Included. (#3784)

Pleasing Near-Gem Proof 1888 Three Cent Nickel

20865 **1888 PR64 NGC.** Essentially brilliant surfaces with just a hint of pale gold on the highpoints. The design elements are frosty, a feature which nicely complements the reflective fields. (#3785)

Attractive Near-Gem Proof 1889 Three Cent Nickel

20866 **1889 PR64 NGC.** Pale golden-gray toning ornaments the centers; the peripheries are brilliant. Striking softness is noted at the obverse rim between 10 o'clock and 1 o'clock, but most other design features are sharp. Excellent eye appeal for the grade. Envelope Included. (#3786)

Final Year Proof 1889 Three Cent Nickel PR64 NGC

20867 **1889 PR64 NGC.** Pale golden toning. The devices have a texture intermediate between satiny and frosty. The fields are glittering mirrors. Here's an aesthetic treat sure to find an appreciative home in the cabinet of an alert specialist. Coined during the final year of the three-cent denomination. (#3786)

SHIELD NICKELS

1866 Shield Nickel "Rays" PR64 NGC

20868 **1866 Rays PR64 NGC.** Delicate pewter gray surfaces. The devices are frosty and the fields are reflective, but not deeply so. Most design features are sharp, but slight striking softness is seen on the stripes of the shield and at the tips of the rays in the sunburst pattern around the numeral 5 in the denomination. Shield nickels with Rays are particularly important to collectors because of their status as a two-year design type. They were coined only in the years 1866 and 1867. The 25% nickel alloy used to produce five-cent pieces was new to the Philadelphia Mint in 1866, and it took several decades before the Mint was capable of reliably producing nickel proofs of the same high consistent quality as those made from silver and gold. Even as late as the 1870s and 1880s, nickel proofs were often minted that have subdued mirror brilliance. (#3817)

1867 Shield Nickel "Rays" MS63 NGC

20869 **1867 Rays MS63 NGC.** Pale golden-gray toning complements lustrous surfaces. The die state of the obverse is advanced with several fine die cracks visible. The obverse is sharp. On the reverse a few of the rays show softness at their tips, and some of the stars are flatly struck; almost all of them, however, show their radials. (#3791)

Boldly Impressed 1867 No Rays Near Gem Proof Nickel

20870 **1867 No Rays PR64 NGC.** The fields are moderately reflective, and accentuate the sharply struck design elements. Both sides are enveloped in light gold-tan and sky-blue patination, and reveal a few flecks here and there, as well as some unobtrusive contact marks on the upper part of the shield. NGC has certified 49 pieces finer (12/05). (#3821)

1868 Shield Nickel MS62 NGC

20871 **1868 MS62 NGC.** Somewhat subdued surfaces yield a light gray color and scattered russet toning spots. The design features are well defined, and there are no significant abrasions. Some wispy, unobtrusive slide marks are noted on the reverse. (#3795)

Choice Proof 1869 Shield Nickel

20872 **1869 PR64 NGC.** Bright gray Proof surface on the obverse with champagne toning on the reverse. Several spots are present on both sides, a couple larger ones on the obverse. (#3823)

Sharply Struck Near Gem Proof 1870 Nickel

20873 **1870 PR64 NGC.** The strike is sharp; virtually all design features show bold definition including the foliage elements on the obverse and the star radials on the reverse. The fields are reflective, but not deeply so, a feature characteristic of many proof nickels seen that were issued during the 1870s. A thin layer of sky-blue and beige patina covers both sides, and incorporates several tiny pepper-like spots. (#3824)

Pleasing Proof 1871 Shield Nickel PR62 NGC

20874 **1871 PR62 NGC.** Golden-gray and powder-blue surfaces exhibit mild reflectivity in the fields, which sets off the well struck motifs to present somewhat of a cameo-like effect when the coin is tilted beneath a light source. Charcoal-gray and russet toning spots are intermixed with some flyspecks. (#3825)

1872 Shield Nickel Doubled Die Obverse MS62 NGC

20875 **1872 MS62 NGC.** Doubled Die Obverse. FS-007. Warm golden-gray toning. The devices are frosty and the fields have a texture intermediate between mirrorlike and satiny. Virtually all design features exhibit bold definition including the reverse stars, all of which show their radials. The doubling on the obverse is perhaps most noticeable on the ring-element at the top of the shield, directly beneath the cross. (#3799)

Proof Strike 1873 Closed 3 Shield Nickel

20876 **1873 Closed 3 PR63 NGC.** Sharply struck with virtually all design features showing bold definition including the reverse stars, each of which exhibits its radials. Both surfaces are essentially brilliant with just a hint of pale gold on the highpoints. The devices are frosty and the fields are reflective, but not deeply so. Varieties with both "Closed 3" and "Open 3" are known for the date, but all proofs seen have the "Closed 3" feature. This example is an early strike with the digit 1 clearly recut. (#3827)

Centennial Year Proof 1876 Nickel

20879 **1876 PR63 NGC.** The design features are well impressed, and light gray surfaces are peppered with freckled charcoal-gray specks and a few carbon-like spots, especially on the obverse. There are no significant contact marks to report. (#3830)

Desirable Proof 1874 Shield Nickel

20877 **1874 PR63 NGC.** Partially brilliant with blushes of mottled gray and gold toning. Most design features are about as sharp as could be desired save for slight softness in some of the horizontal lines near the top of the azure portion of the shield. Close examination reveals some die polish lines on the reverse as made, something that inexperienced collectors will occasionally confuse with hairlines. The devices are frosty and the fields are reflective, but not as fully mirrorlike as one would expect to see on proof coins of the era. Short diagonal die lines are noted along the obverse border left of the date. (#3828)

20878 **1875 PR62 NGC.** Design elements are well impressed, save for minor softness in the horizontal shield lines. The obverse in particular reveals numerous russet toning and flyspeck-like spots. (#3829)

Important Proof-Only 1877 Shield Nickel

20880 **1877 PR63 NGC.** Pewter gray toning with delicate gold highlights. The devices are frosty, with most design features showing bold definition. The fields are reflective, but not deeply mirrored. A scattering of flecks on both sides is probably all that prevented NGC from assigning a considerably higher grade. Here's a desirable proof-only issue, with one of the lowest mintage figures in the entire nickel five-cent series. Prior to 1878, the quantity of Proof minor coins produced was not recorded. Although the actual mintage is not known with certainty, the usually reported figure is just 510 pieces, which represents the number that were included in the silver proof sets issued during the year; others were likely distributed individually. (#3831)

Popular Proof 1878 Shield Nickel

20881 **1878 PR63 NGC.** Pale golden-gray toning complements both the obverse and reverse. The design elements are frosty and most features show bold definition. The fields exhibit subdued mirror brilliance as is typical of many nickel proofs of the era. Evidently, the hardness of the nickel metal, unlike silver and gold, caused heavy wear to proof dies, making it difficult to maintain a consistent quality to the mirror finish in the fields. A scattering of flecks on both surfaces accounts for the assigned grade. A desirable proof-only issue with a scant mintage of just 2,350 pieces, the second lowest production figure of any date in the Shield nickel series after the 1877. (#3832)

Choice Proof 1879/8 Overdate Nickel

20882 **1879/8 PR64 NGC.** Pleasing pale golden toning. The devices are sharp and frosty and the fields are nicely reflective, having a texture that is intermediate between satiny and mirrorlike as is characteristic of many and perhaps most proof Shield nickels of the era. A few tiny flecks and spots are all that keep this beauty out of the PR65 category. Walter Breen classifies the variety as very scarce, and notes that it "forms a small minority of proofs." Our experience suggests that this overdate is actually the more available Proof variety of the year and is a wonderful candidate for the type collector. (#3833)

Choice Brilliant Proof 1880 Nickel

20883 **1880 PR64 NGC.** Lightly and evenly toned with nicely reflective mirrors in the fields. A few flyspecks are noted on each side. (#3835)

20884 **1881 PR62 NGC.** Sharply defined but only modestly reflective with numerous carbon spots. (#3836)

Gem Proof 1882 Shield Nickel

20885 **1882 PR65 NGC.** The obverse exhibits pale golden-gray toning. The reverse is pewter gray with delicate pink, blue, and gold iridescent highlights. Virtually all design features are boldly and deeply defined including the horizontal and vertical lines in the shield and the radials of the stars. The devices are frosty and the fields are reflective. Here's a Gem that would enhance virtually any cabinet of nickel five-cent issues. A small area of raised metal is located below the first 8 in the date, and has the appearance of a partially effaced digit. This should be examined carefully by Shield Nickel specialists. (#3837)

Lustrous Gem Mint State 1883 Shield Nickel

20886 **1883 MS66 NGC.** A lovely Gem example. The devices are sharp and frosty and the fields have a texture that is intermediate between satiny and prooflike. The central areas are brilliant, with just a whisper of pale gold at the borders. Coined during the final year of the Shield nickel design type. Late die state with several die cracks on both sides. The obverse is nearly void of border dentils. (#3813)

LIBERTY NICKELS

1883 Liberty Nickel "No Cents" PR64 NGC

20887 **1883 No Cents PR64 NGC.** A lovely example toned in intermingled pastel hues of gold and gray. The frosty devices nicely complement the reflective fields. Only 5,219 proofs of the variety were issued, and although some collectors may regard this as being a large proof mintage for the era, that perception is offset by the fact that the variety is an eagerly sought one-year design type. (#3878)

20888 **1883 With Cents PR63 NGC.** Exquisitely struck with medium olive-champagne toning. There are no significant contact marks to report. (#3881)

20889 **1884 PR63 NGC.** FS-13.8. The 1 in the date is boldly repunched. Rich golden-gray patina overall. Nicely struck and well preserved for the assigned grade. (#3882)

Key Date Gem Proof 1885 Liberty Nickel

20890 **1885 PR65 NGC.** Sharply struck with virtually all design features defined to full advantage including the obverse star radials, the kernels of corn, the veins in the cotton leaves, and the ears of grain. Both surfaces exhibit pewter gray toning with delicate pink, blue, and gold iridescent highlights. The motifs are frosty and contrast nicely with the reflective fields. Setting aside the extremely rare 1913, the 1885 ranks as the celebrated key issue of the series. We can't fathom the reason why the date is so scarce since the mintage figure of 1,476,490 pieces is low, but not low enough to explain the paucity of available specimens. Could it be that there is some error in the recorded mintage statistics for the issue? (#3883)

Proof Near-Gem 1886 Liberty Nickel

20891 **1886 PR64 NGC.** Sharply struck and attractive. The design elements are frosty and the fields are reflective. Both surfaces exhibit pewter gray toning with delicate pink, lilac, and gold iridescent highlights. A tiny spot beneath the N in CENTS is mentioned more for purposes of identification than for any other reason. (#3884)

20892 **1887 PR63 NGC.** Good reflectivity beneath moderate, multicolored patina that covers the majority of either side. Very nearly a Choice specimen. (#3885)

20893 **1888 PR63 NGC.** A non-reflective proof with a moderate coating of rose-gray toning. The details are quite sharp. (#3886)

20894 **1889 PR61 NGC.** Shallowly mirrored and at first glance looking like a fully struck business strike. Lovely multicolored toning covers each side. (#3887)

Proof 1890 Liberty Nickel PR64 NGC

20895 **1890 PR64 NGC.** Pale champagne iridescence. The devices are frosty and the fields are glittering mirrors. We would characterize this piece as a cameo example, but no such designation is present on the NGC label. A touch of striking softness is noted on the highpoints of Liberty's hair and the reverse wreath. Presumably, this piece was one of the first impressions from the dies, before the mirror fields began to lose their blazing reflectivity. (#83888)

20896 **1891 PR62 NGC.** Nicely toned and fully defined with just a few minor dark specks on the reverse. (#3889)

20897 **1892—Environmental Damage—NCS. Proof.** Boldly struck, some tiny specks of corrosion. (#3890)

20898 **1893 PR62 NGC.** Sharply struck, with medium gray-golden toning over the mirrored fields. A few light toning specks are noted on both sides. (#3891)

20899 **1894 PR63 NGC.** Moderate golden-tan and blue-green toning is seen over each side. Several flecks of carbon seem to limit the grade. (#3892)

See the Online Session listings in the back of this volume for additional Reiver selections.

Select Proof 1895 Nickel

20900 **1895 PR63 NGC.** moderately toned, a few olive, rose, and gold accents become visible as the coin is rotated in the light. A few specks of carbon are reported on the reverse. (#3893)

Sharp Choice Proof 1896 Liberty Nickel

20901 **1896 PR64 NGC.** The surfaces are fully mirrored and overlaid in soft yellow-gold and lavender hues. Well struck throughout. (#3894)

20902 **1897 PR63 NGC.** A lightly spotted coin with some milky, multicolored toning obscuring some of the mint reflectiveness. (#3895)

20903 **1898 PR63 NGC.** The nicely reflective surfaces shine powerfully through the rich, streaky antique-gold iridescence. A boldly defined Select example. (#3896)

20904 **1899 PR63 NGC.** Fully struck throughout, even on the left ear of corn, with surfaces that display a slightly variegated coating of gray-tan and golden patina over both sides. The opaque toning prevents the piece from being highly reflective, but it remains a smooth, attractive Select proof. (#3897)

20905 **1900 PR63 NGC.** Rich golden-gray toning is seen on each side of this modestly reflective Select proof example. (#3898)

20906 **1901 PR63 NGC.** Somewhat subdued because of a thin coating of hazy golden-gray patina, the surfaces of this proof Gem are still smooth and lovely. There are some scattered carbon flecks that serve to limit the grade. (#3899)

1902 Proof 63 Nickel

20907 **1902 PR63 NGC.** Sharp with moderately reflective surfaces and some light toning overall. Specks of carbon are reported on the reverse side. (#3900)

20908 **1903 PR63 NGC.** Delicate peach and dove-gray hues make this attractive piece all the more colorfully appealing. (#3901)

Proof Near-Gem 1909 Liberty Nickel

20909 **1909 PR64 NGC.** Intermingled lilac-gray and orange-gold toning complements the frosty devices and reflective fields. Most design features are sharp save for some tresses of hair above Liberty's temple. (#3907)

Near-Gem Proof 1910 Liberty Nickel

20910 **1910 PR64 NGC.** A bold strike with virtually all design features defined to full advantage. Attractively toned in delicate pastel hues of lilac-gray, pink, and gold. The devices are frosty and the fields have a texture intermediate between satiny and mirrorlike, a quality that imparts a subdued reflectivity. (#3908)

Low Mintage Gem Proof 1911 Liberty Nickel

20911 **1911 PR65 NGC.** A bold strike displaying pale gold, pink, and blue iridescence. Both surfaces, in our opinion, show pronounced cameo, but there is no such designation on the NGC label. The proof mintage of 1,733 pieces is one of the lowest production figures of the design type. (#3909)

Near-Gem 1912-D Liberty Nickel

20912 **1912-D MS64 NGC.** Lustrous surfaces. Medium gray toning with vivid blue, pink, and gold iridescent highlights. A few areas of striking softness are noted on the highpoints of the design. (#3874)

1912-S Liberty Nickel MS63 NGC

20913 **1912-S MS63 NGC.** Deep gunmetal gray toning with delicate pink, blue, and gold overtones. Most design features are sharp. The luster is largely subdued. Notable as the only Liberty nickel issue struck at the San Francisco Mint. Only 238,000 were coined, the second smallest production figure in the Liberty nickel series following the exceedingly rare 1913. (#3875)

BUFFALO NICKELS

20914 **1913 Type One MS65 NGC.** Pleasing golden-gray patina bathes lustrous surfaces that exhibit well struck design elements. Some pepper-like spots on each side are mentioned for accuracy. (#3915)

20915 **1913-S Type One MS63 NGC.** Bright, lustrous surfaces are toned light gold, and display well struck design elements, except for weakness in the tops of the letters in LIBERTY and in the lower digits of the date. A few grade-defining marks are noted on the Indian's cheek. An interesting die crack travels from the rim into the lower feather. (#3917)

20916 **1913-D Type Two AU58 NGC.** Relatively clean surfaces display golden-gray patination and sharply defined devices. A pleasing lightly circulated Type Two nickel. (#3922)

Scarce Type Two 1913-S Buffalo Nickel AU58 NGC

20917 **1913-S Type Two AU58 NGC.** Surprisingly lustrous for an AU coin, the surfaces are gray-olive and the striking details are a bit soft, especially on the reverse. Die wear is evident on each of the two sides. Scarce. (#3923)

Satiny Near-Gem 1914 Buffalo Nickel

20918 **1914 MS64 NGC.** Beautifully toned in even olive hues, the features are boldly, if not sharply struck in all areas. Scattered flyspecks prevent the Gem grade, but do little to disrupt the overall eye appeal of this satiny near-Gem. (#3924)

See the Online Session listings in the back of this volume for additional Reiver selections.

Conditionally Challenging 1914-D Buffalo Nickel MS63 NGC

20919 **1914-D MS63 NGC.** Both sides exhibit satiny luster and are tinted a delicate olive-gray with apricot-gold in the recessed areas. A challenging early Buffalo nickel issue at all levels, and a particularly high end example, for the grade. (#3925)

Conditionally Scarce 1914-S Buffalo Nickel MS64 NGC

20920 **1914-S MS64 NGC.** Well struck and displaying pleasing satiny mint luster accented by gray-gold toning on each side. Both obverse and reverse seem blemish-free. Scarce in near-Gem condition, and extremely difficult any finer. (#3926)

20921 **1915 MS64 NGC.** Golden-gray surfaces are imbued with faint ice-blue undertones, and exhibit sharply struck design features. A couple of minute flecks are noted on each side. (#3927)

Scarce 1915-S Buffalo Nickel MS63 NGC

20922 **1915-S MS63 NGC.** Well struck with rich olive coloration and mark-free surfaces that have a moderate number of scattered flyspecks on each side of the coin. The 1915-S is scarce above Fine condition, and especially so in Uncirculated grades. (#3929)

Attractive Near-Gem 1916 Buffalo Nickel

20923 **1916 MS64 NGC.** An attractive 1916 Buffalo nickel, fully lustrous and boldly struck. A bit of olive color is seen on each side. The unabraded surfaces reveal a few scattered flyspecks on obverse and reverse alike, under close inspection with a magnifier. (#3930)

Well Preserved Near-Gem 1916-D Buffalo Nickel

20924 **1916-D MS64 NGC.** Uncommonly well struck, the centers are well defined and the reverse is fully brought up. Lightly toned on both sides with olive-gray and champagne patina, satiny mint luster shines through. The few small flyspecks on each side seem unimportant. A clean, distraction-free example that strongly resembles a Gem. Population: 247 in 64, 40 finer (8/05). (#3932)

Semi-Key Date Near-Gem 1916-S Buffalo Nickel

20925 **1916-S MS64 NGC.** A very well struck example of this semikey date in the Buffalo nickel series. Rich luster is present under a layer of lovely olive and amber-gold toning. Nearly blemish-free and carbonfree on both sides. (#3933)

20926 **1917 MS63 NGC.** Soft luster emanates from somewhat streaked golden-gray surfaces that exhibit sharply struck design elements. Both sides are devoid of significant contact marks, but reveal a few tiny flecks, especially in the lower left (facing) obverse quadrant. (#3934)

Satiny Mint State Example 1917-D Buffalo Nickel

20927 **1917-D MS62 NGC.** A satiny steel-gray example with hints of delicate red-orange color on the bison. Well struck for the issue, if a tad soft on the bison's head and shoulder. Die cracks (as struck) are evident near nine and ten o'clock on the reverse rim, and a grainy, orange-peel texture (as made), near the reverse borders, indicates mild die erosion. (#3935)

Richly Toned 1917-S Buffalo Nickel

20928 **1917-S MS63 NGC.** Deep olive color with rose highlights, this satiny piece is scarce in this grade. An above average strike for the issue, and carefully preserved surfaces. (#3936)

Scarce, Satiny Near-Gem 1918 Buffalo Nickel

20929 **1918 MS64 NGC.** Blushes of delicate golden-green toning accompany intense, satiny luster. Typically struck with two or three minor contact marks on each side. The '18-P is one of the more difficult P-mints from this decade. Population: 175 in 64, 72 finer (8/05). (#3937)

Conditionally Scarce 1918-D Buffalo Nickel MS62 NGC

20930 **1918-D MS62 NGC.** The strike is typically soft for this difficult D-mint issue, which exhibits gray satin luster with olive undertones. There are no distracting marks on either side. With nearly 8.4 million pieces struck, one would think the 1918-D would be a fairly common issue. It is, in fact, readily obtainable in lower circulated grades, but becomes scarce in all grades above VF. Uncirculated coins are very scarce. (#3938)

Popular Overdate Variety 1918/7-D Nickel, FS-016.5

20931 **1918/7-D VG8 NGC.** FS-016.5. The thick crossbar and center stroke of the underdigit 7 is apparent on this circulated but full date example. Lilac-gray in color with hints of charcoal toning in protected areas. Void of relevant marks. A worthy and collectible example of this coveted key date, produced the same year as the also desirable 1918/7-S Quarter. (#3939)

See the Online Session listings in the back of this volume for additional Reiver selections.

Conditionally Scarce 1918-S Buffalo Nickel MS62 NGC

20932 **1918-S MS62 NGC.** A seldom seen issue in Mint State, the '18-S is scarce above VF. This is a fully lustrous coin that shows original gray patina over both sides, along with glowing apricot-gold highlights. There are a few small specks of carbon scattered about, and a number of shallow contact marks on the bison, that account for the grade. The coin is softly struck, as usual for the issue. (#3940)

Pleasing Near-Gem 1920 Buffalo Nickel

20935 **1920 MS64 NGC.** Both sides sport an attractive metallic sheen and original gray and gold coloration. Well struck although not quite full, with scattered flyspecks and a couple of minor contact marks near the obverse center that limit the grade of this generally pleasing near-Gem. (#3944)

Fully Struck 1919-D Buffalo Nickel

20933 **1919-D MS64 NGC.** The typical 1919-D Buffalo Nickel is very weakly struck with miserable detail. Consider the remarks of David Lange in *The Complete Guide to Buffalo Nickels:* "1919-D is one of the more challenging issues to locate fully struck in the period of generally weak coins that extended from 1917 through 1926. It is one of the last holes filled by a discriminating collector, regardless of whether one is collecting XF-AU or Gem Uncirculated." The Reiver Collection coin is an amazing exception to this rule. This is the first essentially fully defined 1919-D Buffalo Nickel this cataloger has ever seen. The surfaces also have exceptional luster with gorgeous light gold toning. For a 1919-D, this is an amazing example that will delight the connoisseur. (#3942)

1920-D Buffalo Nickel MS62 NGC

20936 **1920-D MS62 NGC.** Well struck, satiny and lightly toned on the blemish-free obverse, where a few scattered carbon spots are apparent. The reverse is softly struck on the bison's head, and shows greenish-gray, iridescent coral, and speckled russet patina, along with two or three trivial contact marks. Very scarce in XF and better grades, the '20-D is an important strike rarity in the Buffalo series. (#3945)

Important 1919-S Nickel, MS61 NGC

20934 **1919-S MS61 NGC.** The 1919-S is one of the most highly respected issues in the Buffalo Nickel series. It is scarce in all grades above VF. The strike is soft in places, as typical for the issue, particularly in the TY of LIBERTY and on the bison's head and tail. Semi-bright golden-gray surfaces are free of significant contact marks. (#3943)

Scarce Select 1920-S Buffalo Nickel

20937 **1920-S MS63 NGC.** A scarce issue in Mint State, this glowing example has semi-reflective surfaces with apricot-gray toning and a typically soft strike. An interesting die crack (as struck) extends beneath 192 in the date, and die wear has produced a mild halo effect along part of the Indian's profile. The 1920-S is one of the scarcest coins in the Buffalo nickel series in Uncirculated grades. (#3946)

Premium Gem Quality 1921 Buffalo Nickel

20938 **1921 MS66 NGC.** Examples of this issue are generally well-struck and appear much nicer than most other dates of nearby years. Production of Buffalo Nickels in 1921 was lower than usual, thus high-quality survivors are not all that plentiful. This Premium Gem has fully brilliant light gray surfaces with satiny luster. Both sides exhibit clash marks. On the obverse below LIBERTY and behind the Indian's neck, and on the reverse at E PLURIBUS UNUM. The obverse has a light die crack from the border at 12:30 to the leading edge of the Indian's hair. Numerous die polishing lines are visible in the obverse fields. (#3947)

Low Mintage 1921-S Buffalo Nickel MS63 NGC

20939 **1921-S MS63 NGC.** The low-mintage 1921-S Buffalo nickel is a scarcity, even in moderately worn grades, so the appearance of an Uncirculated piece is not an everyday occurrence. The surfaces on this outstanding coin display an original, glossy luster with an almost semi-prooflike sheen beneath splashes of light toning. The strike is amazingly sharp on the obverse, and bold on the reverse except for the top of the bison's head. A few scattered carbon specks, on the obverse, limit the grade. (#3948)

Lustrous, Well Defined Near-Gem 1923-S Buffalo Nickel

20940 **1923-S MS64 NGC.** An exceptionally well defined specimen showing only the slightest weakness on the bison's head, a normal characteristic of this date. The reverse has a coating of reddish-golden patina; the obverse is primarily a lustrous gray, with iridescent coral and pink undertones near the lower border. A very Choice coin destined for a high grade Buffalo nickel collection. (#3950)

Scarcer 1924 Buffalo Nickel MS64 NGC

20941 **1924 MS64 NGC.** Satiny, lightly toned surfaces could hardly be more vibrant and are particularly nice for the assigned grade. A scarcer Philadelphia Mint issue. Census: 194 in 64, 113 finer (12/05). (#3951)

Choice Mint State 1924-D Buffalo Nickel

20942 **1924-D MS64 NGC.** Even though this issue is not considered a common date, it is more available than most branch mint issues of the decade. Although not fully struck like the '19-D offered above, this example is still sharper than most. A Choice Mint State example with lovely gold toning. Magnification reveals myriad spots on both sides. (#3952)

Low Mintage Semi-Key Date 1924-S Buffalo Nickel MS63 NGC

20943 **1924-S MS63 NGC.** A low mintage issue that is elusive in all grades and especially difficult with a decent strike. This piece has soft, frosted mint luster and is light in color. Unabraded, but showing a handful of carbon flecks on each side. Reasonably well struck on the reverse, the obverse center displays a lack of full highpoint definition. (#3953)

Near-Gem 1925 Buffalo Nickel MS64 NGC

20944 **1925 MS64 NGC.** Very smooth, satiny surfaces that are lightly toned and essentially blemish-free, except for two or three wispy marks on the bison's shoulder and torso. There are scattered flyspecks on each side, and an interesting die crack (as struck) extends from the left reverse rim, through the bison's horn, and to the center of the bison's shoulder. (#3954)

Mint State 1925-D Buffalo Nickel MS62 NGC

20945 **1925-D MS62 NGC.** Quite lustrous under a moderate coating of natural patina with better than average sharpness for this often poorly produced (and scarce) issue. There are a number of small carbon flecks overall that limit the grade. The reverse is rotated 25 degrees counterclockwise in relation to the obverse. (#3955)

Sharply Defined 1925-S Buffalo Nickel

20946 **1925-S MS63 NGC.** Another of the mintmarked issues in the 1920s that is plagued by poor striking quality. Although by no means is this example fully struck, it has considerably more detail than usual. On the obverse, LIBERTY is separated from the rim, and the hair braid exhibits some detail. The reverse is quite well-defined with virtually full head details and a split tail. Extensive clash marks are visible in the obverse fields, with faint clash marks on the reverse. Satiny surfaces are fully lustrous with brilliant pale gold and iridescent toning. A few minor spots kept this from a higher grade, in our opinion. (#3956)

20947 **1926 MS65 NGC.** This Gem exudes considerable flash, as the nearly untoned surfaces radiate dazzling luster. The design elements are nicely brought up. A few minute marks on the Indian's cheek and the bison's left leg and midsection are mentioned for accuracy. (#3957)

Choice Uncirculated 1926-D Buffalo Nickel

20948 **1926-D MS64 NGC.** Remarkably well struck for this notoriously weakly struck issue. Almost completely defined on each side, the surfaces show a smattering of golden-gray patina equally over each side. A small, thin, lateral planchet lamination is seen across the Indian's braid as the coin is turned under a light. (#3958)

Desirable 1926-S Nickel, MS63 NGC

20949 **1926-S MS63 NGC.** This issue is plagued by weak strikes, especially on the reverse. The present example is clearly sharper than usually seen, although it is still a little weak on the reverse. The obverse is actually much sharper than usually encountered. The surfaces have light gray color and full underlying luster. If not for miniscule flyspecks on both sides, this might have been graded MS64. A remarkable example of this highly desirable issue that is seldom found so fine. (#3959)

20950 **1927-D MS63 NGC.** A thin layer of tan-gold toning overlies lustrous surfaces that display a few tiny pepper-like spots over each side. The design features are generally well impressed. (#3961)

Uncirculated 1927-S Nickel

20951 **1927-S MS62 NGC.** Moderately toned and somewhat glossy with above average striking details for this scarce strike rarity. Rose-gray shades overlay each side and a number of carbon flecks are seen over each side. (#3962)

20952 **1928 MS64 NGC.** Splashes of light milky-gold color alternate with ice-blue over radiantly lustrous surfaces that display sharply struck design elements. A few minor ticks on the Indian's portrait help to define the grade. (#3963)

20953 **1928-D MS64 NGC.** As with other Denver issues from the 1920s, the 1928-D is well known as a strike rarity, albeit to a lesser degree than earlier years. The obverse of this piece shows a bit of highpoint softness on the Indian's hair above the knot, but we can find little fault with the definition on the reverse. Each side displays a layer of ice-blue and gold-tan patina over bright, satiny mint luster. Just a few minor ticks preclude a higher grade. (#3964)

Select 1928-S Nickel

20954 **1928-S MS63 NGC.** Well struck and lustrous under a moderate coating of golden-gray toning. A few scattered carbon flecks limit the grade. (#3965)

20955 **1929 MS65 NGC.** Bright lustrous surfaces display a thin veneer of champagne color, and are impeccably preserved. The motifs exhibit quite strong definition. NGC has certified 31 pieces finer (12/05). (#3966)

Gem 1929-D Buffalo Nickel

20956 **1929-D MS65 NGC.** Apricot and sky-blue colors invigorate this splendidly preserved Gem. The centers show the weakness characteristic of the issue, while the bison's head and tail are crisp. A common date in worn condition, but few remain in lofty Mint State grades. (#3967)

Gem 1929-S Buffalo Nickel

20957 **1929-S MS65 NGC.** Glowing luster peeks through golden-gray patination. The surfaces are well preserved and exhibit sharply struck design features. (#3968)

Choice BU 1930-S Nickel

20958 **1930-S MS64 NGC.** Pale rose-gray iridescence overlays the satiny surfaces. The strike is too soft at the centers for a finer grade. (#3970)

Choice Uncirculated 1934-D Nickel

20959 **1934-D MS64 NGC.** Centrally soft with a full, sharp, horn and medium steel-gray toning. A number of small carbon spots litter each side. (#3973)

20960 **1935-D MS64 NGC.** Pleasing champagne-gold patina rolls over both sides of this highly lustrous Near-Gem '35-D. The design elements are well impressed, and there are no significant marks to report. This piece exudes considerable flash. (#3975)

20961 **1935-S MS64 NGC.** Barely perceptible powder-blue and beige patina covers lustrous, virtually unmarked surfaces. The design elements are sharply struck up throughout. (#3976)

20962 **1936 MS66 NGC.** Highly lustrous surfaces are visited by a barely discernible veneer of champagne color, and are impeccably preserved. Strong definition is apparent on the devices. NGC has certified 49 pieces finer (12/05). (#3977)

20963 **1937-D MS65 NGC.** Lovely steel-green and gold-orange color adorns each side of this satiny, crisply struck Gem. Lustrous and nearly pristine, this is an unusually pleasing example of the type. (#3981)

Uncirculated 1937-D Three-Legged Buffalo Nickel

20964 **1937-D Three-Legged MS61 NGC.** Shades of earth tones lay across the surfaces of this vastly popular three-legged bison variety. A nice piece for the grade with only few abrasions visible upon inspection. (#3982)

SEATED HALF DIMES

Popular 1837 Small Date Half Dime

20965 **1837 Small Date (Flat Top 1) MS62 NGC.** Rich chocolate-brown and russet toning blankets this pinpoint-sharp and unmarked early Seated Half Dime. Satin luster sweeps across the open fields. A narrow die break or 'cud' is noted on the obverse between 3 and 5 o'clock. The No Stars type was produced in Philadelphia only in 1837, although a scarce emission was also struck the following year at New Orleans. Envelope Included. (#4312)

Mint State 1837 Half Dime, Small Date

20966 **1837 Small Date (Flat Top 1) MS62 NGC.** Delicate chestnut toning graces this shimmering first year Seated Half Dime. Undisturbed save for a few wispy slide marks on the obverse field. The scarce late die stage with die breaks in the field near Liberty's knee and raised elbow. (#4312)

20967 No Lot.

Scarce Low Mintage 1838-O Half Dime No Stars XF40 NGC

20968 **1838-O No Stars XF40 NGC.** V-1. A pleasing example of this interesting, short-lived type, without any peripheral stars on the obverse. Well struck and lightly worn, with variegated purple, turquoise, and silver-gray coloration, on the obverse, and an untoned reverse center surrounded by mottled green and lilac border toning. Faint wispy hairlines, in the fields, are not particularly distracting. A scarce, low mintage issue. (#4314)

Original Near Gem 1838 Large Stars Half Dime

20969 **1838 Large Stars MS64 NGC.** Pleasing peach and aquamarine colors embrace this lustrous and meticulously struck near-Gem. Unmarked and decidedly attractive. The eighth star is sharply repunched, and the upper left obverse rim has a lengthy slender die break, as made. (#4317)

1838 Half Dime No Drapery Large Stars MS62 NGC

20970 **1838 Large Stars MS62 NGC.** Deep, mottled sea-green, amber, olive, and rose-gold colors enrich this well struck, blemish-free half dime. The Stars, No Drapery type was only struck for three years. Envelope Included. (#4317)

See the Online Session listings in the back of this volume for additional Reiver selections.

Richly Toned 1839 No Drapery Half Dime MS64 NGC

20971 **1839 No Drapery MS64 NGC.** Rich layers of deep-purple, cobalt-blue, and golden-brown toning adorn the obverse. The reverse center is essentially untoned, and surrounded by an even band of russet and golden-tan peripheral patina. Abrasion-free, with faint hairlines in the fields holding it back slightly from the threshold of a Gem grade assessment. Population: 47 in 64, 52 finer (8/05). (#4319)

20972 **1839 No Drapery AU58 NGC.** V-2. Recut 39 in the date was confused with an overdate in the past. This example is well struck and shows just one noticeable mark, in the obverse field to the left of stars 12 and 13. Original toning abounds, beginning with a radiant ring of sky-blue patina, blending into centers of violet and gold. Envelope Included. (#4319)

Splendid Gem 1839-O Half Dime, No Drapery

20973 **1839-O No Drapery MS65 NGC.** A much underrated early New Orleans half dime in uncirculated grades, despite its second year status and mintage of more than a million pieces. This Gem exhibits sparkling luster and tan and cobalt-blue peripheral toning. The design elements are razor sharp, and there are no major abrasions to report. Two vertical die cracks wander there way through the reverse. Census: 3 in 65, 2 finer (10/05). (#4320)

20974 **1839-O No Drapery—Bent—NCS. AU Details.** Nice definition is apparent, and the surfaces are toned electric-blue and lavender. The bend is relatively minor. Envelope Included. (#4320)

20975 **1840 No Drapery AU58 NGC.** Well struck with deep blue-green and salmon-gold colors on the obverse. The reverse displays equally rich magenta, orange, and blue-green toning. Both sides are near-pristine, with just one or two small marks. The Drapery was added to Liberty's elbow late in 1840, which marked an end to the short-lived No Drapery type. Envelope Included. (#4321)

Near-Mint 1840 Half Dime with Drapery

20976 **1840 Drapery AU58 NGC.** V-7. A well known transitional year in the Seated half dime series, the present example is richly toned near the borders in mottled olive and apricot hues. The silver-gray centers are essentially untoned. A superficial yet lengthy pinscratch, in the right obverse field, is the most obvious detraction. Light wear on the highpoints seems appropriate for the assigned grade level. (#4326)

Conditionally Scarce 1840-O Seated Half Dime AU58 NGC

20977 **1840-O Drapery AU58 NGC.** Unlike its No Drapery counterpart, the 1840-O Drapery is an elusive issue that becomes undeniably rare in grades approaching Mint State. A wonderfully original example, the obverse displays mottled orange-russet and sea-green peripheral patina. The reverse, while somewhat lighter over the center, displays dark-green color around the right and lower borders. The strike is bold with the exception of Liberty's head and the reverse center, and there are no unduly bothersome distractions for the grade. Population: 8 in 58, 4 finer (8/05). (#4327)

20978 **1841 AU58 NGC.** V-2. The last 1 in the date is low and recut, and a small lunule appears between stars 10 and 11. Sharply struck, the surfaces have a warm glow, and show a rich band of red-orange color near the obverse borders. Struck from lightly clashed dies, and there are a couple of spurs visible inside the M in DIME. (#4328)

20979 **1842 AU58 NGC.** V-1. This is a richly toned example whose surfaces are colored in very deep shades of red-brown, sky-blue, gold, cobalt-blue and olive-gray. The strong strike and relative lack of abrasions give this coin the look of a higher grade. Envelope Included. (#4330)

Gem 1842 Seated Half Dime MS65 NGC

20980 **1842 MS65 NGC.** V-4. The 1842 is among the more easily obtainable Seated half dimes from the 1840s, and the present example possesses suitable technical quality, as well as a high level of eye appeal, for the Gem level of preservation. We can find no singularly mentionable abrasions, and the sharply impressed features display considerable mint luster beneath bright slate-gray patina. Gold, russet, golden-brown, and cobalt-blue colors are seen near some of the border areas. Population: 15 in 65, 6 finer (8/05). (#4330)

Important 1844-O Half Dime

20981 **1844-O AU53 NGC.** Breen-3037, V-1. Medium O mintmark (Large O per Breen). This is an important date in the Seated Liberty Half Dime series, and is almost always encountered in low grades when it is encountered at all. The surfaces are pale silver-gray with deep and attractive iridescent toning. Myriad abrasions are visible beneath the toning. Most obverse design elements are quite well-defined, including hair details and star centers. The reverse is somewhat weaker in overall definition. On the reverse, a wonderful retained cud joins ME to the rim. (#4334)

Challenging 1846 Half Dime

20982 **1846 AU55 NGC.** V-1. Only one variety of this date was recorded by Valentine, however, a second variety was later described by Walter Breen. The Valentine-1 die combination was used for business strikes, as seen here, while Proofs are the later "Breen-2" variety. Advanced collectors realize that this is the only date in the 1840s where Mint State examples are actually rarer than Proofs. This example is one of the rare business strikes, and is highly prized as such. Heavy date digits slant down to the right, with the 46 extremely close together. Most survivors are in low grade. The Choice AU specimen offered here displays silver-gray surfaces with peripheral gold and green accents, especially on the obverse. Save for wispy ticks and hairlines, the surfaces are devoid of significant abrasions. (#4336)

20983 **1847 AU58 NGC.** Well struck and satiny, with light green-gray toning and clean, unabraded surfaces. A reverse die crack extends from the lower rim through stem and leaves, through D and H, from H to diagonally up through A and L, through the wreath and to the rim between A and M of AMERICA. (#4337)

Extremely Rare Variety 1848/7/6 Half Dime, Breen-3044

20984 **1848 Medium Date MS62 NGC.** 1848/7/6. Breen 3044, described by him as "Extremely Rare." Medium Date. Bright and satiny, with attractive green and russet peripheral toning on the obverse. Die clash marks are noticeable in the obverse and reverse fields, but there are no contact marks to be found. Faint golden color enhances the reverse edges. (#4338)

20985 **1848 Large Date AU50 NGC.** FS-001, Breen-3043. This variety was created when a half dime obverse die was accidentally impressed with a date logotype intended for the 1848 dime. The top of the date overlaps the rock with the 1 almost touching the point of the shield. Deep, variegated electric-green, golden-brown, and lilac toning blankets both sides. The piece seems boldly struck and only lightly worn, with a few very wispy pinscratches located on the obverse, using a magnifier. (#4339)

See the Online Session listings in the back of this volume for additional Reiver selections.

Pleasing Near-Gem 1848-O Seated Half Dime

20986 **1848-O MS64 NGC.** V-6. Large O. A well struck coin that shows full mint luster, clean surfaces and variegated sea-green to russet-gold toning over the obverse and reverse. Minor die clash marks (as struck) are noticeable on the upper obverse, surrounding Liberty's head. A pleasing example that has lovely original toning and noteworthy scarcity as a near-Gem. (#4340)

Scarce 1849 Half Dime MS61 NGC

20987 **1849 MS61 NGC.** Deep rose-gray, copper-orange and electric-blue toning confirms the originality of this nicely defined example. Were it not for deficient luster quality, the smooth surfaces would easily garner a higher grade, as both sides seem entirely blemish-free. This is a scarcer date despite a respectable original mintage of 1.3 million pieces. Envelope Included. (#4341)

Mint State Details 1849/6 Half Dime

20988 **1849/6—Improperly Cleaned—NCS. Unc. Details.** V-1. The 84 in the date exhibit relatively wide repunching, and the 9 in the date is over what appears to be a large 6, or possibly a large 8 with the upper right loop removed through die preparation. While specialists have room for debate, there is no doubt that it is a dramatic variety worthy of its separate *Guide Book* listing. This sharply struck and lightly toned representative has moderately hairlined fields, but there are no contact marks and no indication of wear. Luster dominates the devices and legends. (#4342)

Uncirculated Sharpness 1849/8 Half Dime

20989 **1849/8—Improperly Cleaned—NCS. Unc. Details.** V-4, FS-001.5. Along with its 1849/6 counterpart, the 1849/8 is controversial since there is little consensus among numismatic experts as to what the extra digit represents. It is located, however, southeast of the prominent 9. The 4 in the date is also recut, and the reverse die features a lengthy vertical crack from 6:30 to 10 o'clock and has a narrow cud along the left rim. This sharply struck Half Dime has golden-tan toning throughout the borders, and thorough inspection locates faint hairlines on the steel-gray fields. (#4343)

Pleasing 1849-O Half Dime, AU53

20990 **1849-O AU53 NGC.** A difficult O-mint Half Dime that displays bits of remaining luster beneath deep crimson, lime-gold, and antique-gold highlights. Only 140,000 pieces were struck, few of which survive as nice as this pleasing, original example. (#4344)

20991 **1850 AU58 NGC.** V-5. The date is low with no digits touching the base. The surfaces are covered with deep shadings of sea-green, maroon, and gold that cover both sides of this lightly worn type coin. Envelope Included. (#4345)

Fully Struck 1850 Half Dime

20992 **1850 MS63 NGC.** V-5. The striking details are amazingly full and crisp on this well preserved example. Original charcoal-gray, gold-gray, and electric-blue toning adorns each side, and there are almost no contact marks to be found, even using magnification. Envelope Included. (#4345)

Conditionally Elusive 1850-O Half Dime, AU58 NGC

20993 **1850-O AU58 NGC.** V-2. Large O mintmark. The medium gray-golden surfaces are lighter in color where luster persists. A well struck representative that has light rub on the knee and breast of Liberty. The reverse field has a few wispy abrasions. A scarce issue in Choice AU and above. (#4346)

Scarce Select Uncirculated 1850-O Half Dime

20994 **1850-O MS63 NGC.** V-2. Large O mintmark. A deeply toned, Select specimen with a crisp strike and pleasing surfaces. A small die break is seen near the denticles at 7 o'clock on the reverse rim. The 1850-O is a common issue in VF and lower grades, but Uncirculated survivors are very scarce. Census: 9 in 63, 15 finer (12/05). Envelope Included. (#4346)

Select Uncirculated 1852-O Half Dime

20995 **1852-O MS63 NGC.** The year 1852 offers considerable challenges to the O-mint Seated collector. The '52-O half dime, dime, quarter, and half dollar are all low mintage issues that were heavily melted as a result of escalating silver prices. Writing in 1992, Al Blythe *The Complete Guide to Liberty Seated Half Dimes* assigns the 1852-O half dime an R.6 ranking in Mint State. A sharp example for the grade, the surfaces are smooth and essentially distraction-free beneath mottled olive, rose, and blue-gray patina. This is a well struck, subtly lustrous example that would fit into any advanced Half Dime collection. (#4350)

Important Mint State 1853 No Arrows Half Dime

20996 **1853 No Arrows MS63 NGC.** Sharply struck with reflective silver surfaces and splashes of iridescent toning on the obverse. (#4351)

See the Online Session listings in the back of this volume for additional Reiver selections.

Affordable 1853-O No Arrows Half Dime

20997 **1853-O No Arrows—Improperly Cleaned—NCS. AU Details.** Although 160,000 pieces were minted, most were melted as a result of the weight change effective February 22, 1853. This is a lightly circulated example showing myriad cleaning lines, the result of a harsh cleaning. Excellent detail remains on each side. The lower part of the date is quite weak, a trait common to every surviving example of this issue, and an excellent tool to distinguish between genuine examples, and those of the with arrows type that have had their arrows removed, or those altered from 1858-O. (#4352)

Gem Uncirculated 1853 Arrows Half Dime

20998 **1853 Arrows MS65 NGC.** Bold detail appears on the obverse, the reverse central area appearing to be soft due to noticeable clash marks appearing on both sides of this coin. The reflective mint glow is heightened by a mist of silver-gray toning evenly distributed over the entire surface. (#4356)

Attractive 1854-O Half Dime, MS62

20999 **1854-O Arrows MS62 NGC.** An attractive, Uncirculated example of this important three year subtype, with sharp detail and few abrasions. Wide bands of bold indigo and vivid, watery violet circle the borders, with small areas of lustrous silver at the centers. The reverse was struck with a well worn die showing an "orange-peel" texture at the periphery and several prominent die cracks. (#4359)

Pleasing 1855-O Arrows Gem Half Dime

21000 **1855-O Arrows MS65 NGC.** A thin die crack connects star 7, head, star 8, cap, and stars 9-13. Even though 600,000 pieces were struck of the 1855-O half dime, it is an issue that was heavily circulated with few examples remaining today in the better grades of Mint State. The Gem offered here displays light gold-brown patina with occasional dapples of cobalt-blue. Lustrous surfaces are well preserved, and show no offensive marks. The devices are generally well brought up throughout. Census: 7 in 65, 10 finer (10/05). (#4361)

21001 **1856 MS62 NGC.** The deep cobalt-blue and brick-red colors combine in a variegated fashion. The depth of color is enough to somewhat subdue the underlying mint luster. A well detailed and problem-free type coin whose only flaw is an indistinctness of details around the denticles, which is a common trait on 1856 half dimes. Envelope Included. (#4363)

21002 **1856 MS62 NGC.** The rich multicolored toning scheme does not inhibit one's appreciation of the coin's sharp features. The denticles on both sides are typically weak and the luster is too subdued for a higher grade. (#4363)

Uncirculated 1856-O Half Dime

21003 **1856-O MS62 NGC.** Lightly toned in purple-russet and silver-gray shades with the underlying surfaces being mostly mark-free and lustrous. A scarcer O-mint Half Dime at all levels of Mint State. Population: 10 in 62, 18 finer (8/05). (#4364)

21004 **1857-O MS63 NGC.** With 1.38 million pieces struck, the 1857-O is one of the more frequently encountered O-mint Half Dimes. Both sides are toned in slightly mottled shades of bluish-green and deep golden-violet. Desirable New Orleans issue. (#4366)

21005 **1858 MS63 NGC.** Deep cobalt-blue and crimson-magenta colors collide on each side in a variegated fashion. There are no mentionable marks or spots on either side. Worth a close look. Envelope Included. (#4367)

Gem Proof 1858 Half Dime

21006 **1858 PR65 NGC.** A lovely Gem Proof with cameo contrast on both sides, although not designated as such by NGC. The surfaces are mostly light silver with hints of pale blue on the obverse and light lilac on the reverse. Seldom is this date encountered in Gem Proof quality. Census: 16 in 65, 13 finer (12/05). (#4437)

Uncirculated 1858-O Half Dime

21007 **1858-O MS62 NGC.** V-1. High, open date with diagnostic die crack from toe to rim (but extremely faint), on the reverse die cracks link R and A in AMERICA to the rim. Reasonably well struck with a subdued appearance and mottled charcoal-blue and russet toning and clean surfaces for the assigned grade. (#4369)

Attractive, Lustrous 1859-O Half Dime MS63 NGC

21008 **1859-O MS63 NGC.** Attractive and lustrous, toned a deep gray with shades of gold. A few surface marks are noted, and the piece was struck from noticeably clashed dies. (#4370)

Nicely Toned, Well Defined 1860 Half Dime, MS64

21009 **1860 MS64 NGC.** The upper half of the obverse is a deep brick-red color, the lower half is silver-gray. The reverse displays a pleasant mix of rose-crimson and sea-green color. Well struck with no mentionable distractions. (#4377)

21010 **1860 MS63 NGC.** Both sides are covered in deep sunset-red and blue-green toning that allows the strong underlying luster to still be visible. Envelope Included. (#4377)

1860-O Half Dime MS62 NGC

21011 **1860-O MS62 NGC.** The first year of this design and a fairly scarce coin with only one million examples struck. As it turned out, the '60-O is a one-year type coin from the New Orleans mint which closed the following year for the duration of the Civil War. This is a well struck piece whose surfaces are too dull to grade higher, but nicely toned. Golden-russet hues decorate each side. (#4378)

21012 **1861 MS62 NGC.** Deep lavender and forest-green toning blankets this carefully preserved and satiny Half Dime. The reverse periphery shows moderate striking softness, although the Seated Liberty is generally sharp. The Philadelphia Mint in 1861 produced large mintages of most denominations, however, after 1863, only base coinage was struck in quantity, since a flood of unbacked paper money removed silver and gold from circulation. Envelope Included. (#4379)

See the Online Session listings in the back of this volume for additional Reiver selections.

Choice Proof 1861 Half Dime

21013 **1861 PR64 NGC.** This glittering proof is one of an estimated 400 that were actually released from a mintage of 1,000 pieces, most of which were melted by the mint. Coppery-gold toning shading to blue about the obverse and reverse borders. (#4444)

Uncirculated 1862 Half Dime

21014 **1862 MS62 NGC.** An attractive coin despite scattered abrasions, both sides show deep sea-green and antique-gold toning at the peripheral areas on each side. Suitably lustrous overall. (#4381)

Select Proof 1863 Half Dime

21015 **1863 PR63 NGC.** The 1 in the date is clearly repunched. A popular Civil War era issue because of limited business strike production (18,000 pieces) made necessary by wartime hoarding. This richly toned example displays golden-russet and green hues throughout with flashes of blue and rose iridescence at the margins. An area of weakness is noted at the upper left portion of the wreath. (#4446)

Uncirculated 1863-S Half Dime

21016 **1863-S MS62 NGC.** Sharply struck with a thin layer of gray-golden patina over each side that deepens at the border areas. The underlying surfaces are quite subdued, the grade-limiting factor, but this is one of the few Mint State survivors of this low mintage issue. (#4383)

Scarce Near-Mint 1864 Seated Half Dime

21017 **1864 AU58 NGC.** Myriad clash marks (as struck) are noted on both sides of this minimally abraded example. Golden-brown and turquoise-green iridescence resides near the borders, and the strike is suitable for the series. Wispy hairlines are evident in the obverse and reverse fields. With an original mintage of 48,000 business strikes and a poor rate of survival, this Civil War issue is a well respected rarity in all grades. (#4384)

Scarce Near Mint 1864-S Half Dime

21018 **1864-S AU58 NGC.** A richly detailed and slightly subdued Borderline Uncirculated better date Half Dime. The strike is good if not needle-sharp. A short scratch is east of the denomination, but no other marks are encountered. A mere 90,000 pieces were struck. Census: 6 in 58, 32 finer (12/05). (#4385)

Low Mintage 1865 Proof Seated Half Dime PR63 NGC

21019 **1865 PR63 NGC.** A low total mintage issue with only 13,000 business strikes and 500 proofs produced. Naturally, there is significant date pressure on the few remaining proofs because of the scarcity of high grade business strikes. A diamond sharp strike reveals the most minute details of the elegant design. A small amount of milky toning is present in the field areas, on each side, while sea-green, olive, and coral-red coloration adorns the peripheries. Wispy striations (as struck) reside in the right obverse field, but no bothersome hairlines or contact marks are apparent. (#4448)

Difficult Uncirculated Sharpness 1865-S Half Dime

21020 **1865-S—Obverse Improperly Cleaned—NCS. Unc. Details.** V-4. All date digits are clearly albeit lightly repunched, and the fields exhibit dual sets of mint-made clash marks. A slender diagonal die crack, as struck, descends across the reverse. Light chestnut toning frames the pearl-gray centers. Well struck aside from the upper tips of the wreath, and unmarked save for faint hairlines on the obverse field. The 1865-S is another conditionally rare early S-mint Half Dime; most survivors are in VF and lower grades. (#4387)

Scarce 1866 Half Dime PR64 Cameo NGC

21021 **1866 PR64 Cameo NGC.** The 1866 Half Dime is a scarce issue whether it is in proof or business strike format. Only 10,000 business strikes were produced along with 725 proofs, making the proofs always in demand by collectors who need a high grade example and do not wish to spend the extra money for a more expensive business strike. This coin is clearly superior from a technical standpoint, with deeply reflective fields and a sharp strike. The devices are lightly frosted yielding a noticeable cameo effect. A few wispy striations (as struck) and pinscratches are noted on each side of this near-Gem, but they do little to harm the overall eye appeal of the piece. Population: 6 in 64 Cameo, 4 finer in Cameo condition (9/05). (#84449)

Lightly Circulated 1866-S Half Dime AU58 NGC

21022 **1866-S AU58 NGC.** A very scarce issue with only 120,000 pieces produced. The strike is typical of the series, but there are no mentionable abrasions on either side of the coin, and a mere trace of wear seems evident on Liberty's head. The luster is muted. A bit of speckled green patina appears near the obverse and reverse peripheries. (#4389)

Low Mintage 1867 Proof Seated Half Dime PR62 NGC

21023 **1867 PR62 NGC.** Cobalt-green and purple-rose toning richly adorns each side of this sharply struck proof. A window of brilliance near the reverse center shows bright reflectivity, along with some faint hairlines. Both sides seem contact-free, however. An important date in the series, with only 625 proofs minted, along with a mere 8,000 business strikes. (#4450)

Choice AU58 1867-S Half Dime

21024 **1867-S AU58 NGC.** With a mintage of only 90,000 pieces, this is a much scarcer date from the 1860s. Well struck in the centers, with softly defined dentils, a light coating of milky-beige patina is seen on each side. Faint clash marks are evident, some mottled russet color has settled on the lower half of Liberty, and the otherwise unabraded surfaces reveal one minor contact mark on the reverse, just to the left of DIME. The 1 in the date is recut. Census: 7 in 58, 28 finer (12/05). (#4391)

Gem Proof 1868 V-1 Half Dime

21025 **1868 PR66 NGC.** V-1. Proof examples of the date are more plentiful than business strikes, however, neither are all that common in Gem quality. Two varieties are known, apparently both existing in Proof and business strike format. This specimen is the more plentiful V-1 variety, with a high date that slants down slightly to the right. Breen stated that the top of the 1 in the date almost touches the base of Liberty, however, it appears to us that the date is almost centered between the base and the border. The Reiver Collection coin is a splendid Gem Proof with exceptional lilac, blue, gold, and iridescent toning. The central reverse is mostly brilliant with vivid blue and iridescent toning at the border. Population: 14 in 66, 5 finer (8/05). (#4451)

21026 **1869—Improperly Cleaned—NCS. Impaired Proof.** An intricately struck and untoned piece with slight cameo contrast, particularly on the reverse. Wispy hairlines appear throughout the fields when viewed from select angles. Struck from a lightly rusted obverse die. A scant 600 proofs were coined. (#4452)

Proof 1870 Half Dime

21027 **1870 PR62 NGC.** A richly toned and well struck proof example that seems lightly hairlined and free of contact marks, with noticeable reflectivity remaining in the fields. This issue is much scarcer than the mintage of 1,000 proofs would indicate, with much of the production apparently melted by the mint. (#4453)

Proof 1871 Half Dime

21028 **1871 PR62 NGC.** The proof qualities are somewhat muted beneath charcoal-violet, charcoal-green, and golden-brown toning, but there are no outwardly noticeable handling marks. A few faint hairlines are detected in the fields, using a magnifier. Die rust glitters around Liberty's head, and produces a matte-like texture over her legs and torso. Sharply struck in most areas, as befits a proof of this type. (#4454)

1871-S Half Dime Mintmark Above Bow MS63 NGC

21029 **1871-S MS63 NGC.** Mintmark Above Bow. Speckled plum and electric-blue toning adorns each side of this well detailed example, which has satiny luster and just a few minor surface marks. A tough, lower mintage date. (#4399)

21030 **1872 MS63 NGC.** Aquamarine and golden tones grace the peripheries of this subtly lustrous representative. A solitary vertical hairline crosses the right obverse field, a small mark is seen on the head, and some softness of strike is noted on the extremities of the design. (#4400)

21031 **1872-S Mintmark Above Bow MS62 NGC.** A boldly struck and gently shimmering Half Dime from the final years of the series. Mottled golden-brown and apple-green toning adds to the eye appeal. Clean for the grade, and more attractive than its modest Uncirculated grade suggests. (#4402)

Final Proof Issue 1873 Half Dime PR63 NGC

21032 **1873 PR63 NGC.** A sharply struck example that has mottled turquoise-green and champagne-rose patina. Essentially problem-free, with some minute hairlines in the obverse fields. Only 600 pieces were produced for this final proof issue. (#4456)

21033 **1873-S MS62 NGC.** A thoroughly lustrous piece from the terminal year of the Half Dime denomination, one of the outcomes of the "Crime of 1873", which in effect demonetized silver. Tan-gold and cream in color with a blush of deep gray toning near DIME. The strike is generally sharp, but HALF and the reverse dentils are not conspicuous. (#4405)

SEATED DIMES

Colorfully Toned Near Mint 1837 No Stars Dime

21034 **1837 Large Date AU58 NGC.** Vivid aqua-blue and ruby toning embraces this briefly circulated No Stars Dime. The surfaces are bright but only moderately abraded. An early die state that lacks any indication of the triangular die cracks that eventually dominate the obverse. Similar to the first two years of the Seated Half Dime, the No Stars type consists of common 1837 Large and Small Date varieties and a scarcer 1838-O issue. (#4561)

Mint State 1838 Large Stars Dime

21035 **1838 Large Stars MS61 NGC.** A well struck piece with decent luster and medium russet and blue-green peripheral colors. A faint mark crosses the first star, but on the whole, the surfaces are quite clean for the grade. From the briefly produced Stars, Tilted Shield, No Drapery subtype. (#4568)

21036 **1839 No Drapery AU58 NGC.** Medium chestnut-gray toning enriches this bold piece, which displays pleasing luster for the near-Mint grade. No marks are worthy of discussion, and the eye appeal is pleasing. The 39 in the date is clearly repunched. (#4571)

Choice Fine 'Little Orphan Annie' 1844 Dime

21037 **1844 Fine 15 NGC.** Although the popular 'Little Orphan Annie' 1844 Dime has probably been overly promoted since the 1950s, it is nonetheless a difficult date, due to its small emission of 72,500 pieces. Among early Seated Dime issues, only the 1846 has a lower production. This attractive collector grade example exhibits a sharp LIBERTY, and portions of drapery are still present. Dusky sea-green and steel-blue colors confirm the originality. (#4585)

21038 **1846—Reverse Damage—NCS. VG Details.** Light gray surfaces reveal some fine scratches in the central field. Not as bad as it sounds. (#4588)

Lightly Circulated 1847 Dime

21039 **1847 AU58 NGC.** Golden-orange patina adheres to silver-gray surfaces that are quite clean. The design features are well defined through-out. (#4589)

Pleasing Near-Mint 1848 Seated Dime

21040 **1848 AU58 NGC.** Subdued steely-gray surfaces with speckled darker russet-red and dark-green toning near the borders, and some scattered wispy abrasions. A shallow scratch extends from between the bases of IM in DIME to the wreath. Nonetheless, a nice AU example of this conditional rarity. (#4590)

Scarcer New Orleans Issue 1849-O Seated Dime XF45 NGC

21041 **1849-O XF45 NGC.** Small Mintmark. Greer-101. A bit softly struck under layers of coral-gray and antique-golden patina, but free of marks and evenly worn. A scarcer New Orleans issue. (#4592)

21042 **1852-O—Damaged—NCS. XF Details.** Light to medium gray surfaces show tiny pin prick marks on the reverse. The design elements are well defined. (#4598)

Mint State 1853 No Arrows Dime

21043 **1853 No Arrows MS62 NGC.** Ahwash-2. The skirt pendant is left of center over the digit 5, and tiny die chips appear near several stars on the left, especially outside stars 5 and 6. The late Kam Ahwash, who was the leading student of Liberty Seated Dimes in the 1970s, recorded two different die varieties of this issue. He considered this variety slightly rarer than the other. This example is sharply struck with essentially full detail on both sides. The surfaces, even though lightly abraded, are fully lustrous with satiny brilliance. Traces of gold appear around the obverse border, while the reverse is similar with a large splash of vivid blue. Minor clash marks are visible on the obverse. (#4599)

Desirable 1853 Arrows Dime MS64 NGC

21044 **1853 Arrows MS64 NGC.** A desirable type coin, this example displays mottled toning shades of gold and gray on each side. Well struck from slightly rotated dies, with noticeable die clash marks (as struck) on the obverse, and several faint pinscratches near the center of the reverse, that limit the grade. (#4603)

Tough Low Mintage 1856-S Dime

21045 **1856-S—Damaged—NCS. VF Details.** Important as the first Dime issue from the San Francisco Mint, a combination of low mintage and a poor survival rate ensures that Seated collectors have few examples to select from. This slightly granular and bright representative has a few wispy obverse slide marks, and the slate-gray centers are bounded with hints of golden-brown toning. (#4613)

AU Details 1858 Seated Dime

21046 **1858—Improperly Cleaned—NCS. AU Details.** Luster connects the stars and legends, and is only broken across the open fields. This nicely struck piece exhibits little evidence of its past cleaning, and many collectors would appreciate such an addition to their holdings. Struck from clashed dies, a partial wire rim is noted on both sides. (#4616)

See the Online Session listings in the back of this volume for additional Reiver selections.

Challenging Choice XF 1858-S Dime

21047 **1858-S XF45 NGC.** Primarily dove-gray in color, however, olive-tinged luster outlines the legends and devices. Other than an edge mark at 12 o'clock on the reverse, this rare date Dime is surprisingly unabraded for the moderately circulated grade. Just 60,000 pieces were struck, and unlike the lower mintage dates from 1879 to 1881, few if any pieces were set aside by collectors of the day. (#4618)

Lovely Toned Choice 1859 Dime

21048 **1859 MS64 NGC.** Honey color enriches this crisply struck and vibrant Dime. A small mark in the field near the final star prevents classification as a full Gem. From the final year of the Obverse Stars type. A plentiful date in typical circulated grades, however, lustrous and originally toned near-Gems are both desirable and elusive. Population: 26 in 64, 54 finer (9/05). (#4619)

21049 **1860-S VF20 NGC.** LIBERTY is bold on this deep dove-gray better date Stars Obverse Dime. A diagonal wispy pinscratch across the Seated Liberty will be missed by most observers. Since the San Francisco Mint continued to emphasize larger denominations, only 140,000 pieces were struck, not many of which have survived. Nonetheless affordable in circulated grades. (#4622)

21050 **1860 MS61 NGC.** Light golden toning graces the borders of this mildly prooflike piece, which has frosty devices and a good strike. No distracting marks are detected. (#4631)

Tough VG Details 1860-O Dime

21051 **1860-O—Improperly Cleaned—NCS. VG Details.** A slate-gray example with cloudy surfaces and a hint of granularity. Four of the seven letters in LIBERTY are clear. The date and mintmark are bold. A better date, since just 40,000 pieces were struck, nearly all of which went into circulation. The New Orleans Mint struck the Legend Obverse Dime only in its first and last years of production, 1860 and 1891. The mint closed in 1861, before it had struck Dimes, and after it re-opened in 1879, it was primarily devoted to striking Morgan Dollars. (#4632)

Richly Toned Proof 1863 Seated Dime

21052 **1863—Environmental Damage—NCS. Proof.** Richly patinated in variegated apple-green and peach colors, this assertively struck proof Dime has an attractive and original appearance. There is little indication of environmental damage referred to on the NCS insert. Since only 460 proofs were struck, and the business strike production was limited to 14,000 pieces, this is a desirable Civil War example, and is worthy of bidder evaluation. (#4756)

Collectible Proof 1864 Seated Dime

21053 **1864—Improperly Cleaned—NCS. Proof.** Probably dipped in the past, since the gray fields offer reduced reflectivity. Not offensively hairlined, however, and partly retoned in peripheral golden tones. This sharply struck Civil War proof Dime exhibits a wire rim on both sides. The obverse rim at 4 o'clock has a small mark. A mere 470 pieces were struck, along with just 11,000 business strikes. Philadelphia Mint issues had tiny mintages between 1863 and 1867, since silver coins were hoarded during those years. Their place in commerce was taken by Fractional Currency. (#4757)

Scarce Proof 62 1865 Dime

21054 **1865 PR62 NGC.** Sharply struck. Magnification reveals some scattered mint-made lint marks on both surfaces. The central areas are brilliant. Wisps of blue and violet ornament the rims. From a scant proof mintage of just 500 pieces. (#4758)

Low Mintage AU Sharpness 1866 Dime

21055 **1866—Improperly Cleaned—NCS. AU Details.** A subdued gunmetal-gray key date Dime with tan and russet peripheral toning. Boldly struck, and little wear is evident, even upon inspection with a loupe. Struck from clashed dies. A mere 8,000 business strikes were coined, since Fractional Currency temporarily replaced silver denominations in circulation. (#4643)

Scarce AU Sharpness 1866-S Dime

21056 **1866-S—Stained—NCS. AU Details.** Fortin-101. This lightly circulated golden-brown example has no relevant marks, and is attractive despite a couple of small ebony spots on the Seated Liberty. The S mintmark is faint and can be easily overlooked by a cursory appearance. Likely, many 1866-S pieces have inadvertently been sold as an 1866, a problem since the 1866 is a low mintage rarity. The Fortin-101 variety is interesting for its lengthy vertical die crack (as made) above the shield. (#4644)

Select Cameo Proof 1867 Dime

21057 **1867 PR63 Cameo NGC.** Fortin-103. Light repunching is noted on the bases of the date digits. Nearly fully struck, only a couple of cereal grains on the upper left portion of the wreath are not completely brought up by the dies. Flashy fields, obvious white on black contrast, and rich peripheral gold toning combine to ensure the eye appeal. Proofs and business strikes combined for only 6,625 pieces, the final date in a run of very low mintage P-mint issues. (#84760)

Popular 1870 Dime

21058 **1870—Obverse Improperly Cleaned—NCS. Unc. Details.** Some faint hairlines on the obverse account for the NCS label designation. Attractive blue, violet, and gold iridescence complements both surfaces. (#4651)

Rare 1870-S Seated Dime

21059 **1870-S Fine 12 NGC.** The 1870-S Dime will always stand in the shadow of its unique Half Dime counterpart. Nonetheless, the low mintage of 50,000 pieces ensures that few survivors exist to satisfy the demand from the many collectors of the series. Slate-gray in color with wispy hairlines across the reverse. LIBERTY and the mintmark are sharp, a few central letters in the denomination are worn. Census: 1 in 12, 23 finer (12/05). Envelope Included. (#4652)

See the Online Session listings in the back of this volume for additional Reiver selections.

Elusive 1871-CC Dime

21060 **1871-CC—Damaged—NCS. VG Details.** Medium gray toning with pale gold and lilac highlights. The NCS label designation probably refers to some fine pin scratches which are largely masked by toning. From a tiny mintage of just 20,100 pieces. Eagerly sought and difficult to find in all grades, including at the VG level. (#4654)

1872-S Seated Dime With AU Details

21063 **1872-S—Improperly Cleaned—NCS. AU Details.** Pearl gray toning with some splashes of golden-brown. Traces of satiny luster survive in the protected areas of the designs. The strike is about average with softness noted at the base of the shield and at the top of the wreath. The first S is STATES is broken at the top. (#4658)

Scarce 1871-S Dime

21061 **1871-S AU50 NGC.** Medium gray surfaces with hints of gold. Scarce in AU50 and higher grades; all but a small portion served extensively in the channels of commerce. Most examples encountered range from Good to VF. (#4655)

Scarce 1873-CC Arrows Dime

21064 **1873-CC Arrows VG10 NGC.** Pearl gray toning on the highpoints deepens to charcoal gray in the fields. A scant 18,791 examples of the variety were minted and survivors are elusive in all grades, a claim that's well attested by the NGC *Census Report* data. A prize for the specialist. Census: 7 in 10, 37 finer (12/05). (#4666)

Eagerly-Sought 1872-CC Dime

21062 **1872-CC—Improperly Cleaned—NCS. Fine Details.** Pearl gray toning. Some tiny digs are noted in the obverse field beneath STATES, and magnification reveals two or three fine pin scratches at the obverse rim at eleven o'clock. Scarce and desirable in all grades. Only 35,480 dimes were coined at the Carson City Mint during the year. (#4657)

Choice AU 1874 Arrows Dime

21065 **1874 Arrows AU55 NGC.** Brilliant in the central areas with wisps and tinges of electric blue and golden-brown at the borders. This piece was prooflike at the time of issue and traces of the original mirror surface can be seen in the protected areas, especially near the rims. (#4668)

Popular 1878-CC Dime, XF40 NGC

21066 **1878-CC XF40 NGC.** Gunmetal gray toning with warm golden-brown and navy blue iridescent highlights. The 1878-CC is notable as the final dime issue coined at the Carson City mint. (#4686)

Low-Mintage 1879 Dime

21067 **1879—Environmental Damage—NCS. AU Details.** Charcoal gray toning with hints of pale violet. There appears to be scattered spotting beneath the toning, thus accounting for the NCS label designation. From a tiny mintage of just 15,100 pieces. The small production figure for 1879 suggests that stockpiles from preceding years were essentially adequate for the demands of commerce. Dime mintages remained low until 1882, at which time large-scale production was resumed. (#4687)

Low-Mintage 1880 Proof Dime

21068 **1880 PR60 NGC.** Delicate golden toning. Both surfaces exhibit pleasing cameo contrast, although there is no such designation on the NGC holder. The question that comes to mind after the examination of this piece is whether it's a proof or a prooflike business strike. The mirror quality of the fields and the sharpness of strike proclaims it to be a proof, but on the other hand, a scattering of contact marks on both surfaces look like bag marks to us, a feature which suggests that it's really a prooflike business strike. We invite prospective bidders to decide for themselves. The answer is important because pricing data indicate that Uncirculated business strikes are scarcer than proofs. Only 37,355 dimes were coined during the year of which 1,355 were proofs. (#4777)

Scarce 1881 Seated Dime, XF45

21069 **1881 XF45 NGC.** Intermingled blue and violet toning with some wisps of gold at the borders. Scarce in all grades, only 24,975 pieces were minted. By way of comparison, the 1916-D Mercury dime had a mintage that's more than ten times greater: 264,000 pieces. (#4689)

1884-S Dime

21070 **1884-S—Damaged—NCS. XF Details.** Pale silver-gray surfaces with sharp design features on both sides. The surfaces, and especially the obverse surfaces, have numerous tiny pin pricks. (#4693)

Rare 1885-S Seated Liberty Dime

21071 **1885-S—Improperly Cleaned—NCS. AU Details.** Bright silver surfaces with splashes of dark steel toning on the obverse and pale gold on the reverse. This is an attractive and extremely important Seated Dime, in spite of the minor hairlines that were generated when it was cleaned. (#4695)

Collectible 1886-S Dime, AU55 NGC

21072 **1886-S AU55 NGC.** Satiny luster with very faint speckled green and russet peripheral toning and bold devices. The initial appearance is exceptional for the grade, but each side displays a few wispy hairlines, under close examination with a magnifier. The 1886-S is not a common date, and carries a sizeable premium even in circulated grades. (#4697)

Attractive 1890 Dime, MS62 NGC

21073 **1890 MS62 NGC.** Bright surfaces display soft luster and whispers of gold-tan patina at the borders, and reveal minor handling marks in the right (facing) obverse field. Mild softness in noted in Liberty's hair and in the upper left (facing) part of the wreath. An attractive coin for the grade. (#4704)

1891 Dime With Prooflike Obverse MS64 ★ NGC

21074 **1891 MS64 ★ NGC.** Glimpses of apple-green and plum toning cling to the left obverse border of this boldly struck final year near-Gem. While the brilliant reverse features the usual cartwheel luster, the obverse is decidedly prooflike, which probably compelled NGC to award the star designation. Portions of the drapery near Liberty's shield are absent, and light clash marks are noted near the denomination, all as made. The obverse die was presumably polished to remove clash marks, which inadvertently caused the prooflike surface. (#4706)

BARBER DIMES

21075 **1892 MS62 NGC.** Bright silvery surfaces display peripheral cobalt-blue, golden-brown, and lavender toning, and sharply defined devices. Wispy handling marks are noted on Liberty's cheek and neck. (#4796)

21076 **1892-O AU58 NGC.** Pastel cobalt-blue, olive-green, and lavender toning overlays each side. The design features are sharply struck, and retain ample luster. There are no significant marks to report. (#4797)

21077 **1893 AU58 NGC.** Silver-gray surfaces retain considerable luster and display golden-tan patina around portions of the peripheries. A few minor handling marks are apparent on Liberty's cheek and in t he right (facing) obverse field. (#4800)

Attractively Toned 1894 Barber Dime

21078 **1894 MS62 NGC.** Lime-green and golden-tan patination covers most of the fields, leaving the motifs light silver-gray. All of the design elements are well brought up, and a few minute marks are visible on Liberty's face. (#4803)

Semi-Key Date 1895 Barber Dime AU58

21079 **1895 AU58 NGC.** This coin is a smoky purple-gray color, with a few grade-limiting marks on the cheek and a sharp strike. From a mintage of 690,000 business strikes, the 1895 is considered the rarest P-mint date in the series, and an overall semi-key issue. (#4806)

Sharp 1897 Gem Dime

21080 **1897 MS65 NGC.** Bright lustrous surfaces display splashes of cobalt-blue, lilac, and golden-brown patina, which tends to be heaviest in the border areas. The design elements are exquisitely struck throughout, and the surfaces are devoid of mentionable marks. Population: 47 in 65, 26 finer (9/05). (#4812)

Pleasing Mid-Grade 1897-O Dime

21081 **1897-O VF30 NGC.** A pleasant, circulated example of this key date dime. Strong remaining detail, but there is some evidence of rough handling visible at the center of the obverse. A collector's favorite. (#4813)

Colorful 1904 Near Gem Dime

21082 **1904 MS64 NGC.** Sharply struck, with bright lustrous surfaces that reveal golden-green and lilac on the obverse, and concentric rings of peripheral gold-yellow, light green, and cobalt-blue framing gold-lilac centers on the reverse. Light marks on Liberty's cheek and neck limit the grade. Population: 51 in 64, 14 finer (9/05). (#4833)

Pleasing Near-Gem 1906 Barber Dime

21083 **1906 MS64 NGC.** Boldly struck with full satin luster and light speckled toning near the edges. Just one or two small contact marks are evident on each of the two sides. A very nice coin, for the grade. (#4838)

Colorful and Well Preserved Near-Gem 1908-D Barber Dime

21084 **1908-D MS64 NGC.** Sharply defined throughout and exceptionally clean for this normally well preserved Denver Mint issue. Both sides are adorned near the peripheries in variegated hues of cobalt-blue and crimson, with a bit of olive and gold interspersed as well. The underlying mint luster is especially vibrant. Census: 28 in 64, 30 finer (12/05). (#4847)

See the Online Session listings in the back of this volume for additional Reiver selections.

MERCURY DIMES

Lightly Toned 1909-D Barber Dime

21085 **1909-D MS63 NGC.** This is a surprisingly difficult and elusive date in the Barber Dime series that is only occasionally available in Mint State grades. In fact, it is one of just 12 issues with a mintage below 1 million coins. A pleasing Mint State example with brilliant silver color at the centers, framed by lovely orange and russet toning on the obverse. The reverse is almost entirely brilliant silver with a hint of yellow color along the border. A few faint hairlines appear on the obverse along with a short scratch on Liberty's cheek, perhaps the limiting factors for the quality assessment by NGC. Over the years, since we began tracking our auction sales with our permanent archives, we have only handled 15 finer examples of this date. In an era where multiple examples of rare coins might appear in a single sale, this is a telling statistic. (#4851)

Gem Quality 1911 Barber Dime

21086 **1911 MS65 NGC.** Frosty and highly lustrous with excellent eye appeal. Essentially brilliant with only a wisp of champagne toning. (#4857)

21087 **1911-D MS64 NGC.** A satiny Mint State example with bright silver surfaces and traces of peripheral toning. (#4858)

Pleasing Key Date 1916-D Mercury Dime VF30 NGC

21088 **1916-D VF30 NGC.** An evenly worn light-gray example of this popular key date. The smooth surfaces only reveal faint obverse pinscratches under magnification. Considering the large number of counterfeit and altered versions of this issue, it is wise to pay a premium and purchase one that has already been authenticated, certified, and graded. (#4906)

Gem F.B. 1916-S Mercury Dime

21089 **1916-S MS65 Full Bands NGC.** Sharply struck with satiny silver luster beneath splashes of gold and iridescent toning. (#4909)

Desirable Gem 1919 Mercury Dime, F.B.

21090 **1919 MS65 Full Bands NGC.** Mostly brilliant with streaks and splashes of golden-brown color on each side. (#4923)

Popular AU Details 1921 Dime

21091 **1921—Improperly Cleaned—NCS. AU Details.** This bold P-mint series key has a slate-gray obverse and mottled russet and cream toning on the reverse. Very faint obverse hairlines are not readily detected, and should deter few collectors. The low mintage of the 1921 Dime has long made it a target for speculators, and it is the stopper to a date collection of Mercury Dimes. (#4934)

Brilliant Uncirculated 1925-D Dime

21094 **1925-D MS62 Full Bands NGC.** Both surfaces are essentially brilliant with some wisps of orange-gold at the obverse border. Most design features are boldly and deeply defined. (#4951)

Bright, Choice 1924-D Dime With Full Bands

21092 **1924-D MS64 Full Bands NGC.** Sharply struck and frosty. The reverse is essentially brilliant. The obverse is brilliant at the center with wisps of gold and blue at the periphery. (#4945)

Semi-Scarce 1926-S Dime

21095 **1926-S—Improperly Cleaned—NCS. VF Details.** A semi-scarce issue in the series. (#4958)

Mostly Brilliant 1924-S Dime, MS64

21093 **1924-S MS64 NGC.** Mostly brilliant surfaces with some splashes and blushes of gold, gray, and blue. Although some softness is noted at the central bands on the reverse, most of the other design features are about as sharp as could be desired. (#4946)

Lustrous Full Bands Gem 1927 Dime

21096 **1927 MS65 Full Bands NGC.** Speckled olive-green patina overlays lustrous surfaces on each side. A few minute marks are noted on the fasces. All of the design features are well brought up, culminating in the Full Bands designation. (#4961)

See the Online Session listings in the back of this volume for additional Reiver selections.

Choice Uncirculated 1927-S Dime

21097 **1927-S MS64 NGC.** Delightful satiny luster. Both surfaces exhibit appealing golden-gray toning with blushes of rose and navy blue visible on the obverse. Softness is noted on some of the reverse bands, most other design features are about as sharp as could be desired. (#4964)

Scarce 1942/1 Mercury Dime Overdate

21098 **1942/1—Corroded—NCS. AU Details.** Light silver surfaces with evidence of corrosion on the obverse. A pleasing example with hazy silver color on the reverse. (#5036)

An Attractive 1942/1 Mercury Dime

21099 **1942/1 AU55 NGC.** An attractive example of this popular overdate variety, listed as FS-010.7 in the Fivaz-Stanton reference book; the citation is mentioned on the NGC label. Delicate golden gray toning. Much original mint luster can still be seen around the letters, numerals, and central motifs. The overdate feature shows bold definition. Softness at the highpoints is noted, but it is not clear whether this is due to striking quality or wear. The story behind the 1942/41 overdate is well known, but bears repeating. In the later part of 1941 the die manufacturing department at the Philadelphia Mint continued to make 1941-dated obverse dies for the current coinage, but also prepared 1942-dated dies so that coinage could commence without delay at the beginning of the new calendar year. Evidently, when the overdate die was made, the workers in the die department impressed a hub having one of the dates, removed the die from the press to be annealed (a process required to remove brittleness due to work hardening), and then after annealing, replaced the die back into the hubbing press to receive a second impression. Unbeknownst to them, they had made a mistake by using a hub with the other date. The result was a die that had both a 1 and a 2 in the position of the fourth digit. (#5036)

21100 **1945-S Micro S MS67 NGC.** A lustrous coin with exceptional mint frost and abrasions of any type being held to a bare minimum. Some mottled gray patina is seen on each side. (#5062)

TWENTY CENT PIECES

Splendid Gem Uncirculated 1875 Twenty Cent Piece

21101 **1875 MS65 NGC.** A brilliant splendid Gem example. The devices are frosty and the fields have a texture intermediate between satiny and prooflike. Virtually all design features show bold definition including Liberty's hair and drapery, the obverse stars, all of which show their radials, and the eagle's plumage and claws. The only area that shows softness is the extreme tip of the eagle's left wing (viewer's right), which lacks full definition. A small planchet inclusion, as made, is noted on the reverse just below the juncture of the eagle's wing and body. (#5303)

Beautiful Superb Gem 1875 Twenty Cent Piece

21102 **1875 MS67 NGC.** First year of the type and also of this denomination, which only saw production for circulation in 1875 and 1876. The following two years saw production only of proof examples before the denomination was discontinued in its entirety. The strongly prooflike surfaces are covered with a veneer of medium intensity cobalt-blue and lavender patination. The design elements are sharply struck, except for the star centers along the right border. The NGC Census indicates that four examples of this date have received the coveted MS67 grade, but none have ever been given a higher grading number.

In some instances, the distinction between Mint State and Proof coins is not precise or clearly defined. Jules Reiver included this coin with Proof examples of 1876, 1877, and 1878. On the other hand, this cataloger agrees with the assessment by NGC that it is a superb gem Mint State example of the date. The fields are fully prooflike, but not deeply so, although the toning tends to mask the reflective qualities. The strike is sharp, but not full. Perhaps the biggest distinction is around the periphery, especially the obverse. The border dentils appear to blend into the field. This slight blending or merging is normally not seen on Proof coins, but only on Mint State examples. (#5296)

Select Uncirculated 1875-CC Twenty Cent Piece

21103 **1875-CC MS63 NGC.** Brilliant and lustrous. A typical strike with a few areas of softness noted on the highpoints of the designs. Probably no more than a fraction of 1 percent of the original mintage survives in Uncirculated condition. (#5297)

Blundered Date 1875-S Twenty-Cent Piece

21104 **1875-S—Improperly Cleaned—NCS. Unc Details.** FS-1875S-302. The mintmark is slightly doubled. Most important here, though, is the blundered date. The top of a stray 8 can be seen in the dentils below 18. To the left of this, it appears that the serif of a stray 1 is also visible. (#5298)

PROOF TWENTY CENT PIECES

1875-S Twenty Cent Piece, MS63

21105 **1875-S MS63 NGC.** The obverse is essentially brilliant. The reverse exhibits delicate golden-gray iridescence. The luster is satiny in some areas and frosty in others. Most design features are sharp, save for some softness noted at the eagle's beak and right claw, and two or three obverse stars. (#5298)

Choice Proof 1876 Twenty Cent Piece

21107 **1876 PR64 NGC.** The devices are sharp and frosty and the fields are glittering mirrors. Both surfaces exhibit gunmetal gray toning with delicate pink and blue iridescent highlights. Some die polish lines can be seen in the reverse field as made. Only 1,260 proofs were coined during the year. (#85304)

Well Preserved 1876 Twenty Cent Piece, MS64

21106 **1876 MS64 NGC.** Pewter gray toning with delicate pink, blue, violet, and gold iridescent highlights. The devices are frosty and the fields are satiny. Virtually all design features are boldly and deeply defined, save for some softness noted on portions of the eagle's claws. Not an easy issue to find this nicely preserved. (#5299)

1877 Twenty Cent Piece, Proof 63 Cameo

21108 **1877 PR63 Cameo NGC.** The frosty devices contrast beautifully with the glittering mirror fields. The reverse is fully brilliant. The obverse is brilliant at the center with blushes and wisps of orange-gold at the border. Virtually all design features exhibit bold definition, save for some of the fine details of Liberty's hair. A desirable proof-only issue, with a scant mintage of just 350 pieces, by far the lowest production figure in the short-lived twenty cent piece series; the much rarer 1876-CC had a mintage of 10,000 pieces, but its rarity can be accounted for by the fact that the vast majority of these pieces were melted before they could be issued. (#95305)

SEATED QUARTERS

1878 Twenty Cent Piece, Proof 62

21109 **1878 PR62 NGC.** Delicate pewter gray toning with wisps and tinges of pink and blue at the borders. Virtually all design features are sharply and deeply struck. Some faint hairlines, caused when the coin was wiped with a cloth years ago, account for the assigned grade. (#5306)

Select Proof 1878 Twenty Cent Proof Coin

21110 **1878 PR63 NGC.** Warm gunmetal gray toning with delicate pink, blue, and violet iridescent highlights. The strike is sharp with virtually all design features clearly and boldly defined including the star radials, Liberty's hair and drapery, and the eagle's claws and feathers. Some faint hairlines, visible under magnification, are probably all that prevented NGC from assigning a substantially higher grade. A scarce and eagerly-sought proof-only issue having a tiny mintage of just 600 pieces. (#5306)

Originally Toned Choice AU 1840 Seated Quarter

21111 **1840 AU55 NGC.** Briggs 1-A. This is a very attractive coin for the grade, with a minimum of contact marks and pleasing, iridescent toning that deepens to cobalt-blue about the upper right obverse periphery, with equally pleasing russet-red patina near the remaining borders. Lightly worn on the obverse highpoints, with a few faint pinscratches and scattered minor contact marks on the reverse. The more readily available die variety of this issue, this piece would, nonetheless, make an attractive addition to an advanced type set. (#5397)

Very Rare Large O Drapery 1840-O Quarter

21112 **1840-O Drapery AU53 NGC.** Large O mintmark. Breen-3941, "Very rare." Briggs (1991) states, "Most pieces are low grade... Finest known is XF45... To date this is the rarest collectible Seated Liberty Quarter." A fascinating variety, not only for its distinctive mintmark, but the reverse has two widely separated sets of dentils. Characteristic of the variety, portions of the eagle's body are softly struck, although the shield is relatively sharp. Striking weakness is also noted on Liberty's head and several stars. The gently toned and unmarked surfaces possesses ample luster, and the upper reverse field has myriad tiny planchet flaws. (#5398)

Scarce 1842 Seated Quarter AU50 NGC

21113 **1842 AU50 NGC.** Briggs 2-B. The 8 in the date is repunched. The smooth, problem-free surfaces display an even blanket of slate-gray patina, except for minor russet-red coloration near the obverse peripheries. Richly detailed throughout, the features rise powerfully above the fields despite light wear across the highpoints. Wispy hairlines are noted in the reverse fields, and there are a few small blemishes on the obverse. A pleasing AU example that should elicit strong bids from collectors whose limited budgets rule out the acquisition of a Mint State example. (#5401)

Sharply Detailed 1842-O Small Date Quarter

21114 **1842-O Small Date—Improperly Cleaned—NCS. AU Details.** Nearly all 1842 Quarter Dollars, struck at Philadelphia and New Orleans, employed the Large Date logotype. In Philadelphia, the few quarters struck from dies with the Small Date size were produced only in Proof quality, and today are extreme rarities, with less than 10 examples known today. In New Orleans, the mintage was considerably higher, with a total production of 157,000, and examples are usually available, though far from common. In fact, this issue remains a major rarity in grades better than XF, and even examples at that grade level are elusive. Although it is unquestionably cleaned, with noticeable hairlines on both sides, this is an excellent example with sharp design features and only the slightest wear. The surfaces have reacquired a trace of golden-brown toning. Despite the hairlines, this is an extremely important opportunity for the advanced collector. (#5403)

Patinated Choice AU 1844 Quarter

21115 **1844 AU55 NGC.** Silvery centers are flanked by multicolored peripheral toning, and the design elements are sharply defined. The surfaces are quite clean. Tough to locate this close to Mint State. Census: 6 in 55, 40 finer (12/05). (#5406)

Deeply Toned Near-Mint 1846 Seated Quarter, Repunched Date

21116 **1846 AU58 NGC.** Briggs 2-D, High R.3. Repunched Date. An originally and deeply toned example of this scarce variety that appears Mint State at first glance. Highly attractive and worth a close look from specialists in this area. Population: 14 in 58, 26 finer (9/05). (#5409)

21117 **1848 XF45 NGC.** From an original mintage of only 46,000 pieces, the 1848 is a moderately scarce issue in the Seated quarter series. This example displays lovely, originally toned surfaces that display a rainbow of colors near the obverse peripheries, and greenish-tan patina near the reverse borders. Typically boldly struck and lightly worn, with a few small contact marks in the obverse fields. An attractive example, for the assigned grade level. (#5412)

Collectible Key Date 1849-O Quarter

21118 **1849-O VG10 NGC.** Only the L in LIBERTY is not legible, and this unmarked pearl-gray piece retains pleasing detail on the reverse shield. For whatever reason, the New Orleans Mint did not report a mintage for the 1849-O Quarter. Presumably, the issue was struck in early 1850, and its production included in the reported 1850-O mintage. Briggs (1991) estimates a mintage of 16,000 pieces. A key date to the No Motto series, most survivors are in VF and lower grades. (#5414)

Exceedingly Scarce 1851-O Seated Quarter AU50 NGC

21119 **1851-O AU50 NGC.** A scarce issue at all grade levels, this smooth, unabraded example suffers from little other than a small degree of honest wear, and some wispy hairlines in the field areas. The light-gray surfaces are untoned on the reverse, and just show a small amount of dappled purple toning on the upper obverse. An issue that is seldom offered in any grade, the 1851-O is a low mintage (88,000 pieces), pre-1853 quarter that saw widespread melting during the California Gold Rush era. Population: 2 in 50, 8 finer (8/05). (#5418)

21120 **1852—Improperly Cleaned—NCS. AU Details.** Wispy hairlines are visible on light gray, unabraded surfaces. Nice design detail prevails. (#5419)

Difficult VF Details 1852-O Quarter

21121 **1852-O—Obverse Scratched—NCS. VF Details.** Deep sea-green and lilac-brown colors envelop this evenly circulated rare date Quarter, which bears a bold LIBERTY and substantial plumage detail on the eagle. The right obverse field has a few subdued pinscratches. Tougher than the mintage of 96,000 pieces would suggest, perhaps a portion of the mintage was melted in favor of the lower tenor 1853-O Arrows issue. (#5420)

Elusive 1853 No Arrows Quarter

21122 **1853 No Arrows—Improperly Cleaned—NCS. Fine Details.** Doubling is noted at the 3 in the date, a feature characteristic of all 1853 No Arrows quarters as is attested by Walter Breen's *Complete Encyclopedia*. The scarcity of the issue appears to be greater than the mintage figure of 44,200 suggests, and prompts us to wonder if a large portion of these were melted either before or shortly after the time of issue. (#5421)

Desirable AU53 1853-O Arrows and Rays Quarter

21123 **1853-O Arrows and Rays AU53 NGC.** Brilliant in the central areas with wisps and tinges of golden brown and violet at the borders. This piece was prooflike at the time of issue and traces of mirror surface are still visible in the protected areas, especially on the reverse. The strike is about average with some flatness noted on the obverse stars. Collector demand is boosted by the issue's status as a one year design type. (#5428)

See the Online Session listings in the back of this volume for additional Reiver selections.

Near-Mint 1855 Arrows Quarter

21124 **1855 Arrows AU58 NGC.** The devices are frosty and the fields are satiny. Most design features are sharp save for a touch of flatness on some of the obverse stars. Both surfaces are essentially brilliant with some blushes of pink iridescence at the obverse periphery. Close examination reveals a tiny spot by the fifth obverse star. (#5435)

Rare and Choice Proof 1856 Quarter Dollar

21125 **1856 PR64 NGC.** The estimated mintage for proof 1856 quarters is based upon the number of proof sets distributed that year; that is, approximately 100 sets. Of that number, it is believed that only 25-30 coins are believed extant today. Indeed, NGC and PCGS combined have certified only 39 examples, several of which are likely to be resubmissions. Furthermore, our records indicate that we have handled three specimens over the past 15 years, and the issue has made appearances at 27 auctions within the past 20 years.

The example we offer in this lot is a flashy, deeply mirrored proof that shows pinpoint striking details throughout. Whispers of gold-brown, cobalt-blue, and lavender toning bathe each side. The surfaces are devoid of significant abrasions; some wispy hairlines in the fields preclude an even higher grade. NGC has only certified five finer proof examples of this date. A prominent bulge through the right (facing) wing, from AM to the arrows, is characteristic of all Proof 1856 Quarter Dollars. (#5552)

21126 **1856-S—Improperly Cleaned—NCS. XF Details.** Light gray surfaces reveal light hairlines. The design features are nicely delineated. (#5440)

Important Proof 1858 Quarter Dollar

21127 **1858 PR63 NGC.** Briggs 5-E. Walter Breen, and Larry Briggs after him, recorded the mintage of 1858 Proof Quarters to be 80 coins, undoubtedly borrowing this figure from the long standing historically inaccurate record of 80 Proof Silver Dollars minted. Today, it is believed that the actual mintage of these coins was probably somewhere in the vicinity of 300 or so coins, although this is merely a guess. The 1858 Proof Quarter Dollars are possibly the most poorly made of all Proof issues from that period. Walter Breen reported this in his *Complete Encyclopedia:* "most proofs show multiple lint marks (incuse impressions from lint adhering to dies. Someone failed to wipe them clean before starting the press run)." The Reiver Collection coin shows extensive lintmarks on both sides, including a long depression on Liberty's left (facing) arm, down from the shoulder. Others appear in the fields on both sides. The upper reverse field has a modest lamination defect. The reverse has a die crack from the final S through the bottoms of OF and on to the base of the first A in AMERICA, and another from the border to the point of the top arrow, through the lower to arrows, and into the field above L and O in DOL. The design elements are all fully defined, and the devices are slightly lustrous with considerable cameo contrast, although this example was not designated as a Cameo Proof. Both sides are essentially untoned, save for hints of steel color on the rims. (#5554)

1858-O Quarter With AU Details

21128 **1858-O—Improperly Cleaned—NCS. AU Details.** Pale lilac-gray toning with hints of delicate blue and gold. Faint clash marks can be seen on the reverse. (#5446)

Scarce 1858-S Seated Quarter Fine 12 NGC

21129 **1858-S Fine 12 NGC.** Evenly worn and well detailed, for the grade, with very light toning and a few faint pinscratches on the otherwise smooth surfaces. Scarce at all grade levels, especially Fine and higher. Census: 3 in 12, 25 finer (12/05). (#5447)

Glittering Proof 63 1859 Quarter

21130 **1859 PR63 NGC.** The fields are glittering mirrors and the devices are sharp and frosty; despite this, there's no "cameo" designation on the NGC label. Both surfaces are almost fully brilliant, with wisps and tinges of gold and electric blue noted at the periphery of the obverse. Close examination reveals a tiny mint-caused planchet lamination flaw above the second S in STATES; something mentioned for accuracy's sake. From a proof mintage of just 800 pieces. (#5555)

Choice Cameo Proof 1860 Quarter

21131 **1860 PR64 Cameo NGC.** Frosty devices contrast with nicely mirrored fields. Light golden-brown and rose toning graces the obverse margin. A well struck near-Gem. A tiny reeding mark above the R in QUAR is noted for pedigree purposes. The *Guide Book* reports a mintage of 1,000 pieces. However, a large portion of this emission was reportedly melted as unsold, and low third party populations are in accord. Population: 5 in 64 Cameo, 5 finer (8/05). (#85556)

Lovely Near-Gem 1861 Seated Liberty Quarter

21132 **1861 MS64 NGC.** The 1861 Seated Liberty quarter, in addition to its popularity as a Civil War issue, is one of the few No Motto quarters that is occasionally available in Gem and near-Gem condition for the type collector. This is a dazzling near-Gem coin that is fully struck in all areas. The surfaces are framed in beautiful purple-rose and dark-green toning on the left side of the obverse, and brilliant silver-gray reverse coloration. Well preserved and nearly pristine, save for a few very wispy field marks, the coin has numerous heavy die polish lines (as struck) in the obverse and reverse fields. (#5454)

1862 Proof Seated Quarter PR61 NGC

21133 **1862 PR61 NGC.** Only 550 proofs were struck during this Civil War year. This exceptionally attractive specimen is toned near the obverse borders in shades of cobalt-blue, violet, and apricot, amid nicely reflective fields. The reverse is untoned. A shallow, lengthy vertical abrasion is noted in the right obverse field, and both sides of the coin possess a few faint hairlines. (#5558)

Difficult 1862-S Seated Quarter

21134 **1862-S VF30 NGC.** This Civil War issue had a relatively low production of 67,000 pieces, but this mintage figure only partly explains the scarcity of this issue above basal circulated grades. Silver coins were important to western commerce, and remained in circulation until worn slick. Their numismatic value was not considered for many years after their production. A nicely detailed cream-gray piece with subdued, lightly marked surfaces. Census: 5 in 30, 26 finer (12/05). (#5457)

See the Online Session listings in the back of this volume for additional Reiver selections.

Choice AU 1863 Quarter

21135 **1863 AU55 NGC.** A scarce Civil War issue that is more difficult to locate than its mintage of 191,140 business strikes might indicate. Both sides exhibit a medium silver-gray appearance with a few colorful accents at the borders, and relatively clean surfaces for this often abused issue. A small area of roughness, just above Liberty's flag, appears to be as struck. Numerous wispy hairlines reside in the obverse and reverse fields. (#5458)

1863 Seated Liberty Quarter PR63 NGC

21136 **1863 PR63 NGC.** Pale gray and gold toning covers the reflective surfaces of this popular Civil War issue. Light mottled toning appears at the obverse peripheries. A few hairlines on the reverse keep this example from a higher grade. (#5559)

Low Mintage Proof 1863 Quarter

21137 **1863 PR63 NGC.** An exactingly struck and untoned example that has relatively clean fields. The devices on both sides exhibit noticeable frost; however, NGC has not designated this specimen as Cameo. Just 460 proofs were struck, a nadir for proof production of the denomination between 1859 and 1913. (#5559)

Scarce 1864 Seated Quarter

21138 **1864—Improperly Cleaned—NCS. AU Details.** A sharp example, mostly silver-gray in color although russet and steel-blue patination is located near the rims. The fields are cloudy with hairlines, nonetheless, a collectible representative of this conditionally elusive Civil War issue. (#5459)

Elusive 1864 Proof Seated Quarter PR63 NGC

21139 **1864 PR63 NGC.** Lovely cameo contrast is evident on the obverse, along with some red-gold toning below Liberty, and a few scattered hairlines in the fields. Light silver-gray reverse patina. Elusive Civil War era issue, one of a mere 470 proofs struck. (#5560)

Pleasing Fine 1864-S Quarter

21140 **1864-S Fine 12 NGC.** An untroubled gunmetal-gray rare date Seated Quarter. LIBERTY is fully legible, and all letters are bold except for the L and Y. While 20,000 pieces were struck, few if any West Coast numismatists set aside examples until several decades later. (#5460)

21141 **1865 Fine 12 NGC.** LIBERTY is fully legible if not quite sharp. Some drapery and plumage details remain visible. Blended gunmetal-gray and chestnut colors confer originality. Mintages of Quarters at Philadelphia continued their steady decline from the peak of 4.85 million struck in 1861; only 58,800 pieces were struck in 1865, and production bottomed out at 16,800 coins the subsequent year. (#5461)

Scarce Cameo Proof 1865 Quarter

21142 **1865 PR63 Cameo NGC.** Honey, rose, and pale lavender colors enrich the obverse periphery, while the obverse center and the reverse remain brilliant. Impressive Cameo frost confirms the eye appeal. A few wispy field hairlines are appropriate for the grade. This Civil War date has a low reported proof mintage of 500 pieces. (#85561)

Problem-Free 1866 Seated Quarter With Motto Fine 15 NGC

21143 **1866 Motto Fine 15 NGC.** An attractive specimen with tan-gray toning, enhanced by faint gold and blue accents in the obverse fields. Original, problem-free examples of this issue are difficult to locate, and this is a pleasant exception. From an original mintage of just 17,525 pieces, scarce in all grades. (#5468)

Lovely Select Cameo Proof 1866 Seated Quarter

21144 **1866 PR63 Cameo NGC.** Lovely orange, pink-red, and cobalt-blue toning adorns the obverse borders. Fully struck with gorgeous cameo contrast on each side. As one would expect for the grade, several light hairlines are present in the fields. Population: 4 in 63 Cameo, 12 finer in Cameo condition (9/05). (#85565)

Scarce 1866-S Motto Quarter

21145 **1866-S Fine 15 NGC.** While the 1866-S Half Dollar, Half Eagle, Eagle, and Double Eagle all exist in both No Motto and Motto format, all 1866-S Quarters bear the Motto above the eagle. Apparently, the mintage of 28,000 pieces was struck later in the year, after the new reverse dies had finally reached the westernmost branch mint. This evenly circulated piece has natural steel-gray and charcoal color, and no marks are relevant for the grade. Scarce in all grades. (#5469)

21146 **1867 Fine 12 NGC.** LIBERTY is faint but readable, and IN GOD WE TRUST is also worn but distinct. A slate-gray example, problem-free except for a thin horizontal scratch above the date. A mere 20,000 pieces were struck, in addition to 625 proofs. Census: 1 in 12, 18 finer (12/05). (#5470)

Conditionally Scarce 1867 Proof Seated Quarter PR64 Cameo NGC

21147 **1867 PR64 Cameo NGC.** Deep, variegated, original coloration bathes both sides of this near-Gem cameo proof. All of the design elements are sharply struck. A few wispy hairlines, particularly in the obverse fields, account for the grade. Population: 6 in 64 Cameo, 6 finer in Cameo condition (9/05). (#85566)

21148 **1867-S VG10 NGC.** Briggs 1-A. LIBERTY is fully legible on this circulated silver-gray example. A thin scratch crosses the raised wrist, otherwise problem-free. Very scarce and perhaps underrated. NGC and PCGS combined have certified 31 pieces throughout all grades. To put this small number into perspective, NGC alone has certified 44 examples of the 1916 Standing Liberty Quarter as MS65 Full Head. (#5471)

Low Mintage 1868 Seated Quarter

21149 **1868 VF35 NGC.** Briggs 1-A. Gunmetal-blue and cream-gray colors blend throughout this suitable defined scarce date Seated Quarter. Tiny marks are distributed, none of which distract. Just 29,400 business strikes were coined, a perfunctory production since unbacked Fractional Currency drove out specie during this era. Census: 3 in 35, 25 finer (12/05). (#5472)

Impressive Proof 63 1868 Quarter

21150 **1868 PR63 NGC** The sharp frosty devices contrast beautifully with the glittering mirror fields. We would have cheerfully awarded this piece a "cameo" designation if it were up to us, but there is no such mention included on the NGC label. The central areas are brilliant. Hints of delicate blue, gold, and violet ornament the borders. Some faint hairlines are all that keep this beauty out of the PR65 category. From a scant proof mintage of just 600 pieces. (#5567)

Blazing Proof 64 1869 Quarter

21151 **1869 PR64 NGC.** The design elements are sharp and frosty and the fields are blazing mirrors. There is, however, no "cameo" designation on the NGC label. The central areas are fully brilliant, while delicate pink and gold iridescence can be seen at the borders. Only 600 proof quarters were minted during the year, and collector demand is boosted by the fact that the production figure for 1869 business strikes was a scant 16,000 pieces. (#5568)

Challenging Bold VF 1869-S Quarter Dollar

21152 **1869-S VF30 NGC.** Briggs-1-Die State-A. Dappled gold and pearl-gray color enriches this moderately circulated better date Quarter. Faint handling marks are noted on the eagle's shield and the right obverse field. Difficult to find, even more so than suggested by the low mintage of 76,000 pieces. (#5475)

Desirable Cameo Proof 63 1870 Quarter

21153 **1870 PR63 Cameo NGC.** The devices are sharp and frosty and the fields are blazing mirrors. The central areas are brilliant changing to a vivid orange-gold at the borders. A mere 1,000 proof quarters were minted during the year. Population: 5 in 63, 6 finer (9/05). (#85569)

Rare 1870-CC Quarter, AU Details

21154 **1870-CC—Improperly Cleaned—NCS. AU Details.** Specific die characteristics, especially the mintmark, should be understood by anyone who is thinking of buying an 1870-CC Quarter Dollar. Altered dates and added mintmarks, while not a major problem today, still exist. The top of C in AMERICA is straight, except for a slight indentation at the right side of that letter. The two elements of the mintmark are widely spaced with the first C lower than the second. This reverse die continued in use through early 1873.

The premier issue from the Carson City Mint, generally considered to be the most challenging in the Seated Quarter series. Only 8,340 pieces were struck, and very few are known today in any grade. Indeed, only 65 specimens have been certified by NGC and PCGS combined (some of which are undoubtedly resubmissions) and just one of these is in Mint State. The AU details specimen offered here exhibits semi-bright silvery surfaces that are moderately hairlined. A few small toning spots are noted in the upper right (facing) obverse field. (#5477)

21155 **1871 XF45 NGC.** Slate-gray in color with faint russet color at the margins. Briggs obverse 3 or 4, the BER in LIBERTY is faint due to the die preparation and not because of wear. An attractively detailed and untroubled Choice XF representative of this scarce but collectible issue. Census: 3 in 45, 26 finer (12/05). (#5478)

Popular Proof 61 1871 Quarter

21156 **1871 PR61 NGC.** Mostly brilliant surfaces with blushes of gold, pink, and blue at the obverse border. Although the reverse is Gem-quality, or close to it, the obverse shows a scattering of contact marks suggesting that this piece may have been kept face up in a dresser drawer or jewelry box during several years of its existence. Perhaps one of the greatest benefits provided by NGC and PCGS holders is that it makes the preservation task much easier for today's generation of numismatists, something we should all be grateful for. Only 960 proof quarters were minted in 1871. (#5570)

Very Rare 1871-CC Quarter

21157 **1871-CC—Improperly Cleaned—NCS. VF Details.** Faint hairlines on the obverse account for the assigned NCS label designation. Both surfaces exhibit medium gray toning with pale gold and lilac highlights. Only 10,890 examples were minted and survivors are very rare in all grades, a claim that's attested by both the NGC and PCGS population data. We can only infer that all but a tiny percentage of these were reclaimed into bullion before the time of issue or shortly thereafter. Here's one of the landmark rarities in the Seated Liberty quarter series. (#5479)

Collectible Fine 1871-S Quarter

21158 **1871-S Fine 12 NGC.** Briggs 1-A. Pearl-gray devices and fields contrast with dusky tan toning near the rims. Circulation damage is not present. A worthy example of this scarce issue. Only 30,900 pieces were struck, the lowest Motto S-mint production except for the 1866-S. As a result, the 1871-S is sought in all circulated grades by Seated specialists. (#5480)

Lovely Cameo Proof 64 1872 Quarter

21159 **1872 PR64 Cameo NGC.** The sharp frosty design elements contrast beautifully with the blazing mirror fields. The surfaces are mostly brilliant with blushes and wisps of orange-gold, blue, and violet. Here's one of the nicest survivors from an original proof mintage of just 950 pieces. Population: 6 in 64, 17 finer (9/05). (#85571)

See the Online Session listings in the back of this volume for additional Reiver selections.

Rare 1872-CC Quarter

21160 **1872-CC Good 6 NGC.** Medium gray toning with delicate gold and lilac iridescent highlights. Only 22,500 quarters were minted at the Carson City Mint during the year, and survivors are elusive in all grades. (#5482)

Impressive XF 1872-S Quarter Dollar

21161 **1872-S XF40 NGC.** A mere 83,000 quarters were struck at the San Francisco Mint in 1872. A low mintage, combined with heavy attrition of coins in California during this period make this an especially scarce issue. It has been some time since we have seen this issue in one of our sales that has not been damaged or cleaned in some way. This example displays silver-gray surfaces that are devoid of mentionable abrasions. Perhaps lightly cleaned with some wispy hairlines on each side. Advanced Seated Quarter collectors and specialists are keenly aware of the difficulty locating examples of this issue. In the past 12 years, since we started maintaining our auction archives, we have handled just 17 examples of this date, and only four of those were nicer than this example. (#5483)

Attractive Proof 63 No Arrows 1873 Quarter

21162 **1873 No Arrows PR63 NGC.** Here's yet another lovely proof that shows pleasing contrast between the sharp frosty devices and fiery mirror fields, but without any "cameo" designation on the NGC label. The central areas are brilliant. Wisps and blushes of gold, blue, and violet ornament the rims. A mere 600 proofs of the variety were minted, one of the lowest proof production figures of the era. (#5572)

Desirable Proof 1873 Arrows Quarter

21163 **1873 Arrows PR63 NGC.** Peach and lemon tints endow the margins of this sharply struck and carefully preserved example. The Arrows, With Motto proof type has a combined mintage of merely 1,240 pieces, and the 1873 Arrows has the lesser of the two productions. The present proof reverse die is identified by its die scratch through the left shield lines, and was intermittently used to strike proofs between 1872 and 1880. (#85574)

Rare 1873-CC Arrows Quarter

21164 **1873-CC Arrows Fine Details, Reverse Damage, NCS.** Since only five 1873-CC No Arrows Quarters are known, collectors will have to settle for only the 1873-CC Arrows variety, the scarcest issue with the Arrows type. Just 12,462 pieces were struck, and surprisingly few have survived, even by chance. This slate-gray representative displays a full LIBERTY, although the L and Y are somewhat faint. The reverse retains some plumage definition. A broad scratch and a minor scratch pass through the UA in QUAR, these two marks account for the Damage designation. (#5492)

Frosty Cameo 1874 Arrows Quarter

21165 **1874 Arrows PR62 Cameo NGC.** Undeniable white frost dominates the devices, and only light sea-green and gold peripheral color prevents full brilliance. A few faint hairlines, but less than expected for the conservatively assessed grade. The proof mintage of 700 pieces is certainly low, but the importance of the 1874 Arrows rises when it is understood it represents a short-lived type. (#85575)

Scarce 1874 Arrows Quarter PR63 NGC

21166 **1874 Arrows PR63 NGC.** Rose and gold color illuminates the date and left side stars, and accompanies UNITED on the reverse. A bold and untroubled piece with an especially clean reverse. Proof type collectors soon discover how elusive the Arrows Quarter is, since it was struck in limited quantities for just two years. Minor strike doubling affects the stars and Liberty's profile. (#5575)

Gently Toned AU 1874-S Arrows Quarter

21167 **1874-S Arrows AU50 NGC.** Aqua and gold hues converge upon the faintly toned centers. Several bold die lines pass through Liberty's waist, leg, and shield, all as made. The more available of the two Arrows, Motto S-mint issues. According to Briggs (1991), "a hoard of 80-100 pieces were discovered in a west coast bank in 1949. Almost all UNC.'s on the market today have come from this disposal..." (#5495)

Gem Cameo Proof 1875 Seated Liberty Quarter

21168 **1875 PR65 Cameo NGC.** Type II Reverse. An interesting research piece from the new hub with TATE clearly separated. This is known as the Type II reverse in Seated Liberty Quarter parlance. In his reference on the subject, Larry Briggs noted that two obverse and two reverse dies were combined in parallel marriages to create two different Proof varieties, both from the Type I reverse hub, with TATE virtually touching. The obverse appears to be Briggs obverse die 4 but in a later state with little recutting of the 7 or 5, while the reverse is similar to his reverse die E, except that it is a Type II reverse. A lovely Gem Cameo Proof with mostly brilliant silver-white surfaces accented by peripheral gold, lilac, green, and iridescent toning, mostly on the obverse. The fields have a few faint hairlines, but these are mostly hidden beneath the toning. A scarce Proof issue in an uncommon grade. Population: 6 in 65, 1 finer (8/05). (#85576)

Original Gem 1876 Seated Quarter

21169 **1876 MS65 NGC.** Type Two Reverse. A lustrous and clearly original Gem with lovely apple-green, pearl-gray, and golden-brown toning. Sharply struck and undisturbed. The borders on both sides exhibit lengthy, slender die cracks. 1876 was the high water mark for Seated Quarter production, more than 30 million pieces were struck. The Philadelphia Mint alone struck close to 18 million pieces. However, high grade Mint State pieces are scarce, and in demand from type collectors. Census: 38 in 65, 21 finer (12/05). (#5501)

See the Online Session listings in the back of this volume for additional Reiver selections.

Originally Toned Cameo Proof 1876 Quarter

21170 **1876 PR62 Cameo NGC.** Type Two Reverse. This penetratingly struck specimen features glowing white devices and pleasing cherry, honey, and ocean-blue peripheral toning. Minor obverse hairlines determine the grade. The 1876 had the highest proof production prior to 1880, partly because of the Centennial exposition held in Philadelphia that year, where the Mint had an exhibit and sold proof sets. (#85577)

Borderline Uncirculated 1877 Quarter

21171 **1877 AU58 NGC.** Type Two Reverse. Delicate gold color enriches the borders. This well struck and still flashy example has the look of a briefly circulated proof, but has been designated a business strike by NGC. Wispy blemishes accompany the obverse field, but there are no distracting marks. A light die crack is noted through AR DOL. (#5504)

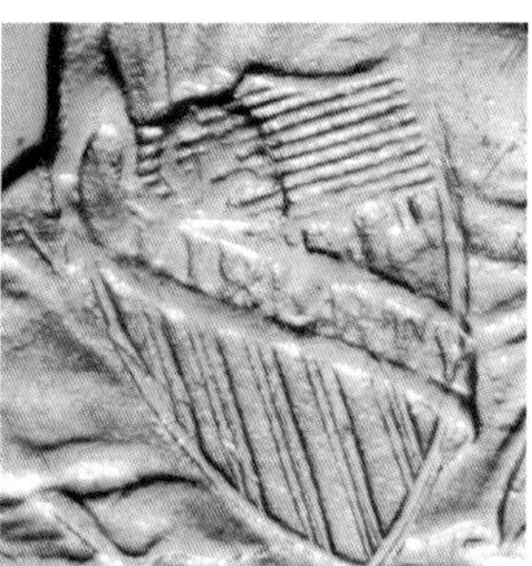

Uncirculated 1877 Quarter, Briggs 2-C

21172 **1877 MS61 NGC.** Type Two Reverse. Briggs 2-C. Honey-gold and apple-green colors enrich the peripheries, while the frosty devices and nearby fields remain untoned. The grade is determined by wispy slide marks on the obverse field and a light vertical pinscratch near the base of the pole. Briggs 2-C is identified by a large die break above LIBERTY and a small area of unfinished surface beneath the right (facing) armpit. (#5504)

Gorgeously Toned 1878 Proof Seated Quarter PR63 NGC

21173 **1878 PR63 NGC.** Crisply struck with sharply reflective fields and lovely cameo contrast on the obverse. The reverse is untoned, while the obverse displays beautiful burnt-orange toning near the peripheries. The glassy surfaces reveal a few grade-defining hairlines on each side. (#5579)

Pleasing 1878-CC Quarter, MS63 NGC

21174 **1878-CC MS63 NGC.** Like the other mints, coinage production in 1878 consisted primarily of the new "Bland Dollars," although other denominations were produced, mostly in limited quantities. The Carson City Mint coined 996,000 quarters in 1878, the second highest mintage denomination. Struck from the so-called "canceled dies" that show a long die scratch from the right knee cap up into the left arm of Liberty. The design features are well brought up, and the lustrous surfaces display a delicate layer of ice-blue, lavender, and golden-brown patina. A few minor handling marks in the fields define the grade. A highly desirable example, and an important opportunity for the advanced Seated Liberty collector. (#5509)

21175 **1878-S Fine 12 NGC.** Briggs 1-A. A subdued slate-gray piece that has a mere hint of granular surface. The 1878-S Half Dollar is a famous rarity within the Seated denominations, but its Quarter counterpart is also scarce. The production of 140,000 pieces was presumably completed early in the year, before the arrival of Morgan Dollar dies. It would be ten years before San Francisco struck additional Quarters. Census: 2 in 12, 25 finer (12/05). (#5510)

21176 **1879—Polished—NCS. AU Details.** Briggs 1-A. Bright and hairlined from polishing, and a pinscratch journeys through the I in LIBERTY. Nonetheless, a sharp representative of this low mintage issue. A scant 13,700 pieces were produced, since the mints were busy churning out Silver Dollars to comply with the Bland-Allison Act. (#5511)

Gem Cameo Proof 1879 Quarter Dollar

21177 **1879 PR65 Cameo NGC.** Breen-4105, Briggs 2-B. Type II Reverse. Official Mint Records state that only 250 Proofs were coined, but as Breen noted: "The low mintage has not been taken seriously." Today, the *Guide Book* shows a mintage of 1,100 Proofs, in line with the production of other silver denominations, and probably closer to the real production total. Today, some prooflike business strikes have been certified as Proof and vice-versa. This is a lovely Cameo Proof with exceptional contrast. The devices are frosty and lustrous with white color. The fields are deeply mirrored and the whole is accented by peripheral rose, lilac, and blue color, mostly on the obverse. Population: 7 in 65, 11 finer (8/05). (#85580)

Collectible Proof 1880 Quarter

21178 **1880—Improperly Cleaned—NCS. Proof.** Type One Reverse. Delicate hairlines suggest a long-ago wipe, but this exactingly struck specimen is partly retoned in chestnut and pearl-gray colors. After the Morgan Dollar was introduced in 1878, mintages of the other silver denominations drastically declined. The Dime returned to mass production in 1882, but it was not until 1888 that a reasonable mintage of Quarters took place, not in Philadelphia but at the San Francisco Mint. (#5581)

Charming Choice Cameo 1880 Quarter

21179 **1880 PR64 Cameo NGC.** Type One Reverse. Lovingly toned in lemon and electric-blue colors, this needle-sharp Choice Proof possesses icy devices and only faintly hairlined fields. A radiant example of this scarce issue, limited to a combined proof and commercial production of 15,000 pieces. Portions of the drapery near the Y in LIBERTY are absent, as made from a lapped die. (#85581)

21180 **1881 VF20 NGC.** Briggs 1-A. LIBERTY is crisp, although a few letters within IN GOD WE TRUST are well worn. This cream-gray piece has even wear and no detracting marks. A mere 12,000 pieces were coined, as the Quarter denomination continued to be neglected by the mints, which instead struck vast quantities of Morgan Dollars. (#5513)

See the Online Session listings in the back of this volume for additional Reiver selections.

Splendid 1881 Quarter, PR66 Cameo NGC

21181 **1881 PR66 Cameo NGC.** Briggs 2-B. There are a pair of short die scratches from the top of Liberty's right (facing) knee into the drapery—a diagnostic feature of the proof die marriage of this issue. Frosty devices stand out against the mirrored fields, and delicate lavender, cobalt-blue, and gold-brown toning gravitates to the borders. A truly splendid example with very few peers. (#85582)

Lovely Select 1883 Proof Seated Quarter

21184 **1883 PR63 NGC.** A pinpoint-sharp Quarter, nicely frosted but without a Cameo designation from NGC. A hint of apricot color prevents full brilliance. An occasional wispy hairline in the fields decides the grade. The Philadelphia Mint was busy making other denominations in 1883, and less than 15,500 Quarters were struck, a figure that combines proofs and business strikes. (#5584)

Scarce Borderline Uncirculated 1882 Quarter

21182 **1882 AU58 NGC.** A charming silver-gray example of this scarce issue. Lightly marked and crisply struck. The 1882 has the highest Philadelphia Mint production of its decade, yet only 15,200 pieces were struck. Light clash marks (as made) outline the central devices. (#5514)

Icy Cameo Gem Proof 1883 Quarter

21185 **1883 PR65 Cameo NGC.** Radiant snow-white devices contrast with seamless fields. Plum and honey colors occupy portions of the obverse border. This intricately struck Gem has a splendidly preserved reverse and only the faintest handling marks on the obverse field. Population: 13 in 65 Cameo, 13 finer (9/05). (#85584)

Pleasing Cameo Proof 1882 Seated Quarter

21183 **1882 PR63 Cameo NGC.** Attractive golden-brown color enriches the borders of this meticulously struck and reasonably preserved specimen. Icy devices display undeniable contrast with the mirrored fields. The obverse is lightly die doubled, most evident along the left border of Liberty's shield. With the exception of the 1888-S, all Quarters from the 1880s are very scarce. (#85583)

Elusive Business Strike 1884 Quarter

21186 **1884 VF30 NGC.** A scant 8,000 Quarters were struck. Aside from the 1886, this was the lowest Philadelphia Mint business strike production of the Seated Quarter series. Some of these pieces were set aside, but most entered circulation, such as the present nicely detailed and problem-free slate-gray representative. (#5516)

Cameo Near Gem Proof 1884 Quarter

21187 **1884 PR64 Cameo NGC.** Orange and pale mauve tones embrace the obverse exergue and the upper reverse rim. Luminous white devices exhibit obvious contrast with the undisturbed fields. The 1884 had the lowest proof mintage since 1878, presumably because proof-only Trade Dollars were no longer part of the silver set. (#85585)

21188 **1885 VF25 NGC.** Briggs 2-A. Mostly slate-gray in color, with a hint of ebony debris here and there. IN and the S in TRUST are weak, but the legends, including LIBERTY, are otherwise sharp. Dimes and Silver Dollars were coined in quantity in 1885, but Quarters and Half Dollars continued their recent year pattern of limited production. A mere 13,600 commercial strikes fell from the dies. (#5517)

Choice Cameo Proof 1885 Quarter

21189 **1885 PR64 Cameo NGC.** Gold, magenta, and ocean-blue colors frame the untoned centers. Frosty devices affirm the Cameo designation. A few wispy slide marks on the obverse field, the reverse is quite clean. The 1885 is within a run of low mintage dates. 930 proofs and 13,600 commercial strikes were issued. (#85586)

Select Cameo 1886 Quarter

21190 **1886 PR63 Cameo NGC.** Vivacious orange, russet, and navy-blue patination hugs the borders but cedes to untoned centers. A few nearly imperceptible hairlines above the denomination and on the right obverse field determine the grade. The Cameo contrast is unmistakable. The lowest mintage year within the series, only 886 proofs and 5,000 business strikes left the dies. (#85587)

Borderline Uncirculated 1887 Quarter

21191 **1887 AU58 NGC.** Satin luster penetrates the exposed fields, and no obvious highpoint friction is apparent, but the obverse has a few faint slide marks associated with momentary circulation. The rose, golden-brown, and pearl-gray toning is original. A scant 10,000 pieces were struck, since the Mint was obligated to strike Silver Dollars in vast quantities. (#5519)

Promising Select Proof 1887 Quarter

21192 **1887 PR63 NGC.** Ruby, blue-green, and honey colors adorn the borders. The frosty devices and legends would appear to merit a Cameo designation, but NGC is not forthcoming. Careful rotation does not reveal any hairline patches to limit the grade. A miserly 710 proofs were struck. (#5588)

Cameo Proof 1888 Seated Quarter

21193 **1888 PR63 Cameo NGC.** Russet and cobalt-blue colors embrace the reverse periphery, however, the obverse is nearly untoned, as is the central reverse. This sharply struck and carefully preserved specimen has good eye appeal, and is one of just 832 proofs produced. (#85589)

See the Online Session listings in the back of this volume for additional Reiver selections.

Beautiful 1888 Quarter, PR66 Cameo

21194 **1888 PR66 Cameo NGC.** This beautiful cameo displays rich peripheral cobalt-blue, golden-brown, and lavender toning, especially on the obverse. Great cameo contrast is evident on both sides. Sharply struck with impeccably preserved surfaces. Only 832 proofs were struck, and the business strike production was also very low. Census: 12 in 66, 1 finer (10/05). (#85589)

Tied For Finest Certified Superb Gem 1888-S Quarter

21195 **1888-S MS67 NGC.** The popularity of this date among Seated Quarter collectors is unflagging due to its status as the only branch mint issue from the 1880s. While some catalogers have emphasized the rarity of the 1888-S (1.2 million pieces produced), it is actually one of the more readily obtainable issues in the entire series (per Larry Briggs, 1991). Superb quality Gems, however, are conditionally rare. Indeed, this specimen is one of just two pieces certified at this grade level by NGC; PCGS has seen no coins of this issue higher than MS66 (10/05). The present coin is sharply struck with impeccably preserved lustrous surfaces visited by whispers of golden-brown and lavender, joined by cobalt-blue on the reverse. (#5521)

Low Mintage Near Mint 1889 Quarter

21196 **1889 AU58 NGC.** Barely detectable wear on Liberty's arms and chest denies an Uncirculated assessment, but this satiny steel-gray example has substantial luster and no relevant marks. The final date in the 1879 to 1889 era of ultra low mintage Philadelphia issues. Business strikes never exceeded 15,200 pieces during that span. (#5522)

Near-Gem Cameo Proof 1889 Quarter

21197 **1889 PR64 Cameo NGC.** The 1889 is a low total mintage issue with 12,000 business strikes produced and only 900 proofs. This is an exceptionally attractive example that has deeply mirrored fields and significant mint frost over the devices. The centers are brilliant with russet-brown accents around the peripheries. Population: 8 in 64, 22 finer (8/05). (#85590)

Collectible 1890 Seated Quarter, AU55 NGC

21198 **1890 AU55 NGC.** A collectible and affordable example of this lower mintage issue (80,000 pieces struck). This is a reasonably well defined example that has oyster-gray surfaces overall with reddish accents around the peripheries. (#5523)

Lovely Cameo PR64 1890 Quarter

21199 **1890 PR64 Cameo NGC.** Glimpses of honey-gold and cherry-red color adorn the borders of this otherwise stone-white near-Gem. The radiant, icy devices exhibit formidable contrast with the carefully preserved fields. The penultimate proof issue of the type, scarcer than most due to a scant emission of 590 pieces. (#85591)

Creamy, Select Uncirculated 1891 Seated Quarter

21200 **1891 MS63 NGC.** Thick, creamy luster with just the lightest bit of color over both sides. Some softness of strike is noted on the highest portions of the design. (#5524)

Beautiful 1891 Quarter PR64 Cameo NGC

21201 **1891 PR64 Cameo NGC.** Blended golden-brown and rose colors endow the borders of this lovely final year Seated Quarter. A meticulously struck and flashy near-Gem, thick frost on the devices and legends ensures the Cameo designation. A pinpoint spot is centered on the right obverse field. Just 600 proofs were produced. (#85592)

Difficult Choice VF 1891-O Quarter

21202 **1891-O VF35 NGC.** Briggs 1-A. After a gap of 32 years, caused by the Civil War and a mint preference toward Silver Dollars, the New Orleans Mint finally struck Quarter Dollars in 1891. Since the Barber design was introduced the subsequent year, the 1891-O is the sole Motto issue from the southern branch mint. Unlike the 1891-O Dime, the Quarter is very scarce, due to its small production of 68,000 pieces and a local indifference to mintmark varieties. This nicely detailed piece is higher grade than the typical 1891-O. The dove-gray centers are bounded by peripheral orange and aqua tones. (#5525)

BARBER QUARTERS

Beautiful 1892 Near-Gem Proof Cameo Quarter

21203 **1892 PR64 Cameo NGC.** Type Two Reverse. The crossbar of the E in UNITED is fully concealed by the eagle's left (facing) wing, confirming the Type Two variety. Beautiful cameo contrast is evident on both sides as the frosted design elements appear to ride over deep watery fields. Delicate cobalt-blue, golden-brown, and lavender toning gravitates to the rims, highlighting the central areas. The design elements are sharply impressed throughout, and the surfaces are devoid of mentionable marks. A few minor scuffs on Liberty's cheek define the grade. (#85678)

Select 1892-O Barber Quarter

21204 **1892-O MS63 NGC.** Type One Reverse. A lustrous first year Barber Quarter, delicately toned near the margins in tan-brown tints. Sharply struck, and the portrait and reverse are quite clean for the Select grade. A couple of minor luster grazes in the lower right obverse field prevent a higher numerical assessment. The introductory Type One Reverse shows the middle serif of the E in UNITED; this design feature is completely covered by the wing for the Type Two subtype, used for the remainder of the series. (#5602)

Mint State Type Two 1892-S Quarter

21205 **1892-S MS62 NGC.** Type Two Reverse. Original peach, lilac, and ocean-blue colors envelop this splendidly struck and satiny S-mint Quarter. A few faint slide marks on the cheek are of little account. The mintage of nearly 1 million pieces would appear to be plentiful, but like most Barber Quarter issues, the 1892-S is very scarce in Uncirculated grades. Population: 11 in 62, 39 finer (8/05). (#5603)

Colorfully Toned 1893 Quarter, PR64 NGC

21206 **1893 PR64 NGC.** Turquoise, golden-brown, and lavender toning encircles the borders of this lovely Near-Gem proof. The design elements are sharply impressed and lightly frosted, offering a cameo-like effect, particularly on the obverse. A few minor marks on Liberty's cheek and neck limit the grade. From a mintage of 792 pieces. (#5679)

Choice Mint State 1893-O Barber Quarter

21207 **1893-O MS64 NGC.** Although the mintmark is right of center below the tail, it is not the variety that Breen described with the mintmark far to the right. Overall a sharply struck example of this date. The obverse appears to have full detail throughout, including all star details. The reverse is similarly sharp with only a hint of weakness at the eagle's claw and arrow feathers. Both sides are fully lustrous and brilliant with peripheral rose and blue on the obverse. The reverse does not exhibit any sort of toning. (#5605)

Conditionally Scarce 1893-S Barber Quarter MS62 NGC

21208 **1893-S MS62 NGC.** The obverse is toned charcoal-gray, with golden-brown and green patina at the lower and right side peripheries. The reverse displays champagne color, with speckled russet-brown and green border toning. The luster is muted somewhat on the reverse, perhaps precluding the coin from a higher grade, as the surfaces are quite clean. A conditionally scarce item in Mint State. (#5606)

21209 **1894 MS62 NGC.** Apple-green, ruby-red, and gold colors endow the reverse. The moderately abraded obverse is draped in dappled chestnut, aqua, and pearl-gray tones. This well struck piece displays vibrant cartwheel shimmer. Scarce in Mint State, although not rare by the standards of the series. (#5607)

Pretty 1894 Quarter, PR63 NGC

21210 **1894 PR63 NGC.** Turquoise and lilac patination graces the obverse periphery, while the reverse margins are visited by electric-blue, lavender, and golden-brown toning. The design features are sharply impressed over each side. Wispy slide marks are noted on Liberty's cheek and neck. From a mintage of 972 pieces.. (#5680)

Near Mint 1894-S Quarter

21211 **1894-S AU58 NGC.** A nearly fully lustrous example with light hairlines and a couple of minor marks on the obverse, and a modest amount of russet-red peripheral toning on each side. Somewhat scarce in high grades, despite a hefty original mintage. (#5609)

Select 1895 Barber Quarter

21212 **1895 MS63 NGC.** Fully struck and highly lustrous, with attractive golden-tan color near the obverse borders, and a bright, untoned reverse. Hardly any marks are seen on either side. A pleasingly Select example. (#5610)

Pleasing 1895 Barber Quarter, PR63 NGC

21213 **1895 PR63 NGC.** Dappled electric-blue and crimson colors dance over luminous surfaces that exhibit sharply struck design features. An interesting lint mark is noted on Liberty's nose just beneath the eye. A few wispy handling marks occur on Liberty's cheek and neck. From a mintage of 880 pieces. (#5681)

21214 **1895-O AU58 NGC.** Luster beckons from the borders but does not penetrate the right obverse field. This nicely struck slider shows golden-brown and navy-blue color near the rims. More than 2.8 million pieces were struck, but these were not generally saved, confirmed by the difficulty of obtaining Uncirculated survivors. Census: 14 in 58, 56 finer (12/05). (#5611)

Pleasing 1896 Quarter

21215 **1896 MS62 NGC.** Well struck with bright satiny luster and pleasing purple-rose toning near the obverse borders. A few wispy slide marks are evident, also on the obverse. (#5613)

Sharp Near-Gem Cameo Proof 1896 Quarter

21216 **1896 PR64 Cameo NGC.** Deep, glassy mirrored fields provide characteristic (for late 1890s issues) contrast with the major design elements. Delicate touches of cobalt-blue, gold-brown, and lavender patina travel over the fields, further heightening the contrast with the mildly frosted motifs. All devices are razor sharp, enhancing the coin's overall eye appeal. A couple of minute milling marks in the upper right (facing) obverse field are all that prevent a higher grade. A high quality survivor from a mintage of 762 proofs. (#85682)

Semi-Key 1896-S Barber Quarter Good 6 NGC

21217 **1896-S Good 6 NGC.** Rare in all grades, this is a well worn light-gray example that shows deeper color around the margins. Essentially unmarked, save for a few wispy pinscratches across Liberty's head. (#5615)

Lusciously Toned 1897 Barber Quarter MS64 NGC

21218 **1897 MS64 NGC.** The rich burnt-orange, red-purple, and cobalt-blue patina, on the right side and near the peripheries of the obverse, is unquestionably original. A shallow planchet flaw (as struck) rests between the eagle's wing and the arrowheads, on the reverse, but no other defects exist, on that side of the coin, and the obverse only shows minor slide marks on the portrait. A well struck near-Gem that has good luster and very impressive surfaces overall. Population: 41 in 64, 23 finer (9/05). (#5616)

1897 Premium Gem Cameo Proof Quarter

21219 **1897 PR66 Cameo NGC.** This beautiful Premium Gem features razor-sharp striking details on the frosted design elements, glassy, highly reflective fields, and gorgeous ruby-red, violet, gold-brown, and cobalt-blue toning around the borders. The cameoed surfaces are well preserved, and devoid of major contact marks. Proof mintage was 731 pieces this year. Census: 11 in 66, 11 finer (10/05). (#85683)

21220 **1898 MS63 NGC.** Booming luster sweeps across this medium golden-brown and steel-blue Barber Quarter. The strike is intricate, and only trivial marks are detected on the portrait, nearly imperceptible due to the attractive original toning. (#5619)

Appealing 1898 Quarter, PR62 Cameo NGC

21221 **1898 PR62 Cameo NGC.** A nicely contrasted specimen, with very strong eye appeal. Peripheral toning is evident on the peripheries, with turquoise, lavender, and gold-brown toning dominant. The design elements are exquisitely struck in all areas. A few wispy handling marks are noted over each side. From a mintage of 735 pieces. (#85684)

21222 **1899 PR64 Cameo NGC.** This piece is one of only 846 pieces issued in Proof. It exhibits full frost bloom on all of the devices with deep mirror fields. Whispers of cobalt-blue, gold-brown, and lavender toning are confined mostly to the margins. Sharply struck design elements enhance the overall eye appeal of this Near Gem. Some wispy handling marks are noted on Liberty's cheek and neck. (#85685)

21223 **1900 AU58 NGC.** A richly toned near-Mint representative of this popular turn-of-the-century date. Golden-brown, sea-green, amber, and electric-blue colors adorn both sides. Nearly full satin luster illuminates the deep patina, and there is only a trace of highpoint wear on the obverse to restrict the grade of this problem-free example. (#5625)

Attractive 1900 Quarter, PR62 NGC

21224 **1900 PR62 NGC.** Dappled cobalt-blue and olive-brown coloration over both sides is joined by a swath of rainbow toning along the lower left (facing) obverse border, and all of the design elements are well brought up. Some wispy handling marks are noted on Liberty's cheek and neck. A total of 912 proofs were struck this year. (#5686)

Pleasing Near-Mint 1900-S Barber Quarter

21225 **1900-S AU58 NGC.** Boldly struck and lightly worn, with speckled olive and iridescent gold-orange coloration. Essentially blemish-free on both sides. Census: 18 in 58, 30 finer (12/05). (#5627)

Beautifully Toned 1901 Gem Proof Quarter

21226 **1901 PR65 NGC.** Only 813 proofs were struck of this popular date. This bright specimen displays a cameo-like effect and beautiful turquoise, lavender, and gold-brown toning. The design elements are sharply struck, with only the upper right (facing) corner of the shield and the eagle's left claw revealing minor weakness. The surfaces are of high quality throughout, and exhibit no significant marks. (#5687)

An Original Example of the 1901-S Barber Quarter

21227 **1901-S Fair 2 NGC.** An original, uncleaned coin. Heavily worn into the rims, but the date and mintmark are still clearly defined. (#5630)

Sharply Struck 1902 Gem Proof Quarter

21228 **1902 PR65 NGC.** Dappled pastel cobalt-blue and russet toning on the obverse is complemented by deeper speckled russet on the reverse. The design features are sharply impressed, and the surfaces are well preserved over both sides. From a mintage of 777 pieces. (#5688)

21229 **1903 AU55 NGC.** Lovely rose, steel-gray, and gold-orange patina adorns both sides of this lightly worn example. A well struck Choice AU coin with good luster and generally clean surfaces. One of many seemingly common issues in the series that are in fact quite scarce in AU or Mint State. (#5634)

Proof 1903 Barber Quarter

21230 **1903 PR61 NGC.** Pastel gold and aqua-blue colors visit the borders of this exquisitely struck proof Barber Quarter. Wispy hairlines emerge on the obverse field, however, the reverse on its own has the appearance of a finer grade. A scant 755 pieces were struck. Envelope Included. (#5689)

21231 **1904 AU58 NGC.** Mottled rose and dark-green patina decorates the obverse. The reverse displays dove-gray toning with hints of speckled russet color. A well struck near-Mint example, with substantial luster and faint traces of highpoint wear. Both sides of the coin are free of distracting contact marks. (#5637)

Peripherally Toned Near-Gem 1904 Proof Quarter

21232 **1904 PR64 NGC.** Blushes of golden-brown, electric-blue, and lavender patina around the borders encroach upon the essentially untoned centers. The design features are exquisitely struck, and the surfaces are devoid of mentionable contact marks. A patchy of wispy hairlines in the right obverse field defines the grade. From a mintage of 670 pieces. (#5690)

Select Toned Proof 1905 Barber Quarter

21233 **1905 PR63 NGC.** A spectacular toned example with lovely electric blue, lilac, and iridescent color, mostly on the obverse. Faint hairlines on both sides have kept this from a higher grade. (#5691)

Outstanding 1906 Premium Gem Proof Quarter

21234 **1906 PR66 NGC.** A technically outstanding proof Barber quarter that displays razor-sharp impressions on the design features. The bright surfaces are delicately toned in dappled russet and cobalt-blue colors, and are impeccably preserved. This Premium Gem will fit nicely into a high grade proof type set. Census: 43 in 66, 32 finer (10/05). (#5692)

See the Online Session listings in the back of this volume for additional Reiver selections.

Sharp 1907 Quarter, PR66 NGC

21235 **1907 PR66 NGC.** The design elements exhibit sharp delineation, are mildly frosted, and offer a notable contrast with the glassy, reflective fields. Both sides are bathed in splashes of cobalt-blue, golden-brown, and lavender, and are devoid of any mentionable marks. Only 575 proofs were struck, a low mintage number even for a Barber Quarter issue. Census: 30 in 66, 24 finer (10/05). (#5693)

Attractively Toned Proof 1908 Quarter

21236 **1908 PR62 NGC.** Orange, ruby, and electric-blue colors invigorate the obverse periphery, while the reverse rim displays honey-brown hues. The strike is virtually unimprovable. Wispy horizontal hairlines are detected on the portrait and right obverse field. A scant mintage of 545 pieces is among the lowest within this scarce but collectible proof series. Envelope Included. (#5694)

Collectible 1908-D Quarter, MS63 NGC

21237 **1908-D MS63 NGC.** Bright, satiny luster with peripheral golden and deep blue accents particularly on the obverse. A few tiny marks on the portrait limit the grade. (#5650)

Near-Gem 1908-O Quarter

21238 **1908-O MS64 NGC.** Mostly brilliant with a faint hint of golden and sea-blue at the margins. A bit softly struck, as often seen, bur still a worthwhile example. (#5651)

Lightly Toned 1909 Quarter, PR63 NGC

21239 **1909 PR63 NGC.** Light transparent toning consisting of dappled orange, cobalt-blue, violet, and lime-green colors visits both sides of this luminous proof. The design elements are sharply struck, except for minor softness in the upper right (facing) corner of the shield. A few wispy, hardly noticeable hairlines are noted on the obverse. There are no mentionable abrasions to report. From a mintage of just 650 pieces. (#5695)

Highly Attractive 1910 Premium Gem Cameo Proof Quarter

21240 **1910 PR66 Cameo NGC.** A mere 551 proofs were struck during 1910, few of them able to claim a Cameo designation. The devices are well frosted on this Premium Gem specimen, and are handsomely contrasted by the deeply mirrored fields. In fact, the obverse comes close to a Deep Cameo. The strike is excellent, with all the design elements showing sharp definition. Dapples of cobalt-blue, orange, mauve, and lime-green display deeper shades on the obverse. The surfaces are well preserved on both sides. Census: 13 in 66, 18 finer (10/05). (#85696)

Attractive 1911 Near-Gem Proof Quarter

21241 **1911 PR64 NGC.** This lovely Near-Gem proof quarter exhibits relatively strong field-motif contrast. The mildly frosted design elements are sharply struck in all areas. The obverse is layered in medium intensity cobalt-blue, golden-brown, and lavender patination, which takes on lighter hues on the reverse. Both sides are impeccably preserved. From a mintage of just 543 pieces. (#5697)

Select 1911-D Barber Quarter

21242 **1911-D MS63 NGC.** Splashes of sea-green and russet toning accompany the obverse perimeter. Good luster and clean surfaces confirm the Select grade. The lowest mintage D-mint issue of the series; no Quarters were struck in Denver the following year. Difficult to locate in Mint State, which is more the rule than the exception for this challenging series. Population: 11 in 63, 17 finer (9/05). (#5660)

21243 **1912 MS62 NGC.** Modestly lustrous under a coating of steel-gray toning. Minimally marked for the assigned grade. (#5662)

Lightly Toned Gem Proof 1912 Quarter

21244 **1912 PR65 NGC.** In addition to this specimen's peerless reflective surfaces, both sides are endowed with an enticing blend of speckled gold-brown, lavender, sea-green, lavender, and olive-green coloration. The design features are sharply impressed, and both sides are free of mentionable abrasions. From a mintage of 700 pieces. Census: 35 in 65, 36 finer (10/05). (#5698)

Important Gem 1912-S Barber Quarter

21245 **1912-S MS65 NGC.** A scarce issue in Gem condition, and very seldom seen any finer. Highly lustrous with light ivory color and no other evidence of toning. Several fine die cracks are visible on both sides. Population: 15 in 65, 5 finer (8/05). (#5663)

21246 **1913 VF35 NGC.** Naturally toned, essentially mark-free surfaces show moderate wear. (#5664)

Magnificently Toned 1913 Premium Gem Proof Quarter

21247 **1913 PR66 NGC.** Only 613 pieces were struck of the 1913 proof issue. This magnificently toned example has bright russet, crimson, violet, and cobalt-blue toning in the fields, highlighting the silvery design elements. Sharply struck, except for a touch of softness in the eagle's left claw and in the upper right corner of the shield. The coin is further enlivened by the unfathomable depth of mirrored reflectivity seen in the fields. The surfaces are devoid of significant abrasions. Census: 35 in 66, 22 finer (10/05). (#5699)

Near-Gem 1913-D Barber Quarter

21248 **1913-D MS64 NGC.** Satiny and extremely close to Gem status, with specks of natural russet toning in selected peripheral areas of the obverse. A more challenging D-mint issue in Choice and better condition. Census: 34 in 64, 25 finer (12/05). (#5665)

See the Online Session listings in the back of this volume for additional Reiver selections.

Ultra Low Mintage 1913-S Quarter

21249 **1913-S Good 4 NGC.** The 1913-S is famous for its mintage of 40,000 pieces, the lowest mintmarked twentieth century silver issue. The mintage is even lower than the coveted 1916 Standing Liberty Quarter, and is more than six times less than the popular 1916-D Dime. Nonetheless, the 1913-S remains affordable, particularly in VG and lower grades, which encompass the majority of survivors. This cream-gray example has wisps of original charcoal toning in protected areas. The date and mintmark are bold, and only traces of the right side reverse legends are threatened by the rim. (#5666)

Attractive 1914 Near-Gem Proof Quarter

21250 **1914 PR64 NGC.** The proof mintage for the 1914 Quarter of 380 pieces is the lowest recorded for any date within the series. Most of the obverse is bathed in a lovely melange of cobalt-blue, lavender, golden-brown, and crimson, while a similar color scheme is confined to the rim areas on the reverse. All of the design features are well impressed, and some cameo-like characteristics are noted. A few luster grazes on Liberty's cheek account for the grade. (#5700)

21251 **1914-D MS63 NGC.** Slightly speckled steel-gray patina is seen over the soft, frosted mint luster that characterizes this original piece. The arrow feathers are softly struck, but the devices are relatively sharp. An original and very attractive example. (#5668)

Choice Proof 1915 Quarter

21252 **1915 PR64 NGC.** Blue-green, rose, and lemon patination invigorates this well preserved and suitably struck near-Gem. White on black contrast is apparent, but only from selected angles. The 1915 has the second lowest proof production of the series, only the 1914 has a smaller emission. Population: 30 in 64, 57 finer (9/05). Envelope Included. (#5701)

21253 **1915-S AU58 NGC.** Only the slightest wear shows on the highpoints of this untoned example. A few minor slidemarks on Liberty's cheek hardly detract. (#5672)

21254 **1916 MS63 NGC.** A wonderful strike, including full detail on the normally softly struck eagle, displayed on moderately toned surfaces. This is a Select example of the final year of issue for this design. (#5673)

Choice Uncirculated 1916-D Quarter

21255 **1916-D MS64 NGC.** Well struck with deep gray-golden patina on each side and a few small surface marks on the obverse. (#5674)

STANDING LIBERTY QUARTERS

Pleasing 1916 Standing Liberty Quarter, AU58 NGC

21256 **1916 AU58 NGC.** The Philadelphia Mint produced the first Standing Liberty Quarters between December 16 and 31 of this year. The total number of 1916-dated coins struck was just 52,000 pieces, and these were released to the public early the next year. The limited original mintage of the 1916 propelled it to instant stardom among numismatists, a position that it has retained ever since. This lightly circulated example retains considerable luster, and is sharply defined on the motifs. Both sides are covered in mottled electric-blue, lavender, and gold-brown patination. The surfaces are quite well preserved, revealing just a couple of small milling marks in the fields above the juncture of the eagle's wings. (#5704)

Lovely Full Head Gem 1917 Type One Quarter

21257 **1917 Type One MS65 Full Head NGC.** A gorgeous chestnut-gray Gem. Vibrant luster sweeps across the nearly unmarked surfaces. A pinpoint strike is characteristic of the Type One design. A high mintage for the era and a dynamic new design led to a quantity of quality Mint State survivors, but these are always in demand as a short-lived type. (#5707)

Handsome 1917-D Type One Quarter MS63 Full Head NGC

21258 **1917-D Type One MS63 Full Head NGC.** Tan-gold and aqua colors adorn the peripheries, along with a few freckles of ebony patina. Sharply struck, as is usual for the transitional type. An unmarked example with impressive luster and attractive eye appeal. (#5709)

21259 **1917-S Type One AU58 NGC.** Only the slightest hint of rubbing is reported on the highpoints of this originally toned piece. Golden-brown and sea-green colors are slightly deeper at the borders. (#5710)

Eye Appealing 1917 Type Two Quarter

21260 **1917 Type Two AU58 Full Head NGC.** Creamy luster rolls across this nicely struck Type Two example. Golden-brown, russet, and apple-green toning enriches the borders. A hint of friction on the knee and the inner shield denies a Mint State assessment, but the eye appeal is that of a higher grade. (#5715)

Choice Uncirculated 1917-S Type Two Quarter

21261 **1917-S Type Two MS64 NGC.** Both sides are slightly subdued by a uniform layer of golden-gray patina. Despite a substantially higher mintage, fewer Mint State examples were saved of this type than the Type One S-mint. (#5718)

See the Online Session listings in the back of this volume for additional Reiver selections.

Splendid Full Head Near-Gem 1918 Quarter

21262 **1918 MS64 Full Head NGC.** Original light cream-gray and apricot colors illuminate this lustrous and unusually well struck near-Gem. Not only is the head intricately defined, but the shield rivets and waist are bold and the date is also relatively crisp. A beautiful representative of this conditionally scarce World War I issue. (#5721)

21263 **1918-D AU55 NGC.** Barely circulated with no detracting blemishes, a moderate amount of golden-russet patina can be seen over each side. (#5722)

Full Head Gem 1919 Quarter Dollar

21264 **1919 MS65 Full Head NGC.** Although many 1919 quarters (and other dates as well) have been certified with Full Head details, few actually qualify. This is one of those few and not only is the head detail sharply defined, but every rivet in the shield is completely outlined. In fact, this is so sharply struck that even the crest at the center of the shield exhibits considerable detail. That is almost never the case. In addition to the exceptional strike, the obverse has ivory luster accented by rich gold and iridescent toning at the border. The reverse is mostly brilliant silver color with just a touch of gold along the inside of the border. A delightful and highly important Gem. (#5729)

Elusive Near Mint 1919-D Quarter

21265 **1919-D AU58 NGC.** Pearl-gray and pastel gold tones grace this lightly marked better date Quarter. Mint luster is essentially complete, but inspection beneath a loupe locates friction on the shield, the right (facing) wing, and selected other highpoints. A lower mintage issue scarce even in well worn grades, particularly since the date was not recessed until 1925. (#5730)

Challenging 1919-S Quarter

21266 **1919-S VF30 NGC.** Mostly pewter gray surfaces with wisps and tinges of orange-gold and blue on the obverse. The 1919-S ranks as one of the scarcest Standing Liberty quarter issues in VF and higher grades. (#5732)

Attractive Mint State Example 1920-S Standing Liberty Quarter

21267 **1920-S MS62 NGC.** Lightly toned with slightly subdued luster for the grade. Attractive mottled charcoal and russet patina adorns the obverse peripheries. Both sides seem blemish-free. A scarce issue and a more affordable example. Well but not fully struck. (#5738)

Unc Details Low Mintage 1921 Quarter

21268 **1921—Improperly Cleaned—NCS. Unc. Details.** Although the sprigs on the helmet are not fully defined, the strike is generally impressive. The steel-gray fields are faintly hairlined, but the only detectable marks are trivial pinscratches on the left (facing) wing. A key date to the series, even in lower circulated grades, since the date wore off many survivors. Less than 2 million pieces were struck, the lowest of the pre-recessed date issues aside from the 1923-S, the heavily saved 1917-D Type One, and the famous 1916. As is the case with Dimes and Half Dollars of the date, the mintage of Quarters was low because of the Pittman Act, which compelled the Mint to strike Silver Dollars in quantity. (#5740)

Dandy MS63 1923 Quarter, Full Head

21269 **1923 MS63 Full Head NGC.** Sharply struck and fully lustrous. Lovely rosy-gold iridescence enhances both surfaces. A dandy coin suitable for inclusion in either a 20th-century type set or outstanding quarter dollar collection. (#5743)

Sharp Premium Gem Full Head 1923-S Quarter

21270 **1923-S MS66 Full Head NGC.** The 1923-S Quarter, one of the most asked-for issues in the entire series regardless of grade, is an elusive coin from the standpoint of both absolute and condition rarity. Only 1.36 million pieces were struck and the majority of the Uncirculated survivors fail to qualify for full head status. The sharp strike on this specimen transcends the Full Head. The inner shield displays the vertical stripes, and all of the rivets with the exception of one are bold. Intense luster radiates from the well preserved surfaces that are bathed with speckled cobalt-blue, lavender, and gold-brown patination. Census: 21 in 66, 4 finer (10/05). (#5745)

Near-Gem 1924-D Quarter Dollar, MS64 FH

21271 **1924-D MS64 Full Head NGC.** This is one of those hidden surprises among the coins from the Jules Reiver Collection. Examples of this issue are nearly always weakly struck, with only a partial date visible, and with little detail in Liberty's head. The example offered here is an exception to both of those points. Only the extreme tops of the digits in the date are a little weak. The head details are sharp and boldly detailed. Except for a tiny cheek chip, the head is essentially perfect. Fully brilliant and lustrous surfaces with a satiny cartwheel appearance and light ivory color. Splashes of yellow and orange toning are present on both sides, down the center of the obverse and primarily along the border of the reverse. Just a single point shy of being a landmark offering in the present collection. (#5749)

See the Online Session listings in the back of this volume for additional Reiver selections.

Lightly Toned 1925 Quarter MS63 Full Head

21272 **1925 MS63 Full Head NGC.** Silver-gray surfaces display soft luster and faint speckles of light tan color, along with some charcoal-gray peppering on the lower reverse. The design elements are sharply struck throughout, except for weakness in a couple of the lower rivets. (#5753)

Boldly Struck 1927 Quarter MS62 Full Head

21275 **1927 MS62 Full Head NGC.** A conservatively graded example with full satin luster and minimal abrasions for the grade. Essentially untoned, save for traces of mottled olive and russet patina near the peripheries. Very sharply struck. (#5761)

Full Head Mint State 1926 Quarter

21273 **1926 MS62 Full Head NGC.** Sharply struck and lightly toned with few post-striking impairments. The satiny surfaces are free of contact marks, and show scattered charcoal-brown mottling on both sides, which is noticeable mainly on the upper half of the reverse. A pleasing Full Head example. (#5755)

Lustrous Premium Gem 1928-D Standing Liberty Quarter

21276 **1928-D MS66 NGC.** Lovely golden-orange obverse peripheral patina adds to the eye appeal of this lustrous Premium Gem. Well preserved and attractive, with bold striking details that include nearly full definition on Liberty's head. (#5768)

Frosty, Untoned Gem 1926-D Quarter

21274 **1926-D MS65 NGC.** Frosty-white surfaces are a trifle mushy on the highpoints, but still well above average for this famously ill-defined issue. (#5756)

Attractive Gem 1928-S Standing Liberty Quarter

21277 **1928-S MS65 NGC.** Slightly soft on the eagle, and on Liberty's head, but reasonably sharp elsewhere, this attractive Gem is lustrous and lightly toned, showing speckled multicolored patina near the borders. There are no mentionable marks on either side of the coin. (#5770)

Satiny Gem 1929 Standing Liberty Quarter with Full Head Details

21278 **1929 MS65 Full Head NGC.** A satiny Gem that combines pinpoint detailing with nearly mark-free surfaces. Some speckled russet patina is seen near the obverse borders. Population: 119 in 65 Full Head, 59 finer (9/05). (#5773)

Well Preserved Gem 1929-D Standing Liberty Quarter

21279 **1929-D MS65 NGC.** Boldly struck, with only minor weakness on Liberty's head, the shield rivets, and the eagle's breast. There is scattered, slight russet color on the mostly untoned surfaces, and pleasing, full satin luster. Both sides of the piece seem well preserved and essentially blemish-free. (#5774)

Conditionally Scarce Premium Gem 1929-S Standing Liberty Quarter

21280 **1929-S MS66 NGC.** Lustrous and satiny, with subtly variegated steel-blue and peach pastels, and a slight degree of speckled russet patina, over the obverse and reverse surfaces. Very well preserved, with just a couple of minor marks on each side. An attractive and conditionally scarce Premium Gem. Census: 97 in 66, 23 finer (12/05). (#5776)

Virtually Pristine Premium Gem, F.H. 1930 Standing Liberty Quarter

21281 **1930 MS66 Full Head NGC.** Well struck and virtually pristine, this satiny Premium Gem displays lovely gray-silver toning and impeccable surface preservation. Some russet patina has settled over the top of Liberty's head. Just seventeen pieces have been graded finer, by NGC (8/05). (#5779)

Glowing Premium Gem 1930-S Standing Liberty Quarter

21282 **1930-S MS66 Full Head NGC.** Both sides of this satiny Premium Gem exhibit full glowing luster and attractive light toning, with pastel rose-gray color in the fields and a dash of russet patina along the side of Liberty's head. The reverse also has a light coating of speckled reddish toning. Well preserved and virtually blemish-free, a beautiful example of this final year issue. Population: 78 in 66 Full Head, 17 finer (9/05). (#5781)

WASHINGTON QUARTERS

Series Key 1932-D Quarter

21283 **1932-D MS62 NGC.** An original, lightly toned example of this key date, the surfaces show good luster characteristics overall beneath layers of creamy toning. There are surprisingly few marks, for the grade, and none of them are overly distracting. Quite a nice example, and worthy of inclusion in a Mint State set of Washington quarters. (#5791)

Satiny Key Date 1932-S Quarter

21284 **1932-S—Improperly Cleaned—NCS. Unc. Details.** This satiny and relatively unmarked key date Quarter has delicate tan toning and good eye appeal for the conservatively assessed grade. A short pinscratch northeast of the eye is not significant. The lowest mintage issue in the business strike series, although the 1932-D is considered tougher in Mint State. (#5792)

Popular Choice 1934-D Heavy Motto Quarter

21285 **1934-D Heavy Motto MS64 NGC.** Unlike its Philadelphia Mint counterpart, the Denver Mint did not produce Light Motto Quarters in 1934, but both Medium and Heavy Motto pieces were struck. Since the 1934-D is already a better date due to its low mintage, the presence of two distinctive varieties only increases the demand for quality Mint State examples. This lustrous and nearly brilliant near-Gem has clean surfaces, and only minor striking incompleteness along the obverse periphery. (#85796)

Elusive Choice 1935-D Quarter

21286 **1935-D MS64 NGC.** Well struck and virtually blemish-free, save for two or three pinpoint-sized marks on the obverse, this scarcer Denver Mint near-Gem has a coating of milky grayish-white patina over both sides. There are a few faint striations (as struck) on the obverse, along with trace amounts of mottling near the peripheries. (#5798)

Low Mintage 1936 Quarter PR63

21287 **1936 PR63 NGC.** Faint tan and milky toning are seen over bright, glassy proof surfaces that are essentially devoid of contact marks. Fingerprint remnants are seen on the left side of the obverse. (#5975)

Scarce Near Gem 1936-D Quarter

21288 **1936-D MS64 NGC.** One of the scarcer dates in the series to locate in high grades. Lightly toned with plenty of original mint frost. Well struck and carefully preserved, as well. (#5801)

Pleasing Premium Gem Proof 1937 Washington Quarter

21289 **1937 PR66 NGC.** Sharply struck and seemingly pristine, this lovely Premium Gem has a layer of milky and speckled toning over both sides. No bothersome hairlines or contact marks seem evident, either on the obverse or the reverse. Population: 168 in 66, 85 finer (9/05). (#5976)

21290 **1937-D MS65 NGC.** Well struck and lustrous, with a small amount of scattered russet-red and olive patina on each side, and a couple of tiny contact marks, on Washington's cheek and eyebrow. Very scarce any finer. (#5804)

Low Mintage Gem 1937-S Washington Quarter

21291 **1937-S MS65 NGC.** The 1937-S is a very appealing issue, inasmuch as the original mintage is a limited 1.6 million coins. This lot offers a bright, satiny Gem whose surfaces present as essentially untoned. Both sides are expectantly well preserved, with a small contact mark on Washington's lower bust being mentioned solely for the sake of accuracy. (#5805)

Seemingly Flawless Premium Gem Proof 1938 Washington Quarter

21292 **1938 PR66 NGC.** Fully struck, brilliant, and pristine, with highly reflective fields. A lovely representative of this scarce early Proof issue in the Washington quarter series. (#5977)

21293 **1938-S MS66 NGC.** Well struck and satiny, with a light coating of milky patina on the obverse, and some speckled iridescence near the obverse borders. The carefully preserved surfaces are near-pristine. A scarce S-mint quarter from the 1930s, and seldom seen in MS66 condition. (#5807)

Gently Toned Choice 1939-S Quarter

21294 **1939-S MS64 NGC.** Nearly imperceptible golden-gray patina bathes lustrous surfaces. The design elements are well struck on both sides of this near Gem. A few minor marks are noted on Washington's cheek and neck, and on the eagle's right leg. (#5810)

21295 **1942-S MS66 NGC.** Trumpet tail S, one of two mintmark styles used for this issue. A satiny premium Gem, originally toned in light pearl-gray and tan colors. Well struck aside from a couple of left side letters in the motto. A single tiny reeding mark on the left wing, otherwise essentially pristine. (#5819)

End of Session Five

SESSION SIX

Public-Internet Auction #390
Thursday, January 26, 2006, 6 PM CT, Lots 21296-21909

A 15% Buyer's Premium ($9 minimum) Will Be Added To All Lots.

Visit HeritageGalleries.com/Coins to view full-color images and bid.

SEATED HALF DOLLARS

Choice AU 1839 Drapery Seated Half

21296 **1839 Drapery AU55 NGC.** 1839 was the first year of the Seated Half design, and drapery was added beneath the elbow after about half of the annual mintage had been struck. The No Drapery pieces are not particularly scarcer, but are popular as a separate design type. This makes the nearly equally elusive Drapery examples the better value, and despite a high mintage, the 1839 Drapery is difficult to find in better circulated grades. The present piece possesses medium apricot and blue-green color, and the crisply impressed devices exhibit ample shimmering luster. A few minor field marks are not of importance. (#6232)

Near Mint WB-102 1840 Half Dollar

21297 **1840 Reverse of 1839, Small Letters AU58 NGC.** WB-102. The 0 in the date is widely recut southeast. Peach, sky-blue, and olive-gray colors endow this briefly circulated but unblemished scarcer date representative. The Wiley-Bugert reference lists WB-102 as Low R.5 in XF/AU and High R.6 in Mint State. (#6234)

Scarce AU 1840-O Half Dollar

21298 **1840-O AU53 NGC.** WB-104. Large O mintmark, one of three different sizes in use at New Orleans that year. This sharply struck example displays olive and stone-gray color, and no obtrusive marks are present. A few specks of charcoal patina near OF do not distract. (#6235)

Lovely Borderline Uncirculated 1841 Half Dollar

21299 **1841 AU58 NGC.** Dusky and original olive, steel-blue, and tan tints enrich this satiny and briefly circulated scarcer date Seated Half. No marks are readily detected, and the eye appeal is undeniably pleasing. The 1839 to 1841 issues are interesting for their Small Letters reverse, which features wider spacing between the letters than the 1842 and later Large Letters reverse design, more familiar to collectors. (#6236)

21300 **1841-O XF45 NGC.** This is a challenging date, but a 40-piece hoard found on the site of Fort Harrison in Florida several years ago has helped the availability. This example displays obviously original golden-brown, cobalt-blue, and reddish-gold toning, and well struck features that only exhibit a slight degree of wear, for the assigned grade level. A wispy die crack (as struck) connects the eagle's left (facing) talons to the lower reverse rim. There are no more than a handful of trivial marks on either side of the coin, and only one or two of these are individually noticeable. (#6237)

1842 Medium Date Half With Widely Repunched Date

21301 **1842 Medium Date, Large Letters—Environmental Damage—NCS. AU Details.** WB-105. The date is broadly repunched, most evident beneath the prominent 8. On the reverse, heavy die cracks (as made) atop UNITED and along the base of HALF DOL reach the rim and threaten to form retained breaks. This sharp representative is deeply toned in mauve and apple-green toned. Environmental damage appears minor, but some roughness is noted above the eagle's right (facing) shoulder. (#6239)

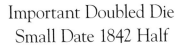

Important Doubled Die Small Date 1842 Half

21302 **1842 Small Date, Large Letters AU55 NGC.** WB-103. Listed by Wiley-Bugert as High R.7 in XF/AU grades. The upper reverse is widely die doubled, prominent on the tops of STATES OF, but even more significant on the top of the eagle's shield and shoulders. An important find for the Seated Half specialist, this sharply struck piece has substantial mint luster and no untoward marks. Chestnut and sea-green colors invigorate the borders. (#6240)

Scarce 1842-O Small Date Half Dollar, XF Details

21303 **1842-O Small Date, Small Letters—Improperly Cleaned—NCS. XF Details.** Several times scarcer than its 1842-O Medium Date, Large Letters counterpart, the Small Date has a low emission of 203,000 pieces and is difficult to locate in all grades. This specimen displays silvery surfaces that are finely hairlined, and a narrow band of pale blue, lavender, and golden-brown patina hugs the rims. (#6238)

Charming Near Mint 1843 Half Dollar

21304 **1843 AU58 NGC.** Light golden-brown color graces this sharply struck Seated Half. No wear is apparent on the devices, however, the luster is diminished across the open fields. Many of the vertical lines on the eagle's shield extend deeply into the horizontal stripes, a minor but interesting engraving error found on many issues and denominations of the era. (#6243)

Conditionally Rare 1843-O Seated Half

21305 **1843-O MS62 NGC.** An exquisitely struck and satiny representative that displays delicate tan and navy-blue color, mostly near the borders. A small handling mark above the eagle's head and a few wispy slide marks on the right obverse field determine the grade. A common date in VF and lower grades, but Mint State survivors are elusive. Population: 11 in 62, 17 finer (8/05). (#6244)

See the Online Session listings in the back of this volume for additional Reiver selections.

Promising AU Details 1844 Half Dollar

21306 **1844—Improperly Cleaned—NCS. AU Details.** Assertively struck aside from the eagle's left (facing) claw, this bagmark-free example is essentially untoned and has noticeable luster in the open fields. Friction is limited to Liberty's thigh, and the past cleaning is mild and inoffensive. (#6245)

Popular Near Mint No Drapery 1845-O Half Dollar

21307 **1845-O No Drapery AU58 NGC.** A boldly struck cream-gray example, unworn but without the full cartwheel luster necessary for Mint State classification. This 'No Drapery' variety has only a trace of drapery folds beneath the elbow. Liberty's foot and rock have also been dramatically attenuated by lapping of the obverse die. Her sandal is removed, and the left and right borders of the rock are mere pointed stumps. (#6250)

Challenging Mint State 1846 Medium Date Half

21308 **1846 Medium Date MS62 NGC.** Freckles of apple-green and electric-blue toning enrich the margins of this meticulously struck Seated Half. The fields possess delicate slide marks, and the reverse is curiously prooflike, but few abrasions are apparent to the unaided eye. Multiple sets of clashmarks, as struck, are encountered in the fields. Population: 19 in 62, 28 finer (8/05). (#6251)

Choice AU 1846-O Medium Date Half

21309 **1846-O Medium Date AU55 NGC.** WB-104. The 1 in the date is nicely recut, and the 6 has a mysterious die lump within the loop, similar to that seen on certain 1846 Philadelphia Mint Half Dollars and the so-called 1846/5-O Eagle. The Wiley-Bugert reference discusses these lump varieties, and concludes that they are caused by "poor relief on the punch used to form the 6." This somewhat bright Choice AU example exhibits glimpses of russet toning near the rims, and has a minor obverse ding at 10 o'clock. A broad die scratch is seen beneath the eagle's right (facing) wing, similar to the 1890-CC Dollar 'Tail Bar' variety. (#6255)

Attractively Toned Near Mint 1847 Half Dollar

21310 **1847 AU58 NGC.** Rich tan-gold, plum, and forest-green colors embrace the borders, and frame the untoned centers. This well struck and lightly marked piece does not display full mint luster, but only has a trace of wear on the Seated Liberty. Minor buildup is noted near the eagle's beak. Population: 16 in 58, 28 finer (8/05). (#6257)

Problem Free 1847-O Half Dollar AU58 NGC

21311 **1847-O AU58 NGC.** Ocean-blue and golden-brown toning graces the margins. This suitably struck piece has no relevant marks despite its brief circulation. Lightly repunched above the crossbar of the 4, and unlisted as such in the Wiley-Bugert reference. Population: 10 in 58, 21 finer (8/05). (#6259)

About Uncirculated 1848 Half Dollar

21312 **1848 AU50 NGC.** Peach and honey colors make occasional visits the borders. Liberty's chest and legs are lightly worn, but ample luster emerges from recessed areas. No obtrusive marks are present. A small cud is noted on the obverse rim at 7 o'clock. Obtainable without difficulty in VF and lower grades, however, XF and AU examples are undeniably scarce. (#6260)

21313 **1848-O AU53 NGC.** Attractive peripheral gold toning on both sides, surrounded light silvery-gray surfaces. (#6261)

21314 **1849 AU50 NGC.** Traces of olive-green color gravitate to the borders of this half dollar. The design elements are well defined, and luster is apparent in the protected areas. A few minute marks do not distract. (#6262)

Near Mint 1849-O Half Dollar

21315 **1849-O AU58 NGC.** Under close examination, there are no unusual die characteristics on this example. The date appears to slant down ever so slightly to the right. The reverse has a medium sized O mintmark close to the junction of the stem and tip of the lowest arrow feather, and the mintmark appears to lean very slightly to the left. The reverse die is rotated clockwise about 45 degrees. Randy Wiley and Bill Bugert do not mention any individual varieties in their *Complete Guide* to the series. While the characteristics of this example do not constitute a special die variety, they may be important to the researcher who is trying to track all individual die characteristics. In their reference, Wiley and Bugert indicate that 15 individual die marriages have been documented. Walter Breen records two varieties in his *Complete Encyclopedia*, a doubled date and a normal date.

Although the mintage of this issue was well over 2 million coins, it is still quite rare in Mint State grades, with only 61 such pieces certified by PCGS and NGC combined. Even this AU58 example is important to the specialist or the avid collector. Probably once cleaned, the central obverse and reverse are mostly light silver in color with pale gold and peripheral toning on both sides. A few faint scratches and abrasions are visible, but these are by know means significant. This is a pleasing example with only a trace of wear on the highest design points. Population: 18 in 58, 19 finer (8/05). (#6263)

Well-Detailed 1850 Half Dollar

21316 **1850—Improperly Cleaned—NCS. AU Details.** Iridescent pale peach, steel-blue, and olive-brown colors embrace this sharply struck representative. Near Mint in terms of wear, but the fields are cloudy with faint hairlines. The matte-like texture on the Seated Liberty is as made. The 1850 had the lowest Philadelphia Mint production since a fire at the mint prevented coinage of the denomination in 1816. This reduced mintage was likely due to the success of the California gold mining camps, which affected the relative gold and silver valuation. There was little economic sense in striking silver coins with a bullion value above face. (#6264)

Borderline Uncirculated 1851 Half Dollar

21317 **1851 AU58 NGC.** Russet, plum, and electric-blue colors invigorate the peripheries. The fields and devices are essentially untoned. Mint luster is ample but does not extend into the open fields. Wear is slight, limited to the thigh and a few other obverse highpoints. No relevant marks are detected, and the eye appeal is substantial. A pleasing example of this conditionally scarce issue. (#6266)

Scarce AU Details 1851-O Seated Half

21318 **1851-O—Improperly Cleaned—NCS. AU Details.** Rich peach, mauve, and blue-green toning dominates the peripheries. A slightly bright example, the fields have wispy hay marks but the devices possess vibrant luster. Liberty's drapery folds are clashed within the shield, as made and not unusual for the type. New Orleans mintage of Half Dollars in 1851 was the lowest since 1841, undoubtedly due to the rising value of silver relative to California-mined gold. (#6267)

See the Online Session listings in the back of this volume for additional Reiver selections.

Charming 1852 Half Dollar MS62 NGC

21319 **1852 MS62 NGC.** This crisply struck low mintage Seated Half has good luster and original golden-gray color. A few faint slide marks in the fields, but refreshingly clean overall. The Wiley-Bugert reference states "one interesting marriage can be found with a bounced die doubled date; has very heavy diagonal die lines in the recessed area of the shield." No machine doubling is present, but this lot is the variety with the heavy die lines within the reverse shield. Just 77,130 pieces were struck, likely because silver coins were contemporaneously hoarded from circulation since their bullion value was greater than face. High mintages followed in 1853 once the silver weight was decreased. (#6268)

Golden Brown AU 1852-O Half Dollar

21320 **1852-O AU53 NGC.** Rich peach-gold toning outlines the rims and encroaches upon the lightly patinated centers. This pleasing Seated Half briefly entered Southern commerce prior to the Civil War, but has since been carefully saved. No singular marks require mention, and the eye appeal and originality are unmistakable. The 1852-O was limited to 144,000 pieces. Silver coins did not circulate in 1852, since an influx of west coast gold had increased the relative value of silver, and removed the latter metal from commerce. Population: 4 in 53, 13 finer (9/05). (#6269)

Desirable Choice 1853 Arrows and Rays Half Dollar

21321 **1853 Arrows and Rays MS64 NGC.** Light olive-gold in color, this impressive Choice type coin features creamy mint luster and an intricate strike. A single small reeding mark on the thigh, otherwise magnificently void of contact. The Arrows and Rays type was produced only in 1853; the dramatic Rays probably reduced reverse die life. Arrows remained on the obverse through 1855. Although struck in generous quantities to replenish hoarded old tenor silver, the 1853 is important for type purposes, and relatively few pieces have survived in better Mint State grades. (#6275)

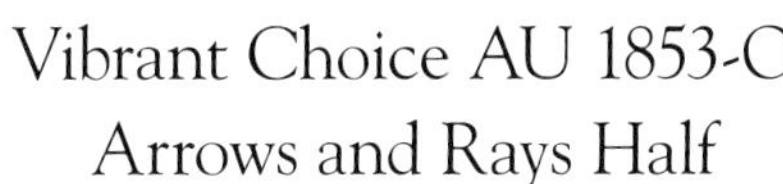

Vibrant Choice AU 1853-O Arrows and Rays Half

21322 **1853-O Arrows and Rays AU55 NGC.** Medium russet patination encroaches upon the lightly toned centers. This bold single year type coin displays substantial luster, and only the upper right obverse field has marks detectable to the naked eye. The bullion content of Half Dimes through Half Dollars was reduced nearly 7% early in 1853 to return those denominations to circulation, and arrows and rays were added to the design to indicate which 1853-dated pieces were new tenor. The rays were dropped in 1854, but fortunately for type collectors, the 1853 and 1853-O Arrows and Rays issues are available due to plentiful productions. (#6276)

Borderline Uncirculated 1854-O Arrows Half

21323 **1854-O Arrows AU58 NGC.** Dusky coffee-brown toning confirms the originality of this mostly lustrous near-Mint type coin. An occasional stray contact mark is of little import. Presumably, the rays were removed on Quarters and Half Dollars in 1854 because they reduced die life, and the arrows by the date were sufficient to indicate their lower bullion value. The Arrows type was struck only in 1854 and 1855, but type collectors should not be deterred, since only the scarce 1855-S is costly to acquire. (#6280)

Extremely Rare Proof 1855/54 Half Dollar

21324 **1855/54 PR63 NGC.** Walter Breen knew of just three Proof examples of this issue, stating that Proofs were discovered by Q. David Bowers. Perhaps a couple additional examples have been found since the time of his *Proof Encyclopedia*. We sold an example in our September 2002 Long Beach sale, the second example that we have handled prior to the current offering. At the time, we noted both the diagnostics, and the current roster as best we could determine.

Diagnostics of this rare proof delivery are:

1. Upper and lower loops of the 8 in the date are open.
2. Tiny rust pit on the upright of the 1 in the date to the right of the crossbar.
3. Scattered die file marks within the white stripes of the reverse shield (these fade on later strikings).
4. Die file marks in the reverse field between the tip of the eagle's left (facing) wing and the olive leaves.
5. Eagle's right (facing) wingtip is joined to the uppermost arrow shaft.

The present coin from the Reiver Collection displays all of these diagnostics, except the first, with remnants of the underdate evident under the final three digits. This example also exhibits remnants of the previous date *on the top surface* of the final digits, as well as the arrowheads.

It is believed that approximately 23 proof 1855 Arrows Seated Halves are extant, at least three of which (per Wiley and Bugert) are from the 1855/54 overdate die. This pleasing Proof is appreciably bright in the fields with hazy silver toning on both sides. All devices are sharply impressed, and we can find no outwardly distracting blemishes. A tiny diagonal mark in the reverse field, between the top of the left (facing) wing and the beak, will serve for pedigree purposes.

We are aware of the following proof 1855/54 Half Dollars:

1. Ex: FUN 2001 Signature Sale—The Richard Allen Collection (Heritage, 2/01), lot 7822. Certified PR61 by PCGS. Is this the "impaired" example that Breen (1977) says was once owned by Ted Clarke?
2. Ex: The Chicago Sale (Superior, 8/91), lot 516. Certified PR63 by PCGS.
3. Ex: E. W. Ropes Collection (New York Stamp and Coin Co., 2/1899); J. M. Clapp; John H. Clapp; Clapp Estate (1942); Louis E. Eliasberg, Sr.; Louis E. Eliasberg, Sr. Collection (Bowers and Merena, 4/97), lot 1962. The coin was described as PR64 by Bowers in the Eliasberg catalog.
4. Ex: The Rarities Sale (Bowers and Merena, 8/96), lot 137; The Dr. Juan XII Suros Collection of United States Overdate Coinage (Superior, 2/99), lot 200; October 2000 Pre-Long Beach Sale (Superior, 10/2000), lot 4378.
5. Ex: The Norweb Collection (Bowers and Merena, 11/88), lot 3166; Baltimore '93 Auction (Superior, 7/93), lot 428. Certified PR65 by PCGS at the time of the latter sale. (#6409)

21325 **1855 Arrows AU53 NGC.** Whispers of electric-blue and reddish-gold patina line the peripheries. Nicely defined, with remarkably clean surfaces that display luster in the protected areas. (#6281)

Richly Toned 1855-O Arrows Half Dollar

21326 **1855-O Arrows—Improperly Cleaned—NCS. AU Details.** Deep ocean-blue, olive-green, and apricot colors blanket this partly lustrous O-mint type coin. The devices exhibit little indication of wear. Close inspection yields faint vertical hairlines on the obverse field. (#6283)

Challenging AU Details 1855-S Arrows Half Dollar

21327 **1855-S Arrows—Improperly Cleaned—NCS. AU Details.** The initial S-mint issue, since the San Francisco Mint concentrated on the production of high denomination gold during its inaugural year of coinage. The 1855-S is also significant as the only Arrows, No Motto issue from that facility. The production of nearly 130,000 pieces is not especially low, but is deceptive, since few pieces were set aside. This bold but somewhat granular example has tan-gray color. The left obverse is thickly hairlined and has been smoothed. (#6284)

Important Proof 1856 Half Dollar

21328 **1856 PR63 NGC.** It is not known how many of these early Proofs were coined, and it is similarly difficult to determine how many different examples are known today. Walter Breen estimated 20 to 25 coins in his 1988 *Complete Encyclopedia*. Today, we believe that the number might be a little greater, but this is not known with certainty. The only way to have a good count of the survivors is to create a comprehensive Condition Census or roster of all early proof coins known. Essentially fully struck, save for only the slightest design weakness on the feathers above the eagle's left (facing) claw. The fields are deeply mirrored on both sides, with light cameo contrast, especially on the obverse. That side of the coin has pale gold toning throughout, while the reverse is essentially brilliant silver, tending toward faint gray color. Both sides have light hairlines in the fields, and these limit the grade of this example. (#6410)

Borderline Uncirculated 1856-O Half

21329 **1856-O AU58 NGC.** This sharply struck and pleasing near-Mint O-mint Half Dollar features gentle peripheral chestnut toning, and only a few stray slide marks on the right obverse field are remotely worthy of discussion. Only partial drapery beneath Liberty's elbow, not unusual for the type. (#6288)

Scarce Uncirculated Sharpness 1857 Half

21330 **1857—Improperly Cleaned—NCS. Unc. Details.** Bright from a relatively mild polishing, this intricately struck example is lightly toned and has detectable hairlines only on the field near the eagle's beak. Traces of chocolate-brown, rose, and sea-green color outline design elements near the rims. (#6290)

Memorable Uncirculated 1857-O Seated Half

21331 **1857-O MS61 NGC.** WB-103. A rare issue in Mint State condition, although VF and lower examples are not difficult to locate. Light tan toning endows this lustrous and attentively struck Seated Half. A few wispy field hairlines are expected of the grade. Traces of a prior date logotype are noted, particularly near the ball of the 5 and above the serif of the 1. Population: 2 in 61, 7 finer (8/05). (#6291)

Difficult AU Details 1857-S Seated Half

21332 **1857-S—Improperly Cleaned—NCS. AU Details.** WB-103, traces of a 1 from a blundered date are northwest of the prominent 1. Medium S mintmark. Olive, blue-green, and plum colors embrace this partly lustrous representative. Slightly subdued in appearance, but certainly an above average example of this tough early S-mint issue. (#6292)

Elusive Brilliant Proof 1858 Half Dollar

21333 **1858 PR62 NGC.** WB-101. Type One Reverse. A brilliant and carefully preserved piece that has chrome-like fields, as made. Cameo contrast is present but is prominent only when viewed from selected angles. The strike is good but not razor-sharp, a few stars and the eagle's left (facing) claw have not received a full blow from the dies.

In terms of their distribution, 1858 proofs are transitional. Proofs were struck in prior years, generally for presentation purposes rather than for sale to collectors. Select issues, such as 1856 Flying Eagle Cents, were restruck by the Mint for well placed collectors. Beginning in 1859, proofs were struck for distribution to collectors, and are scarce but affordable for modern numismatists. The 1858 proofs have an unknown mintage, and are significantly scarcer than the 1859 and subsequent issues. However, they are obtainable, while pre-1858 Seated Half proofs are very rare. Perhaps the decision to strike proofs for collectors was made in the later part of 1858, which would explain the small but collectible number of proof survivors. Population: 8 in 62, 38 finer (9/05). (#6412)

Significant Mint State 1858-S Half Dollar

21334 **1858-S MS61 NGC.** Splashes of golden-brown and ocean-blue color overlay the gunmetal-gray fields. This pinpoint-sharp representative has unbroken satin sheen and only one handling mark worthy of mention, beneath the D in UNITED. Although not a rare date in VG and lower grades, the 1858-S is seldom encountered in Uncirculated condition. Population: 2 in 61, 9 finer (9/05). (#6295)

See the Online Session listings in the back of this volume for additional Reiver selections.

Brilliant Proof 1859 Seated Half

21335 **1859 PR62 NGC.** Type One Reverse. This powerfully struck specimen is fully brilliant and is only lightly hairlined for the assigned grade. White on black contrast is substantial, but apparently insufficient to command a Cameo designation from NGC. A mere 800 proofs were struck. Several issues of Seated Halves from 1858 to 1864 come with either Type One or Two reverses, which are best distinguished by the spacing between LF in HALF at the top. (#6413)

AU Definition 1859-S Half

21336 **1859-S—Improperly Cleaned—NCS. AU Details.** WB-101. Large S. Richly detailed, but evaluation beneath a lens reveals dense hairlines. Partly retoned in peripheral chestnut hues. Ample luster illuminates the devices. Not a low mintage issue, but surprisingly scarce in XF and higher grades. (#6298)

Magnificent Gem Proof 1860 Half Dollar

21337 **1860 PR65 NGC.** Type Two Reverse. Plum, gold, and forest-green hues enliven the peripheries. The radiant, icy devices appear to demonstrate cameo contrast, but NGC has not been generous. An exquisite strike and undisturbed fields ensure the quality. The *Guide Book* reports a proof mintage of 1,000 pieces, however, Breen estimates about 525 proofs were actually sold by the mint, and the remainder melted. Certainly, 1860 Halves are scarcer in proof format than many subsequent Seated proof issues with smaller mintages. Population: 13 in 65, 7 finer (9/05). (#6414)

21338 **1860-O AU58 NGC.** A lustrous, sharply struck half with rich, original patina over the obverse and much lighter color on the reverse. Envelope Included. (#6300)

21339 **1860-S—Improperly Cleaned—NCS. AU Details.** WB-101. Large S mintmark. A mild past cleaning has subdued the surfaces of this richly detailed pearl-gray Seated Half. A partial drapery variety, only a wisp of drapery is beneath the elbow. Although collectible, Partial Drapery varieties are the result of a mint worker lapping the die, perhaps to remove clashmarks, and do not represent a design modification. (#6301)

Beautifully Toned Gem Proof 1861 Half Dollar

21340 **1861 PR65 NGC.** Original powder-blue, magenta, and peach-gold toning enriches the borders, while the mildly frosty devices are nearly untoned. A few wispy hairlines are of little concern. Dazzling mirrors and an above average strike provide exceptional eye appeal. In his 1988 Encyclopedia, Breen noted, "Of 1,000 proofs struck, fewer than 400 were sold, the rest melted." Population: 14 in 65, 4 finer (9/05). (#6415)

Mint State Details 1861-O Seated Half

21341 **1861-O—Obverse Scratched—NCS. Unc. Details.** WB-104. The 'speared olive bud' variety. Sharply struck and satiny, this chestnut and pearl-gray piece has reasonable eye appeal. A short horizontal scratch reaches the third star, and the reverse has a rim ding at 12 o'clock. A famous issue, since a portion of 1861-O Half Dollars were struck after Louisiana seceded from the Union. (#6303)

Conditionally Elusive 1861-S Half Dollar

21342 **1861-S—Improperly Cleaned—NCS. AU Details.** WB-101. Large S. Golden-brown hues overlay the dove-gray surfaces of this well struck Half Dollar. Luster glints from protected areas, and no unpleasant marks are detected, although the fields are cloudy from cleaning. (#6306)

Quality Proof 64 1862 Half Dollar

21343 **1862 PR64 NGC.** A gorgeous, razor-sharp Choice Seated Half, originally toned in dappled orange, aquamarine, and pearl-gray colors. Obviously beautifully preserved since its day of production. The upper left tip of the F in OF is defective, a hub defect that appears on some (but not all) neighboring No Motto dates and mintmarks. A stingy 550 proofs were delivered for this Civil War issue. Population: 54 in 64, 29 finer (9/05). (#6416)

21344 **1862-S XF45 NGC.** Light friction is seen over the highpoints. Light gray patina deepens slightly around the devices. (#6308)

Delightful Gem Proof 1863 Half Dollar

21345 **1863 PR65 NGC.** Ruby, gold, and sea-green toning hugs the obverse border, and the reverse has consistent light chestnut color. The Seated Liberty displays pleasing frost. This well struck Gem is refreshingly void of contact, and is a worthy addition to an important cabinet. Unlike other silver denominations, Half Dollars were coined in quantity at Philadelphia throughout the Civil War, perhaps for bank reserves. Half Dollars were the highest 'new tenor' silver denomination, since Silver Dollars retained their heavy pre-1853 weight. A mere 460 proofs were struck. Population: 13 in 65, 8 finer (9/05). (#6417)

Die Doubled Mint State 1864 Half Dollar

21346 **1864 MS62 NGC.** A lustrous medium golden-brown Civil War Half Dollar, well struck and clearly original. A couple of moderate handling marks on the upper obverse limit the grade, but not the eye appeal. The upper obverse is nicely die doubled, most apparent on Liberty's eyebrow. Population: 5 in 62, 42 finer (9/05). (#6311)

Originally Toned Choice Proof 1864 Seated Half

21347 **1864 PR64 NGC.** Dappled golden-brown and aquamarine colors grace this impressive Half Dollar, which is fully struck save for a trace of softness on the eagle's left (facing) ankle. Careful rotation beneath a light does not display any detectable hairlines. For this Civil War issue, a mere 470 proofs were produced, and high quality pieces are very scarce. Population: 47 in 64, 17 finer (9/05). (#6418)

See the Online Session listings in the back of this volume for additional Reiver selections.

Exquisitely Toned Gem Proof 1864 Half Dollar

21348 **1864 PR65 NGC.** Lush apple-green, olive, and peach colors interchange throughout this essentially unblemished and magnificently preserved Gem. The strike is penetrating except on the eagle's left (facing) ankle. The Jules Reiver Collection features many outstanding proof Seated Half Dollars, which makes the Reiver pedigree all the more desirable. One of a mere 470 pieces struck. Population: 8 in 65, 9 finer (9/05). (#6418)

Important Cameo Gem Proof 1865 Half

21349 **1865 PR65 Cameo NGC.** This desirable Cameo Gem features impressive white on black contrast and lovely peripheral peach, rose, and navy-blue toning. Well struck, and thorough evaluation locates only a small number of barely perceptible hairlines. One of the most important years in American history, 1865 witnessed Lincoln's assassination and the end of the Civil War. Population: 5 in 65 Cameo, 7 finer (9/05). (#86419)

Choice XF 1866-S No Motto Half

21350 **1866-S No Motto XF45 NGC.** Tan-brown luster accompanies steel-gray fields and highpoints. A richly detailed and relatively unmarked example. Only 60,000 No Motto 1866-S Halves were struck, apparently coined early in the year prior to the arrival of Motto dies made at the Philadelphia Mint. The No Motto variety is scarce in all grades, and the Wiley-Bugert standard reference estimates XF/AU pieces as Rarity 5. (#6315)

Impressive PR66 ★ 1866 Half Dollar Motto

21351 **1866 Motto PR66 ★ NGC.** A scarce date and the first year to show the new reverse motto above the eagle. This lovely piece displays a cameo-like effect on both sides. Exquisitely struck, with near-pristine surfaces. Delicate lavender, gold-brown, and cobalt-blue patina encircle the rims. Census: 1 in 66 ★, 0 finer (10/05). (#6424)

21352 **1866-S Motto AU53 NGC.** First year of issue for the With Motto type, this piece is deeply and evenly toned over each side. (#6320)

Attractively Toned Proof 1867 Half Dollar

21353 **1867 PR62 NGC.** Thin bands of ice-blue and golden-brown color grace the obverse margin, and the reverse has similar but deeper toning. The Seated Liberty is nicely frosted, however, the reverse is sufficiently toned to deny Cameo status. Intricately struck and attractive. The right obverse field has a patch of vertical hairlines and a possible fingerprint fragment. Just 625 proofs were struck. (#6425)

21354 **1867-S—Improperly Cleaned—NCS. AU Details.** WB-102. Die doubling is evident on the right side of the letters T in TRUST, and on the stripes within the eagle's shield. Subdued by a mild cleaning, this ivory-gray piece is generally unabraded. A prominent clashmark connects the left scroll end to the olive branch. (#6322)

Vibrantly Toned Cameo Gem 1868 Half

21355 **1868 PR65 Cameo NGC.** Warm honey, ruby-red, and powder-blue border tints encroach upon the brilliant fields and icy devices. A boldly struck beauty, undisturbed and undoubtedly original. Only partial drapery beneath Liberty's elbow, and some plumage detail is absent on the eagle, all as made from polished dies. One of a mere 600 pieces struck. Population: 3 in 65 Cameo, 2 finer (9/05). (#86426)

21356 **1868-S XF45 NGC.** Autumn-brown toning approaches the rims, while the centers offer ivory-gray color. A few light handling marks on the obverse field and the eagle, but the overall appearance is impressive for the grade and issue. A plentiful production, nonetheless underappreciated in better circulated grades. Census: 5 in 45, 27 finer (12/05). (#6324)

Lovely Patinated Near Gem Proof 1869 Half

21357 **1869 PR64 NGC.** Vibrant blue-green, plum, and orange colors endow this boldly struck and beautifully preserved near-Gem. An aesthetic treat for the eyes, and also desirable for its scarcity. Only 600 proofs were struck. Population: 45 in 64, 29 finer (9/05). (#6427)

Outstanding 1869-S Half Dollar, MS64

21358 **1869-S MS64 NGC.** A lightly toned and splendidly unabraded near-Gem. Rich cartwheel luster is unencumbered by contact, and the strike is sharp except for Liberty's hair and the two stars that bookend her head. Delicate tan toning denies full brilliance. Virtually a No Drapery variety, since only a faint fragment of the drapery below the elbow remains present, as made from a lapped die. The Wiley-Bugert reference states that the 1869-S is High R.6 in Mint State. An opportunity for the determined specialist. Population: 4 in 64, 11 finer (9/05). (#6326)

Richly Toned 1870 Proof Half Dollar

21359 **1870 PR62 NGC.** Blue-green, apricot, and ruby tones endow the borders. Not fully impressed on the eagle's left (facing) leg, this beautiful Half Dollar has intricate definition on Liberty's head and the stars. Significantly scarcer than the mintage of 1,000 pieces suggests, perhaps unsold examples were melted by the Mint as was done with the 1861 proof issue. (#6428)

21360 **1870-S AU50 NGC.** Olive color graces the margins, while the fields provide sky-gray toning. A whisper of PVC between the pole and the arm, otherwise a well defined example with noticeable remaining luster. Scarce in better grades despite a reasonable production. Census: 3 in 50, 10 finer (12/05). (#6329)

Elusive 1870-CC Half Dollar, VF35 NGC

21361 **1870-CC VF35 NGC.** The survival ratio of the 54,617 pieces struck at the Carson City facility in this initial year of production is extremely low, making it one of the most sought-after issues in the entire Seated Liberty series in any grade. This specimen displays medium golden-gray toning with iridescent highlights. The design elements are sharply defined, and the surfaces exhibit just a few minute, inoffensive contact marks. Census: 4 in 35, 12 finer (10/05). (#6328)

Vividly Toned Gem Proof 1871 Half Struck Thru Wire Obverse

21362 **1871—Obverse Struck Thru—PR65 NGC.** Dusky peach toning consumes much of this meticulously struck Gem, but mauve, electric-blue, and apple-green colors adorn the rims. Apparently struck through a thin, lengthy, and horizontally placed wire, which came between the planchet and the obverse die from 8 o'clock to Liberty's right (facing) leg. Such a strike-thru is very unusual for a 19th century proof. 960 proofs were struck, only a portion of which have survived unimpaired. Population: 12 in 65, 7 finer (9/05). (#6429)

21363 **1871-S—Improperly Cleaned—NCS. AU Details.** WB-103. The "Incomplete mintmark" variety, the mintmark apparently entered into the die at an angle such that the upper half was only faintly entered. No hairlines are readily evident, but the tan and steel-blue surfaces are slightly glossy from a mild cleaning. Boldly struck, and luster is evident throughout the devices. (#6332)

Tough Very Fine 1871-CC Half Dollar

21364 **1871-CC VF25 NGC.** In the early years of the Carson City Mint, Half Dollars tended to have larger productions than the other silver denominations. Nonetheless, survivors are surprisingly scarce, since few if anyone collected such pieces from circulation within a generation of their issue. Dusky apricot and gunmetal-gray toning embraces this inoffensively abraded example. Ample drapery and plumage details and a clear LIBERTY confirm the VF grade. (#6331)

Richly Toned 1872 Seated Half PR65 Cameo NGC

21365 **1872 PR65 Cameo NGC.** Lemon-gold color endows the reverse, but gradually gives way to an untoned center. Dramatic electric-blue, russet, and plum toning enriches the obverse border. The Seated Liberty, in particular, displays prominent frost. This lovingly preserved Cameo Gem will be a standout within an advanced proof Half Dollar cabinet. A scant 950 proofs were struck. Population: 4 in 65 Cameo, 4 finer (9/05). (#86430)

21366 **1872-CC Fine 15 NGC.** The E in LIBERTY is very faint, however, all other letters are crisp. Deep earth tones blanket this moderately abraded Seated Half Dollar. The devices exhibit pleasing definition for the assigned grade. Although available by the standards of early Carson City Mint coinage, the 1872-CC is very scarce by nearly any other standard, and survivors are eagerly pursued in all problem-free collector grades. Census: 2 in 15, 44 finer (12/05). (#6334)

21367 **1872-S XF40 NGC.** WB-102. Medium-Small S mintmark. Well struck with light even wear and a small degree of satiny luster still remaining. The surfaces are lightly toned in pink-gray, russet, and red-orange coloration, and both sides are free of distracting marks. A very attractive example, for the grade. Census: 2 in 40, 25 finer (12/05). (#6335)

Exceptional Cameo Gem 1873 Arrows Half

21370 **1873 Arrows PR65 Cameo NGC.** WB-106. Large Arrows. Splendid ocean-blue, apricot, and mauve colors adorn the margins of this assertively struck Cameo Gem. Only fragments of the drapery beneath the elbow are present, due to die lapping that also weakened several feathers on the left (facing) wing. Two varieties of proof Half Dollars were struck in 1873. 600 Closed 3, No Arrows pieces were produced early in the year. After the date logotype modification, and a change to metric weights, 550 Open 3, Arrows proofs were struck. Although the proof mintages are relatively close in quantity, the Arrows pieces are in greater demand, since they represent a two year proof type. Population: 6 in 65 Cameo, 7 finer (9/05). (#86434)

Beautifully Toned Proof 1873 No Arrows Seated Half

21368 **1873 No Arrows PR64 NGC.** Orange and plum colors invigorate the obverse border, while rich honey toning endows the reverse margin. A partial drapery variety, the folds beneath the elbow are attenuated from die polishing, as produced. The right obverse field has a couple of light handling marks. Proof 1873 Half Dollars come with and without arrows, the former is moderately scarcer but priced much higher due to its value as a proof type. (#6431)

Choice VF 1873-CC Arrows Half Dollar

21371 **1873-CC Arrows VF35 NGC.** WB-102. Small CC mintmark. Tan and sky-gray tints envelop this richly detailed representative. A scarce issue requisite for a Carson City type set, since the only other Arrows issue, the 1874-CC, is even more difficult to find. No handling marks are remotely worthy of mention. The weight of silver coins was slightly increased in early 1873 to conform with the metric system, the Half Dollar standard raised to 12.50 grams. (#6344)

Difficult XF Sharpness 1873-CC No Arrows Half

21369 **1873-CC No Arrows—Improperly Cleaned—NCS. XF Details.** The 1873-CC No Arrows Dime is unique, and the 1873-CC No Arrows Quarter is extremely rare. Fortunately for collectors, the mintage of 1873-CC No Arrows Half Dollars was sufficient to make the variety collectible, but survivors are nonetheless very scarce. Cloudy from a moderate cleaning, this chestnut-gray Seated Half has impressive definition for this generally well circulated issue. (#6338)

Affordable 1874 Arrows Seated Half

21372 **1874 Arrows—Improperly Cleaned—NCS. AU Details.** WB-103. Large Arrows recut over Small Arrows. Minutely granular in places from a chemical cleaning, this richly detailed type coin nonetheless displays noticeable luster and has no obtrusive marks. Arrows bookend the date on some 1873 and all 1874 Half Dollars, to indicate a slight gain in weight from 12.44 to 12.50 grams. (#6346)

Impressively Toned Near Gem 1874 Arrows Half Proof

21373 **1874 Arrows PR64 NGC.** WB-101. Small Arrows. Lemon, ruby, ocean-blue, and plum colors illuminate the borders but cede to nearly untoned and lightly frosted devices. This suitably struck near-Gem has a pleasing appearance to the naked eye, and is desirable as a member of the two year Arrows proof type. (#6435)

Challenging 1874-CC Arrows Half Dollar

21374 **1874-CC Arrows—Improperly Cleaned—NCS. XF Details.** For the Half Eagle through Double Eagle denominations, the 1874-CC is among the most available Carson City issues from its decade. However, the same rule does not apply to the 1874-CC Half Dollar, which had a low mintage of 59,000 pieces. Most survivors are in low circulated grades, unlike the present full LIBERTY example. Traces of luster beckon from recesses of the devices, and no hairlines are apparent, although the subdued appearance implies a past chemical dip. A bold diagonal die line (as made) crosses the final S in STATES. (#6347)

Desirable Choice 1874-S Arrows Half

21375 **1874-S Arrows MS64 NGC.** WB-103. Minute S. The Philadelphia Mint produced more than four million Motto, Arrows Half Dollars. The branch mints were not as prolific, and only 622,000 pieces of the type were struck at San Francisco. Close to 400,000 pieces were 1874-S Half Dollars, the more available of the two S-mint issues. Since no one collected by mintmark in 1874, and few collected on the west coast, Mint State survivors are scarce, especially with clean surfaces. Not quite fully struck, but the strike is above average, and the vibrant luster and the lightly dappled tan-gray toning are attractive. Population: 9 in 64, 3 finer (9/05). (#6348)

1875 Half Dollar, MS62 NGC

21376 **1875 MS62 NGC.** Lustrous surfaces are occupied by low intensity golden-tan patina, and exhibit well struck design elements. Light contact marks on the central devices and in the right (facing) obverse fields limit the grade. (#6349)

Vibrantly Toned Proof 1875 Seated Half

21377 **1875 PR62 NGC.** Golden-brown toning, joined by electric-blue on the obverse, gravitates to the borders. The design elements are sharply struck, and the surfaces display a cameo-like effect, which is more noticeable on the obverse. The fields reveal fine grade-defining hairlines, particularly on the obverse. (#6436)

Impressive Choice 1875-S Half Dollar

21378 **1875-S MS64 NGC.** WB-101, Very Small S. Dazzling luster and light tan-gray toning provide pleasing eye appeal. Well struck in the centers, the obverse periphery is not sufficiently complete in strike to fully remove some light mint-made roller marks. A tiny spot is noted above the elbow, however, no unpleasant marks are located. 1875 through 1877 were heavy mintage years for the denomination at San Francisco, since no production of Silver Dollars competed for mint resources. (#6351)

Charming Choice Cameo Proof 1876 Half

21379 **1876 PR64 Cameo NGC.** Type One Reverse. Tawny-gold and rose-red colors enrich the peripheries of this lovely Near Gem. Examples of this issue were sold by the U.S. Mint on the grounds of the Centennial Exposition held in Philadelphia in 1876. Liberty has only partial drapery beneath her elbow, as made. Tiny spots on the D in DOL and near the elbow prevent a finer grade. Population: 4 in 64 Cameo, 11 finer (8/05). (#86437)

Rare Prooflike 1876-CC Half Dollar

21380 **1876-CC MS61 Prooflike NGC.** WB-102. Medium CC mintmark. Type One Reverse. Gentle honey-gold toning endows the borders and visits the centers. The flashy fields, assertive strike, and noticeable frost on the devices all suggest proof manufacture, but the presence of the Carson City mintmark instead confirms a prooflike business strike. Some delicate hairlines appear on the right obverse field upon proper rotation beneath a light, and these are conservatively assessed by NGC. As of (8/05), the only 1876-CC designated as Prooflike by NGC. (#6353)

Charming Proof 1877 Half Dollar

21381 **1877 PR62 NGC.** Type Two Reverse. Invigorating golden-brown, ocean-blue, and ruby-red colors endow the margins of this lightly marked specimen. Generally well struck, only the lower knee and the left (facing) eagle's ankle lack pinpoint detail. The devices are quite frosty, but apparently not sufficiently so to command a Cameo designation from NGC. A scant 510 pieces ensures the scarcity. (#6438)

Pleasing Choice AU 1877-CC Seated Half Dollar

21382 **1877-CC AU55 NGC.** Peripheral aquamarine and olive-gold colors embrace this intricately struck and nearly unabraded Carson City half dollar. There is only slight highpoint wear, and the surfaces only show one slender pinscratch, on the upper reverse, connecting the eagle's neck to the lower edge of the scroll. Wispy hairlines are evident, in the obverse fields. A pleasing Choice AU representative. (#6356)

21383 **1877-S AU55 NGC.** A lightly toned and satiny representative that has a reasonable strike and no detrimental abrasions. Wispy hairlines in the fields define this as a lightly circulated example, but it is certainly one with ample eye appeal. (#6357)

See the Online Session listings in the back of this volume for additional Reiver selections.

Near Gem Proof 1878 Half Dollar

21384 **1878 PR64 NGC.** Type Two Reverse. Freckles of golden-brown, powder-blue, and ruby toning visit the margins of this assertively struck and attractive near-Gem. A hint of granularity at 1:30 on the reverse does not distract. Only 800 proofs were struck. 1878 was a transitional date for the denomination. Business strikes were curtailed once the Morgan Dollar began heavy production, and a series of low mintage Philadelphia Mint issues ensued. (#6439)

Scarce XF Details 1879 Half Dollar

21387 **1879—Obverse Scratched—NCS. XF Details.** Type Two Reverse. Glimpses of luster persist throughout this steel-gray example. Close evaluation locates a horizontal pinscratch above Liberty's rock. A popular date because of its scant commercial production of 4,800 pieces. (#6361)

Bold VF 1878-CC Half Dollar

21385 **1878-CC VF30 NGC.** Both sides are blanketed by deep red-dish-brown color, and show a few scattered surface marks and even, honest wear. Desirable mid-grade quality for this final Carson City Half Dollar issue, one of just 62,000 pieces struck. Population: 3 in 30, 17 finer (9/05). (#6359)

Impressive 1879 Seated Half PR65 Cameo NGC

21388 **1879 PR65 Cameo NGC.** Medium golden-brown and navy-blue colors grace the peripheries of this pleasing Gem. Mirrored fields contrast with radiant white devices. Business strikes and proofs combined for less than 6,000 pieces, since the mints were legislatively compelled to strike Silver Dollars in great quantity. Population: 3 in 65 Cameo, 9 finer (8/05). (#86440)

Legendary 1878-S Half Dollar, AU Details

21386 **1878-S—Improperly Cleaned—NCS. AU Details.** A legendary rarity in the Seated half series. The mintage was a mere 12,000 pieces, all struck before the mint's equipment was pressed into full time service producing Morgan dollars. As a result, surviving examples of the half dollars are very rare. According to our records, only 33 specimens have been offered in public sales during the past 30 some years. This specimen displays sharp design detail. The surfaces are bright and finely hairlined, and are retoning aqua marine in isolated areas, particularly along the borders. We also note a horizontal pinscratch across Liberty's midsection between her two arms. (#6360)

Delightfully Toned Cameo Gem Proof 1880 Half Dollar

21389 **1880 PR65 Cameo NGC.** Type Two Reverse. Lovely honey-gold, sky-blue, and magenta colors frame the brilliant centers. Icy devices display obvious contrast with the nearly undisturbed fields. The 1880 has the largest proof mintage of the type, although it is made more desirable by the low business strike production of 8,400 pieces. One reason for the large proof mintages of the era was the contemporary popularity of the proof-only Trade Dollar. (#86441)

Lovely Toned Gem Cameo Proof 1881 Seated Half

21390 **1881 PR65 Cameo NGC.** Possibly a Type Two Reverse hubbed over a Type One Reverse, since the olive above the H in HALF shows characteristics of both subtypes. Beautiful tobacco-brown, electric-blue, and plum colors embrace the margins, while the frosty central devices are generally untoned. This nicely struck Gem has some mint-made roughness on the raised hand, but the eye appeal is certainly imposing. Population: 11 in 65 Cameo, 10 finer (8/05). (#86442)

Attractive 1882 Gem Proof Cameo Half Dollar

21391 **1882 PR65 Cameo NGC.** This Gem Cameo Proof is a remarkable example of Christian Gobrecht's original Seated Liberty design, having only been through a few minor adjustments. Virtually full design definition, only a touch weak on Liberty's head. Narrow concentric rings of cobalt-blue, lavender, and gold-brown toning gravitates to the rims, and frosty devices offer a striking contrast to the deeply mirrored fields. There are no mentionable abrasions on either side. Wispy die striations, as well as some minor hairlines, are noted in the fields. An extraordinary attractive coin. (#86443)

Low Mintage 1883 Half Dollar PR61

21392 **1883 PR61 NGC.** Well struck with frosted devices, deeply reflective fields, and numerous grade-limiting hairlines, especially on the obverse, which fail to seriously impair the visual appeal of the piece. The Philadelphia Mint was the only coinage facility that produced half dollars in 1883, and a minuscule total of 9,039 coins were struck, 1,039 of which were proofs. (#6444)

Gorgeously Toned Cameo Proof Near-Gem 1883 Seated Half Dollar

21393 **1883 PR64 Cameo NGC.** An appealing proof, with golden, purple-red, and electric-blue toning at the rims and in some of the fields. The fields are deeply mirrored and the devices partially frosted, yielding a strong Cameo effect. This coin is an exceptional survivor of a late date Seated Half issue, that saw just 8,000 business strikes and 1,039 proofs. Population: 14 in 64 Cameo, 15 finer in Cameo condition (9/05). (#86444)

Appealing 1884 Half Dollar, PR63 NGC

21394 **1884 PR63 NGC.** A nicely struck and lightly toned specimen with good reflectivity and not too many faint hairlines. Proofs and business strikes combined for just 5,275 pieces, the lowest total production of any 19th century Philadelphia Mint Half Dollar issue. Population: 31 in 63, 91 finer (9/05). (#6445)

See the Online Session listings in the back of this volume for additional Reiver selections.

Pleasing 1885 Half Dollar, AU50 NGC

21395 **1885 AU50 NGC.** Bright silvery surfaces display traces of luster in the protected areas, and wisps of light to medium russet gravitate to the peripheries. The design elements are well defined, and the few marks scattered about are not offensive. (#6367)

Gorgeous 1886 Premium Gem Proof

21398 **1886 PR66 NGC.** The 1886 is one of several low mintage P-mint issues at the end of the Seated Half Dollar series. In this particular year, only 5,000 business strikes and 886 proofs were produced. This is among the finest certified survivors of the latter delivery. The design elements are exquisitely struck, and the frosted obverse motif contrasts with deeply mirrored fields. Wisps of blue, russet, and lavender toning gravitate to the rims. (#6447)

Richly Toned Near-Gem Proof 1885 Seated Half Dollar

21396 **1885 PR64 NGC.** Deeply mirrored with a moderate amount of frost on the obverse devices. The obverse exhibits rich russet-rose and cobalt peripheral toning, with a noticeable cameo effect, while the reverse is more darkly hued in russet, crimson, smoky-lilac and electric-blue coloration. A popular, low total mintage date. (#6446)

Vividly Toned Gem Proof 1887 Half Dollar

21399 **1887 PR65 NGC.** Luminous golden-brown, mauve-red, and ocean-blue colors adorn the borders. The centers are brilliant, a classic 'album toning' pattern seen on many silver pieces in the Jules Reiver Collection. This carefully preserved Gem delivers irrefutable contrast between the frosty Seated Liberty and the reflective obverse field, but the eagle is not as icy-white, which precludes a Cameo designation. The strike is reasonable albeit not sharp. Proofs were limited to 710 pieces, with extra demand from those unable to secure quality examples of the mere 5,000 business strikes coined. (#6448)

Elusive XF Details 1886 Half Dollar

21397 **1886—Improperly Cleaned—NCS. XF Details.** A richly detailed and only lightly marked example of this popular low mintage issue. Minor hairlines on this slate-gray and honey-brown Half Dollar are no more than is expected from moderate circulation. Proofs and business strikes combined for less than 5,000 pieces. (#6368)

Low Production 1888 Proof Half Dollar

21400 **1888—Improperly Cleaned—NCS. Proof.** A subdued slate-gray better date Half Dollar with minor granularity beneath the U in UNITED and west of the H in HALF. Faint obverse hairlines belie a long ago cleaning. Another in a series of low mintage dates for the denomination, as the Mint was legislatively compelled to strike Silver Dollars during the era. (#6449)

Charming Cameo Gem Proof 1888 Half

21401 **1888 PR65 Cameo NGC.** Radiant honey, ice-blue, and rose-red colors embrace the peripheries of this meticulously struck and beautifully preserved Gem. The frost on the Seated Liberty is especially thick, although the reverse also exhibits good contrast. As is the case with all Half Dollars produced between 1879 and 1890, business strikes were very low in quantity and limited to the Philadelphia Mint. (#86449)

21402 **1889 VG10 NGC.** WB-101. Normal Date. Evenly worn and unabraded, with hints of light coloration on the essentially color-free surfaces. A scarce late date in the series, with an original mintage of only 12,000 business strikes. (#6371)

Obtainable Proof 1889 Seated Half

21403 **1889—Obverse Improperly Cleaned—NCS. Proof.** A curved swatch of delicate hairlines on the right obverse field are strictly assessed by NCS. Medium golden-brown and mauve-wine hues converge upon the essentially brilliant devices. A mere 711 proofs were coined, along with 12,000 business strikes. (#6450)

Cameo Choice Proof 1890 Half

21404 **1890 PR64 Cameo NGC.** Beautifully toned in lemon-gold, ruby-red, and electric-blue colors that cede to brilliant centers. The strike is razor-sharp aside from a trace of softness on the eagle's left (facing) claw. Cameo frost is particularly evident on the Seated Liberty motif. This carefully preserved Choice proof has no shortage of eye appeal, and is among a low production of 590 proofs. (#86451)

Gorgeous Cameo Gem Proof 1891 Half

21405 **1891 PR65 Cameo NGC.** Impressive cherry-red, golden-brown, and aquamarine colors dazzle both sides of this meticulously struck and splendidly preserved Gem. Light die doubling to the south is noted on HALF DOL. The final year of the long-lived Seated type. Population: 5 in 65 Cameo, 10 finer (8/05). (#86452)

BARBER HALF DOLLARS

Collectible Proof 1892 Half Dollar

21406 **1892—Lacquered—NCS. Proof.** This untoned proof appears to have cameo contrast, and the iridescent layer of lacquer on both sides would likely be removed without unpleasant consequence by a proper dip in acetone. The reverse is lightly die doubled, most apparent on the peripheral legends. (#6539)

Choice AU 1892-O Half Dollar

21407 **1892-O AU55 NGC.** Silvery surfaces exhibit golden-brown patina, which is slightly deeper on the obverse, around the peripheries. Luster is retained in the recessed areas, and there are no significant marks to report. (#6462)

See the Online Session listings in the back of this volume for additional Reiver selections.

Challenging 1892-S Half Dollar

21408 **1892-S—Improperly Cleaned—NCS. AU Details.** A bold cream-gray and tan-brown example of this introductory S-mint issue, the first Half Dollar date struck by the western mint since 1878. Designated as cleaned by NCS, but no hairlines are readily discerned, and the piece is not unattractive. The 1892-S is a key date throughout most circulated grades, and is typically among the last holes to be filled by album collectors of the challenging series. (#6464)

Lustrous 1893 Half Dollar, AU58 NGC

21409 **1893 AU58 NGC.** Considerable residual luster is apparent on the bright silvery surfaces of this high end AU specimen, and traces of cobalt-blue and lavender dance about portions of the margins. The design elements are sharply struck, save for the upper right (facing) tip of the shield. Wispy slide marks on Liberty's cheek and the neck are mentioned for accuracy. (#6465)

Promising Proof 1893 Half Dollar

21410 **1893—Lacquered—NCS. Proof.** This sharply struck and brilliant example appears to have cameo contrast and pleasing surfaces beneath its coat of lacquer, which could presumably be removed without desultory effect by a professional conservator. Mintages of proof Half Dollars dropped substantially from the prior year, perhaps because contemporary type collectors were satisfied with only their 1892 specimen. (#6540)

Attractive 1893-S Half Dollar, MS63 NGC

21411 **1893-S MS63 NGC.** An early branch mint delivery in the Barber Half Dollar series, the '93-S undoubtedly saw extensive circulation at the time of issue. Most survivors are well worn, and the date is scarce in circulated grades above the Fine level. Perhaps needless to say, Mint State survivors are rare. The MS63 coin offered in this lot displays intense luster and sharply struck design features. Whispers of golden-brown and cobalt-blue patina occur around portions of the margins, especially on the reverse. A few minute marks are noted on Liberty's cheek and the rear of the cap. Some as-struck light roller marks are also noted on the upper part of Liberty's cheek. Overall, a very attractive coin for the grade, and may be somewhat conservatively graded. Population: 18 in 63, 10 finer (9/05). (#6467)

Bright 1894 Half Dollar, PR63 NGC

21412 **1894 PR63 NGC.** This near brilliant proof exhibits a cameo-like appearance, especially on the obverse. A few splashes of light milky-gray color are scattered about in limited areas, especially on the reverse. The design elements are exquisitely struck throughout. A few wispy hairlines are noted in the obverse fields. (#6541)

High End AU 1894-S Half Dollar

21413 **1894-S AU58 NGC.** Bright surfaces retain ample luster, and display russet patination around the rims, which is slightly deeper and more extensive on the obverse. The design elements are well defined throughout. A few minor contact marks are present on Liberty's cheek and neck. (#6470)

Attractive 1895 PR63 Half Dollar

21414 **1895 PR63 NGC.** The only factors preventing a higher grade on this lovely Proof are some wispy hairlines in the fields. Otherwise, the design elements are razor sharp, and the bright surfaces are essentially brilliant in the centers. Wisps of golden-brown and electric-blue toning hug the rims. Luster grazes are noted on Liberty's cheek. (#6542)

1895-O Half Dollar, MS62 NGC

21415 **1895-O MS62 NGC.** Sharply struck on the design elements, and brilliant or near brilliant centers are framed by golden-brown, lilac, and cobalt-blue around the rims. Several small abrasions are noted on Liberty's cheek and neck, and edge roughness is visible on the obverse rim between 7 and 9 o'clock. Population: 13 in 62, 32 finer (9/05). (#6472)

Attractive Gem Proof 1896 Half Dollar

21416 **1896 PR65 NGC.** The 1896 and 1898 are two of the best produced dates in the Barber half series. Even though this piece is not labeled as a Cameo, the surfaces display a moderate two-toned contrast between the fields and devices, which is slightly more apparent on the reverse. The fields are especially deep in their mirrored reflectivity. Almost completely brilliant, there is just the slightest hint of barely perceptible champagne toning at the rims. An attractive type coin that represents good value. Population: 33 in 65, 45 finer (9/05). (#6543)

Important Mint State 1896-S Barber Half

21417 **1896-S MS63 NGC.** A rich coating of rose-brown and sea-green toning blankets both obverse and reverse. The underlying surfaces remain vibrant, as luster shines through the deep patina. No distracting marks or abrasions are evident on either side. With a mintage of 1.14 million pieces, one would imagine this to be a more available coin than it is in Mint State. But the surviving examples are thinly spread throughout the various Uncirculated grades. Population: 10 in 63, 23 finer (9/05). (#6476)

Pleasing Cameo Proof 1897 Barber Half

21418 **1897 PR63 Cameo NGC.** A nicely struck representative that has a seemingly pristine reverse, while the obverse has a few wispy slide marks and hairlines. The cameo contrast is irrefutable. Just 713 pieces were produced. (#86544)

Scarce 1897-S Half Dollar

21419 **1897-S—Tooled—NCS. AU Details.** Golden-brown toning clings to the margins. Bright from polishing, the fields are thickly hairlined and exhibit smoothing beneath Liberty's chin and above LAR in DOLLAR. Tiny marks on the portrait are consistent with loose handling as jewelry. The 1897-S is a better date. In fact, in Good condition, only the 1892-O and 1892-S carry a higher premium. (#6479)

Cameo Proof 1898 Barber Half

21420 **1898 PR63 Cameo NGC.** A well struck representative that has faint gold patina. Both sides exhibit lovely cameo contrast, and are free of bothersome handling marks. The obverse has a few unimportant hairlines that limit the grade but not the eye appeal of the piece. (#86545)

Impressive Gem Proof 1898 Half Dollar

21421 **1898 PR65 NGC.** A lovely, deeply toned example of Barber proof coinage. This specimen has deeply mirrored fields with minor cloudiness, few hairlines, and mildly frosted devices. A coin that will do justice to any collection of proof Gems. (#6545)

Better Date 1898-O Half Dollar

21422 **1898-O VF30 NGC.** Typically worn for the grade, with noticeable hairlines in the fields. Attractive red-orange toning adorns the obverse and reverse borders. Remaining luster is extensive for the grade. Like most Barber Half issues, the 1898-O is hard to locate in Fine or better grades. (#6481)

Very Scarce Near-Mint Example 1898-S Barber Half

21423 **1898-S AU58 NGC.** The 1898-S is the scarcest of the three S-mint Barber Half Dollar issues (1898-S, 1899-S, and 1900-S) that were sent to the Philippines in quantity at the time of issue. Mint State examples are very elusive. The currently offered piece displays uniformly deeply toned surfaces, primarily in shades of brownish-gray and gold, that are well struck on the obverse, but slightly weak on the reverse. Negligible wear and few surface blemishes are apparent on either side of the coin. Population: 18 in 58, 29 finer (9/05). (#6482)

1899 Proof Barber Half PR63 Cameo NGC

21424 **1899 PR63 Cameo NGC.** Fully struck with deep mirror fields and nicely frosted devices. A light reddish-tan patina clings to some of the reverse devices. A few wispy slide marks, on the obverse, limit the grade. (#86546)

Scarce Choice AU 1899-S Barber Half Dollar

21425 **1899-S AU55 NGC.** Light-gray, apricot, and sky-blue toning covers both sides. Plenty of luster remains evident, along with slight highpoint wear and a number of trivial obverse contact marks. The 1899-S is a scarcer issue in AU and better condition. (#6485)

Conditionally Elusive Near-Gem Cameo Proof 1900 Barber Half

21426 **1900 PR64 Cameo NGC.** The flashy, deeply mirrored fields of this well made specimen provide an ideal background for vivid cameo contrast with the richly frosted devices. A few minor hairlines and several faint vertical slide marks, on the obverse, limit the coin to near-Gem status. (#86547)

Richly Toned 1900-O Barber Half AU58 NGC

21427 **1900-O AU58 NGC.** Richly toned on both sides in a variety of colors, this example is well detailed on the obverse, but softly struck on the eagle. A few faint hairlines and wispy slide marks are apparent on the obverse, and there are two or three trivial contact marks near the center of the reverse. One of the most elusive of all New Orleans Barber issues in high grades. (#6487)

Scarce 1900-S Barber Half AU55 NGC

21428 **1900-S AU55 NGC.** Highly lustrous, for the grade, and richly toned near the peripheries, this Choice AU example shows a number of small contact marks, and a few vertical slide marks over the obverse portrait, with only the faintest traces of wear on either side. A generally pleasing example of this scarce Barber half issue. (#6488)

Lovely Near-Gem Proof 1901 Barber Half PR64 Cameo NGC

21429 **1901 PR64 Cameo NGC.** A sharply struck near-Gem that has extremely pleasing surfaces. Strong cameo contrast is evident on each side, along with small amounts of scattered orange-tan coloration. Faint obverse slide marks prevent the Gem grade assessment. A scant 813 proofs were minted. (#86548)

Bright 1902 Half Dollar, PR61 NGC

21430 **1902 PR61 NGC.** Essentially brilliant surfaces on the obverse are moderately hairlined, while the reverse displays whispers of milky-tan patination. Sharply struck, with no significant contact marks. (#6549)

1903 Half Dollar, PR62 NGC

21431 **1903 PR62 NGC.** Bright surfaces are virtually untoned on the obverse, and display light brown toning scattered throughout the reverse. The design features are exquisitely struck up throughout. Fine hairline patches are noted on Liberty's cheek and neck and in the right (facing) obverse field. Envelope Included. (#6550)

See the Online Session listings in the back of this volume for additional Reiver selections.

Mint State 1903-O Half Dollar

21432 **1903-O MS60 NGC.** Bright surfaces display decent luster and sharply impressed design features. The only hints of toning occur along the rims, which are a light golden-tan. The reverse of the piece is fairly well preserved, but the obverse reveals several light marks, particularly on Liberty's face, neck, and cap. Envelope Included. (#6496)

Challenging Near Mint 1904-S Half Dollar

21435 **1904-S AU58 NGC.** A scarce, low mintage issue that is difficult to locate above VF. Deeply toned on both sides, especially near the borders, with unabraded surfaces that reveal typical striking softness on the reverse. Population: 4 in 58, 13 finer (9/05). (#6500)

1903-S Half Dollar, AU53 NGC

21433 **1903-S AU53 NGC.** Bright surfaces display traces of luster in the protected areas, and wisps of golden-brown and cobalt-blue patina around the borders. Some small abrasions are scattered about, especially on the obverse. Population: 2 in 53, 47 finer (9/05). (#6497)

1905 Barber Half Dollar AU58 NGC

21436 **1905 AU58 NGC.** With crisp striking detail, minimal wear, and no singularly bothersome handling marks, this coin presents remarkably well. Subtle golden-russet and light-green border toning appears on both sides, while the centers display light-gray color. (#6501)

1904 Proof Barber Half PR62 NGC

21434 **1904 PR62 NGC.** The mirror surfaces are flashy and fully brilliant on the obverse, and lightly toned by scattered reddish-tan patina on the reverse. Wispy hairlines on the obverse limit the grade. One of just 670 proofs struck. (#6551)

Lovely Near-Gem Proof 1905 Barber Half

21437 **1905 PR64 NGC.** Sharply struck with deeply reflective fields and mildly frosted devices. Two or three minute contact marks on Liberty's cheek are mentioned solely for accuracy's sake, and there are also a few wispy hairlines on the obverse. Tantalizingly close to qualifying for the Cameo designation, and a truly lovely near-Gem proof. (#6552)

1906 Proof Barber Half PR63 NGC

21438 **1906 PR63 NGC.** Well struck with exceptional reflectivity in the fields, and attractive golden-tan toning on the obverse and reverse devices. A few wispy hairlines in the right obverse field limit the grade, but there are no troublesome handling marks to be seen. Only 675 pieces were struck. (#6553)

Conditionally Scarce Near-Gem 1906-D Barber Half

21439 **1906-D MS64 NGC.** Softly struck on the eagle, but well detailed otherwise, this satiny near-Gem boasts carefully preserved surfaces that are virtually mark-free on both sides of the coin. Speckled russet patina is noted near the peripheries, and wanders into the reverse fields as well. The first year of issue from the Denver Mint. Census: 24 in 64, 9 finer (12/05). (#6505)

1907 Proof Barber Half PR62 NGC

21440 **1907 PR62 NGC.** Well struck and nicely preserved, with faint cloudiness in the fields and mottled light-green and olive-russet patina near the borders. A few faint slide marks on the obverse restrict the grade, along with noticeable striking weakness on the eagle. (#6554)

Uncirculated Details 1907-D Half Dollar

21441 **1907-D—Improperly Cleaned—NCS. Unc. Details.** A fully lustrous and assertively struck Half Dollar, lightly toned save for blushes of forest-green and tan toning near the borders. A moderate abrasion in the right obverse field limits the grade, since evidence of cleaning is not prominent. (#6509)

About Uncirculated 1907-O Half

21442 **1907-O AU53 NGC.** Partially brilliant with blushes and wisps of gray and gold. Much original mint luster still survives in the fields. (#6510)

21443 **1907-S VF35 NGC.** A moderately circulated Barber Half that retains hints of its original luster within the recesses of the design. Tan toning is light throughout, aside from occasional deeper blushes of blue-green color near IN GOD WE TRUST. A relatively generous mintage of 1.25 million pieces, but these were needed in commerce, and collectors of the day set aside High Relief Double Eagles instead. As a result, even in VF, the 1907-S is very scarce. Census: 1 in 35, 36 finer (12/05). (#6511)

Sharp Proof 61 1908 Half Dollar

21444 **1908 PR61 NGC.** Sharply struck with satiny devices and blazing mirror fields. A scattering of small stains and some old hairlines account for the assigned grade. Only 545 proof half dollars were minted during the year, one of the lowest production figures in the series prior to 1914. (#6555)

See the Online Session listings in the back of this volume for additional Reiver selections.

Uncirculated 1908-D Half Dollar

21445 **1908-D MS62 NGC.** A subdued piece with medium golden-brown patina at the borders and surprisingly minimally abraded surfaces. Boldly struck aside from the right (facing) claw of the eagle. The 1908-D is considered to be a type coin, but it is actually a scarce issue in all Uncirculated grades. (#6513)

Pleasing Select 1908-S Half Dollar

21446 **1908-S MS63 NGC.** A crisply struck and lustrous beauty that appears to be high end for the grade, despite a couple of unimportant ticks on the portrait. Tan and rose hues gradually cede to brilliant centers. The 1908-S follows the pattern of most Barber Half issues, available in Very Good and lower grades but very scarce above Fine. However, aside from the 1892-O Micro O, an Uncirculated collection of Barber Halves remains achievable by the advanced numismatist. Population: 5 in 63, 18 finer (9/05). (#6515)

Brilliant Proof 1909 Half Dollar

21447 **1909 PR61 NGC.** Somewhat cloudy surfaces with a light ring of antique-golden toning around the rims. A moderate number of hairlines are visible on both sides that serve to limit the grade. (#6556)

Patinated Proof 1910 Half Dollar

21448 **1910 PR61 NGC.** Hints of golden and gray patina helps to conceal the scattered grade-defining hairlines. The proof 1910 remains popular among collectors due to the limited original mintage of its business strike counterpart. Only 551 proofs were struck. (#6557)

Challenging Select 1910-S Half Dollar

21449 **1910-S MS63 NGC.** Original charcoal-gray and rose-golden toning adorns both sides, somewhat lighter at the centers. Quite a challenging issue in Select and better grades despite a mintage of nearly two million pieces. Population: 9 in 63, 20 finer (8/05). (#6520)

Choice Uncirculated 1911 Barber Half Dollar

21450 **1911 MS64 NGC.** A well struck specimen that displays an overlay of medium steel-gray toning. A few inconsequential contact marks are seen on the obverse that limit the grade. (#6521)

Select Proof 1911 Half Dollar

21451 **1911 PR63 NGC.** A glowing specimen with reflective qualities, the surfaces are dominated by a thin layer of evenly spread reddish-gold toning, particularly on the reverse. (#6558)

Imposing Gem 1911-D Half Dollar

21452 **1911-D MS65 NGC.** Original cream-gray toning does not deny the ebullient cartwheel shimmer. Splendidly unabraded, but perhaps kept from an even finer grade by the strike, which shows slight softness on the right shield corner and fletchings. Despite a mintage of under 700,000 pieces, the 1911-D is not rare in Mint State, relative to other issues in the series. However, when compared with keys from popularly collected series, the Uncirculated 1911-D is surprisingly competitive in scarcity, and provides excellent value. Population: 11 in 65, 7 finer (9/05). (#6522)

Uncirculated 1911-S Barber Half

21453 **1911-S MS62 NGC.** Just a little softly struck with satiny luster underlying a moderate coating of rose-gray and golden-russet toning. Close examination reveals a few small marks on the obverse. A somewhat subdued appearance limits the grade. (#6523)

Obtainable AU Details 1912 Half Dollar

21454 **1912—Improperly Cleaned—NCS. AU Details.** Mint luster is virtually complete, but friction on the cheek indicates momentary circulation. Light tan and cream colors blend throughout this very lightly cleaned example, which has a good strike aside from the fletchings. The last Philadelphia Mint issue of the series with a production above 1 million pieces, since the 1913 through 1915 all have mintages under 200,000 pieces. (#6524)

Brilliant Proof 61 1912 Half Dollar

21455 **1912 PR61 NGC.** Essentially brilliant surfaces with a dusting of golden-brown. Most design features are sharp. Although the portrait of Liberty on the obverse is satiny, the reverse eagle is frosty and shows pronounced cameo contrast. Some obverse hairlines were probably all that prevented NGC from assigning a substantially higher grade. (#6559)

Frosty MS63 1912-D Half Dollar

21456 **1912-D MS63 NGC.** Frosty luster. Warmly toned in intermingled hues of orange-gold and lilac. The strike is average with sharpness noted in some areas and softness in others. Magnification reveals a small abrasion on Liberty's neck. Here's a specimen that's head and shoulders above most examples seen in terms of quality. (#6525)

See the Online Session listings in the back of this volume for additional Reiver selections.

Desirable Proof 62 1913 Half Dollar

21457 **1913 PR62 NGC.** Mostly brilliant surfaces with a faint dusting of pewter gray and golden-brown. The design elements are boldly defined. Liberty's portrait is satiny, while the eagle motif is frosty. A few tiny handling marks on the obverse account the assigned grade designation. Only 627 proof half dollars were minted in 1913. (#6560)

Scarce AU58 1913-D Half Dollar

21458 **1913-D AU58 NGC.** Warm golden-gray toning with almost all of the original mint luster still surviving in the fields. The strike is average, with softness noted on some of the obverse stars and on the highpoints of the eagle's plumage. Only 534,000 half dollars were coined at the Denver Mint during the year, a figure that's well below average for the Barber design type; indeed, only a few other issues in the series have lower mintages. (#6528)

21459 **1913-S XF40 NGC.** Although it is the 1913-S *Quarter* that makes collectors' hearts beat faster, the Half Dollar of the same date and mint is also scarce. A richly detailed piece with smooth slate-gray surfaces. A trace of dark toning near the 3 in the date is accompanied by a faint mark. (#6529)

Low-Mintage Proof 61 1914 Half Dollar

21460 **1914 PR61 NGC.** Sharply struck with glittering mirror fields. As is typical of many proof Barber half dollars of the era, Liberty's portrait is satiny, while the eagle motif is frosty. The obverse is almost fully brilliant with wisps and tinges of electric blue peripherally. The reverse exhibits pale golden toning. Some faint hairlines on both surfaces are probably all that prevented NGC from assigning a much higher grade. A scant 380 proof half dollars were issued during the year, by far the lowest production figure in the series (the 1915 comes in second with a mintage of 450 pieces). (#6561)

Pleasing MS64 1914-S Half Dollar

21461 **1914-S MS64 NGC.** Pleasing golden-gray toning complements frosty surfaces. Most design features show bold definition save for a touch of softness on some of the obverse stars and on the eagle's right claw (viewer's left). Worth a generous bid from the quality-conscious buyer. (#6531)

Lovely Proof 64 1915 Half Dollar

21462 **1915 PR64 NGC.** A lovely specimen characterized by sharp devices and glittering mirror fields. The portrait of Liberty is satiny while the eagle is frosty, features that are shared by most of the proof 20th-century Barber half dollars from the Reiver Collection. The obverse is brilliant at the center, with wisps and tinges of golden-brown, blue, and violet at the border. The reverse exhibits vivid orange-gold toning. The 1915 half dollar has the second-lowest proof mintage in the Barber half dollar series; a scant 450 examples were coined. 1915 is notable as the final year of production of the Barber half dollar design type. (#6562)

Lustrous MS64 1915-D Half Dollar

21463 **1915-D MS64 NGC.** Lustrous and attractive. Vivid orange-gold iridescence with blushes of navy blue and violet. The strike is good with most features showing bold definition including each of the obverse stars. A touch of softness is noted at the tresses of hair above Liberty's forehead and at a few of the eagle's feather details. Two fine die cracks are noted on the obverse. (#6533)

Frosty MS63 1915-S Half Dollar

21464 **1915-S MS63 NGC.** Frosty luster. Intermingled gold and gray iridescence complements both surfaces. The strike is average with softness noted at the eagle's plumage and claws. Virtually all peripheral design features are sharp including the obverse stars and reverse inscriptions. (#6534)

WALKING LIBERTY HALF DOLLARS

Handsome MS63 1916 Half Dollar

21465 **1916 MS63 NGC.** Fully lustrous and essentially brilliant with just a hint of pale gold. Some wisps of sable iridescence can be seen at the obverse border. Most design features show bold definition. A handsome example coined during the first year of the Walking Liberty design type. (#6566)

Mint State Sharpness 1916-D Walker

21466 **1916-D—Improperly Cleaned—NCS. Unc. Details.** Glimpses of russet toning cling to the upper obverse and lower reverse borders. This lustrous introductory year Walker is otherwise cream-gray in color, and close inspection locates only slight vertical obverse hairlines. One of only four obverse mintmark varieties in the series. (#6567)

Semi-Key 1916-S Half Dollar, AU53 NGC

21467 **1916-S AU53 NGC.** This lightly circulated semi-key displays bright surfaces with grayish-tan toning and remarkably clean surfaces. Nice definition is apparent on the design elements. (#6568)

Choice AU 1917-D Obverse Mintmark Walker

21468 **1917-D Obverse AU55 NGC.** Partially brilliant with blushes of golden-gray. Most of the original mint luster still survives in the fields. A mint-caused planchet inclusion on the flag beneath Liberty's right arm (viewer's left), will enable the identification of this specimen at any point in the future. Walking Liberty half dollars with obverse mintmarks were coined only in the years 1916 and 1917. (#6570)

See the Online Session listings in the back of this volume for additional Reiver selections.

Lovely Mint State Details 1917-D Reverse Half Dollar

21469 **1917-D Reverse—Improperly Cleaned—NCS. Unc. Details.** Freckles of navy-blue and golden toning enliven the margins. This lustrous and crisply struck better date Half Dollar has wispy hairlines visible only beneath a loupe, but is beautiful when beheld with the naked eye. (#6571)

Bold 1917-S Obverse Half Dollar

21470 **1917-S Obverse—Improperly Cleaned—NCS. AU Details.** A bold but subdued and slightly grainy dove-gray representative. Modest friction on the eagle's breast confirms a brief encounter with circulation. Of the four mintmark varieties of 1917 Half Dollars, the 1917-S Obverse is the rarest, and in fact is only exceeded in desirability by the 1919-dated and 1921-dated issues. (#6572)

Scarce MS62 1918 Half Dollar

21471 **1918 MS62 NGC.** Fully lustrous and essentially brilliant with a faint dusting of golden-brown and pewter gray on both surfaces. The 1918 is scarcer in Uncirculated grade than most of the other Philadelphia Mint issues of the design type including the 1916, 1917, and 1920. Indeed, only the 1919 and 1921 are scarcer among the Walking Liberty issues struck in Philadelphia. (#6574)

Scarce AU Details 1918-D Half Dollar

21472 **1918-D—Improperly Cleaned—NCS. AU Details.** A satiny light tan-gray better date Half Dollar, sharply struck and void of unpleasant marks. Slightly glossy on the eagle's breast and leg feathers, however, many collectors would be pleased to present this piece within their collection. (#6575)

Frosty MS62 1918-S Half Dollar

21473 **1918-S MS62 NGC.** Frosty and delicately toned in intermingled hues of pewter gray and olive-gold. Not an easy issue to find this nicely preserved despite a generous mintage of 10,282,000 pieces. (#6576)

Lovely MS64 1919 Half Dollar

21474 **1919 MS64 NGC.** A lovely example and truly scarce at the MS64 level. Pleasing satiny luster. Both surfaces exhibit appealing golden-gray toning. Wisps and tinges of golden-brown, navy blue, and charcoal gray iridescence enhance the obverse border. Most design features are sharp for the type: the majority of the pleats in Liberty's gown are defined to full advantage, and virtually all the details of her sandals are boldly delineated. On the reverse the eagle's plumage is sharp in virtually all areas save for the eagle's left thigh (viewer's right), which seldom shows bold definition. The 1919 in Uncirculated condition ranks as the second scarcest Philadelphia Mint issue in the Walking Liberty series; only the 1921 is rarer. (#6577)

21475 **1919-D Fine 15 NGC.** Sharp for the assigned grade, this apricot and lilac-tinged early branch mint Walker is void of unpleasant marks. For the 1919-D, the Choice Fine grade provides good value relative to XF. (#6578)

Important Choice 1919-S Half Dollar

21476 **1919-S MS64 NGC.** Apricot and silver-gray colors commingle throughout this lustrous, boldly struck, and gorgeous near-Gem. Essentially immaculate, save for a subdued mark to the right of the flag. A famous conditional rarity, the 1919-S is available in Fine or lesser grades but is notoriously difficult to locate above VF. Curiously, the 1919 has the lowest mintage of the three 1919-dated issues, but is more available in better grades than its mintmarked counterparts. This lot provides the dedicated specialist an opportunity to secure a high end example with a significant pedigree. (#6579)

Lustrous MS62 1920 Half Dollar

21477 **1920 MS62 NGC.** Pearl gray toning on lustrous surfaces. An attractive example, with most design features showing bold definition. Very conservatively graded in our opinion. (#6580)

Lustrous Select 1920-D Half Dollar

21478 **1920-D MS63 NGC.** Delicately toned in cream and tan hues, this lustrous low mintage Walker has lovely preservation and only slight striking softness on the branch hand. Those searching for a quality example of the toughest 1920-dated issue need look no further than the present coin. (#6581)

Obtainable 1920-S Half Dollar

21479 **1920-S—Improperly Cleaned—NCS. AU Details.** Slightly glossy but certainly acceptable, this lightly circulated San Francisco Walking Liberty Half has no relevant contact marks, and noticeable luster emerges when the piece is rotated beneath a light. (#6582)

See the Online Session listings in the back of this volume for additional Reiver selections.

AU Details 1921 Walking Liberty Half

21480 **1921 AU Details, Improperly Cleaned, NCS.** Speckles of russet toning cling to the rims, although cream-gray color dominates. The eagle's breast has a trace of wear, but satiny luster extends through the fields, and the cleaning is so mild that most collectors would probably not even notice it. The three 1921-dated issues have a combined mintage of under 1 million pieces, and remain the traditional keys to the Walking Liberty series. (#6583)

Significant Near Gem 1921-D Walking Liberty

21481 **1921-D MS64 NGC.** Creamy luster and light chestnut-gray color confirm the originality of this impressive key-date near-Gem. No marks merit discussion, and a few pinpoint flecks near the right reverse border are of no account. The strike is crisp, although not needle-sharp on the index finger of the branch hand and on the outline of Liberty's helmet near the cheek. The 1921-D has the lowest mintage of the entire series, and unlike the 1938-D, was not contemporaneously hoarded. Only the 1919-D and 1921-S are more coveted in Uncirculated grades. (#6584)

Partly Lustrous XF Details 1921-S Half Dollar

21482 **1921-S XF Details, Improperly Cleaned, NCS.** A bright steel-gray key date Half Dollar, the rims offer luminous golden-brown toning. Traces of luster show despite moderate wear, and contact marks are surprisingly few in number, limited to distributed tiny ticks on the right obverse field. Glossy from a light cleaning, nonetheless desirable since the 1921-S is the unchallenged series key in XF and better condition. (#6585)

Impressive AU58 1923-S Half Dollar

21483 **1923-S AU58 NGC.** Satiny luster. Mostly brilliant surfaces with some blushes and wisps of orange-gold, predominantly at the borders. This piece is so nice for the grade, that we had to view it with a 7x glass for quite a while before we could persuade ourselves that it actually spend so much as a single day in circulation. (#6586)

Frosty MS64 1927-S Half Dollar

21484 **1927-S MS64 NGC.** Appealing frosty luster. Pearl gray toning in the central areas changes to golden-brown peripherally. Wisps of navy blue can be seen at the rims. The strike is about average with softness noted on the highpoints of the designs. Sometimes mints would deliberately reduce striking pressure to extend the life of the dies and thereby reduce operating costs. Walter Breen describes the 1927-S half dollar as "usually weak" in his *Comprehensive Encyclopedia*. (#6587)

Lustrous MS63 1928-S Half Dollar

21485 **1928-S MS63 NGC.** Golden-gray toning on lustrous surfaces with wisps and splashes of orange-gold and violet at the borders. The strike shows softness on the highpoints of the designs as is typical for the issue. We can only infer that the San Francisco Mint was trying to reduce operating costs by reducing striking pressures for half dollars, thereby extending the useful life of the dies. (#6588)

Uncirculated 1929-S Walker, No AW Initials

21487 **1929-S MS61 NGC.** Breen-5154. No AW monogram. Apricot and cloud-gray colors alternate across this interesting Mint State S-mint example. The strike is particularly sharp on the skirt lines, although Liberty's head and branch hand are not quite full. Both dies have numerous light raised striations, as made from die lapping, perhaps to remove clash marks. The AW monogram, raised in low relief on the reverse die, was inadvertently removed by the mint worker. (#6590)

Near Mint 1929-D Half Dollar

21486 **1929-D AU58 NGC.** Intermingled gold and lilac-gray toning on mostly lustrous surfaces. The 1929-D is notable for its status as the only Denver-mint half dollar issue struck between 1921 and 1934. (#6589)

Sharply Struck Premium Gem 1933-S Half Dollar

21488 **1933-S MS66 NGC.** This is an issue of the Great Depression, and is one of the best struck of all Walkers issued up to that point. This example is sharply defined, as expected, with a full thumb. Lustrous surfaces display silver-tan patina and are well preserved. A few luster grazes are noted on Liberty's figure. Census: 28 in 66, 2 finer (10/05). (#6591)

21489 **1934-D MS64 NGC.** Mostly brilliant and a frosty near-Gem save for the usual flatness on Liberty's head and a few unnoticeable obverse marks. This is the small, usual mintmark variety of 1934, as used from 1916. (#6593)

See the Online Session listings in the back of this volume for additional Reiver selections.

Uncirculated Depression Era 1934-S Walker

21490 **1934-S MS62 NGC.** Each side has hints of golden-brown patina. A few small marks and slightly subdued luster combine to limit the grade. A scarcer issue. (#6594)

21491 **1935-D MS64 NGC.** A lustrous and deeply frosted near-Gem that has a typical strike and gorgeously preserved surfaces. An impressive example, and in a grade that provides good value. (#6596)

Lovely MS64 1935-S Half Dollar

21492 **1935-S MS64 NGC.** A lovely lustrous specimen toned in intermingled hues of orange-gold and lilac-gray. An aesthetic treat for the connoisseur. (#6597)

21493 **1936 MS65 NGC.** Excellent strike definition complements fully lustrous surfaces that are essentially untoned. A few minute marks do not distract. (#6598)

Gem Proof 1936 Walking Liberty

21494 **1936 PR65 NGC.** After a gap of some twenty years, the production of proof coins resumed in 1936. Mintages began at low levels, but rose each subsequent year, until World War II terminated proof production after 1942. The 1936 Half Dollar is the most desired proof issue within that span, and since only 3,900 pieces were struck, supply is insufficient to meet the demand from collectors of the popular series. The present razor-sharp Gem displays lovely apricot and pearl-gray toning, and the satiny surfaces are undisturbed. (#6636)

Gem MS66 1936-D Half Dollar

21495 **1936-D MS66 NGC.** Frosty and essentially brilliant with just a whisper of pearl gray. Here's a Gem that's virtually as nice as the day it came from the dies. We expect many generous bids when this beauty crosses the auction block. (#6599)

Desirable Proof 64 1937 Half Dollar

21496 **1937 PR64 NGC.** Brilliant surfaces with just a hint of milky toning, probably a feature that derives from having been stored for many years in a cellophane envelope. It's possible that the full proof splendor of this specimen could be restored by immersing it into an aqueous ammonia solution for one or two seconds, followed by a rinse with pure water. Only 5,728 proof half dollars were minted during the year. (#6637)

Popular Proof 64 1937 Half Dollar

21497 **1937 PR64 NGC.** The devices are satiny and the fields are nicely reflective. Delicately toned in pastel shades of gold, violet, and blue. The 1937 proof half dollar ranks as a perennial favorite with the numismatic community. (#6637)

Flashy 1937-D Gem Half Dollar

21498 **1937-D MS65 NGC.** Brilliant surfaces display radiant luster and sharply struck design elements. A few trivial marks do not disturb. (#6602)

Appealing 1937-S Gem Half Dollar

21499 **1937-S MS65 NGC.** This lesser-seen San Francisco issue displays a strong strike, creamy-white surfaces, and a minimum of abrasions. Great overall eye appeal. (#6603)

Blazing Proof 64 1938 Half Dollar

21500 **1938 PR64 NGC.** The fields are glittering mirrors and the devices have a texture intermediate between satiny and frosty. Both surfaces exhibit pewter gray toning with delicate gold, pink, and violet iridescent highlights. The mintage figure of 8,152 proofs was admittedly high in contrast with previous years, but it's truly infinitesimal in comparison with the production figures of recent times. (#6638)

Satiny MS64 1938-D Half Dollar

21501 **1938-D MS64 NGC.** Satiny and essentially brilliant with just a hint of pale gold. The 1938-D is a scarce issue that ranks high in popularity with collectors because its mintage of just 491,600 pieces ranks as the lowest production figure for any half dollar issue coined subsequent to 1921. (#6605)

Gem Proof 65 1939 Half Dollar

21502 **1939 PR65 NGC.** Fully brilliant. Here's a blazing Gem that is characterized by glittering mirror fields and sharp satiny devices. Certain to delight virtually any numismatist who appreciates outstanding 20th-century proofs. A mere 8,808 proof half dollars were coined during the year. 1939 was the final time in mint history that a proof half dollar's production figure was below the 10,000 mark. (#6639)

21503 **1939-D MS65 NGC.** Excellent strike definition and fully lustrous surfaces that show light gold peripheries. Well preserved throughout. (#6607)

Exquisitely Struck 1939-S Half Dollar, MS66 NGC

21504 **1939-S MS66 NGC.** Highly lustrous surfaces display a splash of orange-gold color on the reverse. The design elements are exquisitely struck, and there are no mentionable abrasions. (#6608)

See the Online Session listings in the back of this volume for additional Reiver selections.

21505 **1940 MS65 NGC.** Radiantly lustrous surfaces display sharply struck design features and are essentially untoned. One minor mark in the right obverse field is inconsequential. (#6609)

Impressive Proof 66 1940 Half Dollar

21506 **1940 PR66 NGC.** A blazing Gem, virtually as nice as the moment it left the dies. The fields are glittering mirrors and the satiny devices are about as sharp as could be desired. Both surfaces are essentially brilliant except for a splash of gold by the date. If you're looking for a piece that combines the dual attributes of outstanding technical quality and superb eye appeal, your search stops here. (#6640)

21507 **1941 MS65 NGC.** Occasional speckles of olive-green and reddish-gold occupy fully lustrous surfaces. The design elements are well struck, and the surfaces are well preserved save for minor handling marks. (#6611)

Gem Proof 1941 Half Dollar

21508 **1941 PR65 NGC.** The highly reflective fields shimmer with intense mint brilliance and are completely white and untoned. Sharply struck throughout with the designer's initials clearly visible. (#6641)

21509 **1941-S MS64 NGC.** A few speckles of gold-tan color on otherwise brilliant, fully lustrous surfaces. A few minor handling marks define the grade. (#6613)

Gem Proof 1942 Half Dollar

21510 **1942 PR65 NGC.** Glassy surfaces with a touch of creamy haze over each side. Very pleasing surfaces with only a couple of very tiny dark toning spots. (#6642)

21511 **1942-D MS65 NGC.** Nearly untoned, save for wisps of light peripheral color. The design elements are sharply struck, and there are just a few minute marks on the reverse. (#6615)

Gem Uncirculated 1944-D Half Dollar

21512 **1944-D MS66 NGC.** Creamy, virtually unmarked surfaces show just the slightest amount of golden color on the right side of the obverse. (#6622)

21513 **1946-D MS66 NGC.** Creamy-white, frosty luster gleams over each side. The shimmering surfaces are fully bright and completely untoned. Well, but not fully struck. (#6628)

PROOF FRANKLIN HALF DOLLARS

Gem Proof First Year 1950 Half Dollar

21514 **1950 PR65 NGC.** A noticeable line of brown color is behind the top of the bust, otherwise this is a pleasing lightly toned specimen. A fully original appearance is presented throughout. (#6691)

Gem Proof 1951 Franklin Half

21515 **1951 PR65 NGC.** Nicely reflective with a partial cameo effect overall. Some opaque-milky toning is seen mostly on the obverse. (#6692)

Bright, Superb Proof 1952 Franklin Half

21516 **1952 PR67 NGC.** Essentially brilliant with just the faintest hint of border color on each side. A Superb, virtually flawless example. (#6693)

Gem Proof 1954 Franklin Half

21517 **1954 PR66 NGC.** A sparkling Gem with some pale peripheral color showing on the obverse. (#6695)

Appealing Superb Gem Proof 1955 Half Dollar

21518 **1955 PR68 NGC.** Near-blinding brilliance emanates from virtually perfect, untoned surfaces. This piece has great eye appeal. (#6696)

21519 **1956 Type Two PR67 NGC.** Fully brilliant without a hint of color. This one looks like it has just been struck. Census: 1262 in 67, 1029 finer (12/05). (#6697)

21520 **1957 PR64 NGC.** A thin coating of opaque-gray patina has gathered over each side. Nicely reflective surfaces appear under the toning. (#6698)

GOBRECHT DOLLARS

Pleasing, Problem-Free 1836 Judd-60 Gobrecht Dollar

21521 **1836 Name on Base, Judd-60 Original, Pollock-65, R.1, PR50 NGC.** Silver. Plain Edge. Die Alignment I. Original Issue of 1836 with the eagle flying upward. Produced during the second striking period in late December and showing the faint die scratch above the eagle's wing. The entire mintage of 600 of these coins were distributed to the public via a local Philadelphia bank, and as a result are often found in less-than-pristine condition. This is an attractive example that has light, even gray toning over both sides. Sharply defined, there is just the slightest bit of friction over the highpoints of the design elements. The only surface irregularity is a circular area of discoloration on Liberty's chest. A very pleasing example of this popular type coin and generally not located in such a superior state of preservation. (#11225)

Heavily Circulated Judd-60 1836 Gobrecht Dollar

21522 **1836 Name on Base, Judd-60 Original, Pollock-65, R.1—Plugged, Repaired—NCS. Circ. Proof.** Silver. Plain Edge. Die Alignment I. Original Issue of 1836 with the eagle flying upward. Because of the heavy wear, there is no way to determine whether this piece had the die scratch above the eagle's wing or not. The extensively worn surfaces would make one lean more toward the second striking period in late December, but there is just no vestige of the die scratch to absolutely confirm that belief. The surfaces show the detail of a PR 8 with extensive wear over each side. Light gray patina with just a hint of darker color around the devices and within the recesses of the design. (#11225)

1838 Gobrecht Dollar
Judd-84, PR63 NGC

21523 **1838 Name Omitted, Judd-84 Restrike, Pollock-93, R.5, PR63 NGC.** Silver. Reeded Edge. Die Alignment III (head of Liberty opposite the E in ONE). Apparently, there are no official mint records that indicate how many 1838 dollars (either originals and restrikes) were produced. However, the total number of 1838s that were eventually struck is probably less than 250 specimens. This is a figure that is smaller than the reported 300 1839 dollars that are officially mentioned as struck in 1839, and the 1,600 Gobrecht dollars that were made in 1836 and 1837. In addition, it appears that Judd-84 dollars do not exist in Die Alignment I (a coin configuration that Walter Breen would have defined as an original). Instead, it appears that all 1838 dollars made in 1838 were struck in Die Alignment IV from uncracked reverse dies. In fact, the 1838 dollar that was placed in the U.S. Mint Collection (begun in 1838), and now held in the Smithsonian Institution, is in Die Alignment IV and has no reverse die cracks. In any case, most 1838 dollars seen today are restrikes made in Die Alignment III. The present coin has very faint die cracks through the tops of MERI (in AMERICA), ITE (in UNITED), and AR (in DOLLAR).

The surfaces are bright and deeply reflective. The centers are generally brilliant with a light accent of golden-brown patina around the margins. The striking details are fully brought up in all areas—even the foot of Liberty is completely defined. Very lightly hairlined with no obvious or detracting contact marks on either side. (#11352)

Rare Judd-104 1839 Gobrecht Dollar, PR64

21524 **1839 Name Omitted, Judd-104 Restrike, Pollock-116, R.3, PR64 NGC.** Silver. Die Alignment III (coin turn, eagle flying level). The majority of 1839 restrikes are found in Die Alignment IV, but a small number, such as this one, are known in Die Alignment III. These pieces have reverse die cracks similar to the Type II coins with a faint crack seen at the tops of MERI in AMERICA on the reverse. It is believed that these coins were most likely struck in the late 1860s (or perhaps slightly later); a time period when the Die Alignment III Judd-60s were being made. In any case, the Die Alignment III dollars are very scarce and are estimated to have a total mintage of approximately 100 pieces.

This is a spectacular coin that is deeply mirrored on each side. Each side shows light, even golden-brown toning that deepens around the obverse to a deep brown and cobalt-blue. Fully struck throughout and lightly hairlined with a couple of small planchet flakes in the left obverse field. (#11446)

SEATED DOLLARS

Near-Mint 1840 Seated Dollar With Prooflike Surfaces

21525 **1840 AU58 Prooflike NGC.** A minimally worn representative and a scarcity as such despite the novelty of its first year status. Original pearl-gray and gunmetal surfaces display a prooflike appearance and a few appreciable marks. (#6926)

Scarce AU58 1841 Seated Dollar

21526 **1841 AU58 NGC.** While there is no lack of 1841 Dollars in worn grades, examples are very elusive in or near Mint State condition. This piece shows only the slightest trace of friction on the highpoints. The surfaces are original with a predominately brilliant appearance over both sides. A bit softly struck on the highpoints of the devices, there are no singularly mentionable marks. A coin that represents good value in this conditionally scarce date. (#6927)

Affordable 1842 Silver Dollar

21527 **1842—Improperly Cleaned—NCS. AU Details.** Numerous small abrasions pepper each side and the surfaces are unnaturally bright from having been polished at one time. Despite a limited original mintage of 184,618 pieces, the 1842 is among the more common Seated Dollars from the 1840s. (#6928)

Charming AU58 1843 Seated Dollar

21528 **1843 AU58 NGC.** Minimally worn, but heavily abraded on both sides. A trace of toning is visible around the rims, but the coin is mostly an even silver-gray color. This date is seldom seen above the AU level. (#6929)

Scarce Near-Mint 1844 Seated Dollar

21529 **1844 AU58 NGC.** A sharply struck pearl-gray representative with glossy surfaces that are seemingly free from contact marks. In his 1993 *Silver Dollar Encyclopedia,* Bowers opines that just a single die pair was used to produce business strikes of this date. Liberty's shield is strongly die doubled and exhibits quad stripes, while bold die polish lines surround the eagle's body. Only 20,000 pieces were struck, and survivors are scarce in all grades. (#6930)

Borderline Uncirculated 1845 Dollar

21530 **1845 AU58 NGC.** Only 24,500 pieces were struck of the 1845 Seated Dollar, most of which entered circulation and stayed there, making Choice AU and BU examples very scarce. Generally well struck, each side is mostly untoned with subtle gray-golden tones that deepen toward the borders. Lightly abraded, the only mark of any note is near the eagle's neck. (#6931)

See the Online Session listings in the back of this volume for additional Reiver selections.

Collectible 1846 Seated Dollar

21531 **1846—Improperly Cleaned—NCS. Unc Details.** Mostly brilliant with a hint of border toning. An especially well detailed example that unfortunately was lightly cleaned at one time. A few hairlines are particularly visible in the obverse field. Affordable quality. (#6932)

Choice AU55 1848 Seated Dollar

21534 **1848 AU55 NGC.** Medium-gray surfaces with some of the original luster intact and minimal abrasions. Only 15,000 pieces were struck for the year and the number of survivors in AU and better condition is extremely limited, perhaps 100 or fewer coins. (#6935)

Bright 1846-O Dollar, AU53

21532 **1846-O AU53 NGC.** Only 59,000 pieces were produced of this issue, one of only four Seated dollars struck in the New Orleans mint. A light, generally untoned appearance greets the viewer on each side. Some of the usual strike weakness is seen on Liberty's head and in the stars along the right border. Relatively clean, nicely preserved surfaces prevail. (#6933)

Near-Mint 1849 Seated Dollar

21535 **1849 AU58 NGC.** Boldly defined with nice luster and partially toned steel-gray surfaces. Light abrasions are evident in the fields on each side, but are not overwhelming. Scarcer than a mintage of 62,600 pieces might suggest. (#6936)

Scarce, Mint State 1847 Seated Dollar

21533 **1847 MS61 NGC.** A moderately scarce date, this 1847 shows semi-reflective surfaces under a layer of gray-golden color with several areas of slightly deeper color. With the exception of the two hoard O-mint dates, Seated Dollars in Mint State are all quite scarce. (#6934)

Uncirculated Details 1850 Dollar

21536 **1850—Improperly Cleaned—NCS. Unc Details.** Breen-5443. The 5 in the date is open, and the base of the 0 is lightly recut. This well struck Seated Dollar offers faint golden hues interspersed throughout the abnormally bright, gray-brilliant surfaces. The upper reverse field has a few notable abrasions. Only 7,500 pieces were struck. (#6937)

AU Sharpness 1850-O Dollar

21537 **1850-O—Improperly Cleaned—NCS. AU Details.** An unnaturally bright O-mint Seated Dollar that has a smattering of gray-gold color on the obverse. Noticeably hairlined from the cleaning, the highpoints of the central designs show only light wear. . (#6938)

Lightly Toned 1851 Proof Restrike Dollar

21538 **1851 Restrike—Improperly Cleaned—NCS. Proof.** The 1851 Restrike silver dollars are differentiated from the Originals by placement of the date. The Originals, struck in 1851, have the date high in the field with the tops of each numeral almost touching the base of Liberty. The Restrikes, minted in the very late 1850s at the earliest, and possibly into the 1870s, have the date almost exactly centered between the base of Liberty and the border. 1851 Original silver dollars exist in both proof and business strike format, while the Restrikes are only known in proof format. The total mintage for the Restrikes is not specifically known, however, it was certainly not a large quantity for these are almost as rare as the Originals. This bright surfaces of this specimen display whispers of light tan color, and are covered with fine hairlines. The design elements are sharply struck throughout, and the surfaces are devoid of significant abrasions. (#6993)

Elusive and Sharply Defined Original 1852 Dollar

21539 **1852—Improperly Cleaned—NCS. Unc Details.** A mere 1,100 original business strike Silver Dollars were produced this year, along with an unknown number of restrikes (in proof format) coined at a later date. This example is one of the original coins produced in 1852, as evidenced by various die characteristics that include an unfinished area under Liberty's chin and numerous short die lines visible within the open vertical spaces of the reverse shield. It is doubtful that more than 40-60 pieces survive in all grades. This example displays fine hairlines on the bright silver-gray surfaces. The design elements are well struck, except for weakness in the star centers along the right (facing) border. A series of unobtrusive linear marks are noted in the left (facing) obverse field. (#6940)

Choice AU 1853 Seated Dollar

21540 **1853 AU55 NGC.** An original example with pleasing surfaces and traces of wear on the highest points and in the fields. Light silver-gray patina graces each side, and a few scattered abrasions are present. Uncleaned Seated Dollars are difficult to locate in high circulated grades. (#6941)

Rare 1854 Dollar, AU58 NGC

21541 **1854 AU58 NGC.** Although this date shows a mintage figure of 33,140 pieces, which is higher than many of its contemporaries, the 1854 has long been recognized as a rarity. One explanation for the scarcity of this date is that most of them were used in quantity for trade with China. Walter Breen noted that 10,000 silver dollars bearing this date were shipped to San Francisco in November, 1854. Whether these remained in California, or were shipped to Asia, we do not know, but it is likely many went overseas. This lightly circulated example displays silvery-gray surfaces with traces of luster in the recessed areas. A few minute marks scattered about do not distract. (#6942)

Very Elusive 1856 Seated Dollar

21543 **1856—Improperly Cleaned—NCS. XF Details.** The 1856 is rare not because of a low mintage, as 63,500 pieces were struck. Rather, most of the business strikes were shipped to the Orient for use as "Trade Dollars," where they were either melted or defaced with chop marks. As a result, the 1856 is a rare coin in all circulated grades, including XF and finer pieces. This is a typically struck coin that has slightly bright surfaces from the stated cleaning. Few abrasions are present on this upper-end Dollar. (#6944)

High Grade 1855 Silver Dollar

21542 **1855—Obverse Repaired—NCS. Unc Details.** As Seated Dollar collectors well know the 1855 is generally not available in mint condition and it is very pricey when it is encountered. This high grade piece represents excellent value for the collector as it retains some of the original mint luster, and there is very little friction evident from circulation. However, the right obverse field shows clear evidence of smoothing in an attempt to remove some ambient marks there. Well detailed and nearly brilliant. (#6943)

Affordable 1857 Seated Dollar

21544 **1857—Improperly Cleaned—NCS. AU Details.** Brightly polished in the fields and untoned throughout with light evidence of circulation on the highpoints. Still, an attractive example that would fit perfectly into just about any collection. (#6945)

Flashy 1858 Dollar, PR63 NGC

21545 **1858 PR63 NGC.** The 1858 Seated dollar is one of the most respected and highly sought-after silver coins in U.S. numismatics. While it is known that no business strikes were produced of this date, it is far from clear just how many proofs were struck. The Mint did not start keeping proof mintage records until the following year. Estimates have ranged from as low as 80 coins (per S. Hudson and Henry Chapman) to as high as 600 coins extant (per the *Gobrecht Journal*, July 1982). All we can do with certainty is quote combined NGC and PCGS population data, which lists about 145 coins in all grades (10/05). Naturally, some of these are likely resubmissions of the same specimens. This particular piece has flashy, deeply reflective fields with just a hint of light golden color on each side. Lightly hairlined on both sides, but there are no mentionable abrasions. The design elements are exquisitely struck. All in all, a very pleasing representative. Census: 17 in 63, 18 finer (10/05). (#7001)

Choice Brilliant Proof 1859 Seated Dollar

21546 **1859 PR64 NGC.** Of the 800 proof Seated Dollars that the Philadelphia Mint prepared in 1859, no more than 450 pieces found their way into collectors' hands. As the anticipated public demand failed to materialize, the remaining pieces met their fate in the melting pot. Over the years, many of the distributed specimens have been mishandled to one degree or another and lowered to less desirable states of preservation.

The present specimen displays repunching on the base of the 1 in the date. Only visible under a loupe, this feature is diagnostic of all proof 1859 dollars. Both the obverse and the reverse show a thin peripheral ring of deep antique-golden color. Modestly reflective and free of all but the most inconsequential distractions, the surfaces adequately support the respected PR64 grade. (#7002)

Brilliant Uncirculated 1859-O Silver Dollar

21547 **1859-O MS61 NGC.** Bright frosty surfaces are essentially untoned, and display a few minute contact marks scattered about, especially on the obverse. The design elements are well defined, though the hair atop Liberty's head is soft, as are most of the star centers. (#6947)

Affordable Uncirculated 1859-O Seated Dollar

21548 **1859-O—Reverse Improperly Cleaned—NCS. Unc Details.** Frosty and completely brilliant overall. A well defined example, save for a bit of Liberty's head detail and several of the obverse stars. Some scuffiness is seen above the eagle on the reverse. This was lightly polished in an effort to minimize its visual effect. (#6947)

Elusive 1859-S Dollar, MS62 NGC

21549 **1859-S MS62 NGC.** The 1859-S is the premier issue of the denomination at the San Francisco facility and the only No Motto S-mint. Ten pairs of seated dollar dies were shipped from the Philadelphia Mint and, since only 20,000 coins were struck, it is highly likely that most dies remained unused. Extensively used for export, only a small percentage of the original production survives, particularly in AU and Uncirculated grades. This specimen displays whispers of light gray, sky-blue, and lavender patination, and the strongest luster in the recessed areas. Sharply struck on the design elements. A few minor scuffs are noted in the fields, and these are strictly consistent with the grade. (#6948)

See the Online Session listings in the back of this volume for additional Reiver selections.

Select Proof 1860 Seated Dollar

21550 **1860 PR63 NGC.** Navy-blue and golden-brown colors congregate along the borders of this well struck and faintly hairlined example. Although a mintage of 1,330 proof pieces is recorded, the NGC and PCGS populations suggest that only a small portion of that production has survived. (#7003)

Handsome 1862 Seated Dollar PR63 NGC

21553 **1862 PR63 NGC.** Light gold toning is generally limited to the rims. A sharply struck and flashy piece, the devices are moderately frosty but a Cameo designation is not forthcoming. Although the 1862 Gold Dollar had a large mintage, above 1.3 million, the 1862 Silver Dollar was not as favored, and just 11,540 business strikes were coined along with a scant 550 proofs. (#7005)

Bright Near-Mint 1860-O Dollar

21551 **1860-O AU58 NGC.** The impact of pinscratches around the eagle's head and upper reverse field is diminished by a bright, original appearance. Hints of golden and blue toning are seen about the borders. LIBERTY and the eagle's plumage are sharp, while the arms and legs of Liberty have light wear. (#6950)

Very Scarce Proof 1863 Seated Dollar PR58 NGC

21554 **1863 PR58 NGC.** Scarce and popular Civil War era issue, one of just 460 proofs struck, and even more elusive as an Uncirculated business strike. This proof example is lightly toned and shows a few scattered handling marks, with numerous small hairlines in the field areas, preventing a higher grade assessment. (#7006)

Challenging Select Proof 1861 Seated Dollar

21552 **1861 PR63 NGC.** Gentle chestnut toning endows this exquisitely struck and conservatively graded specimen. The *Guide Book* states a mintage of 1,000 pieces, however, the net production was significant lower, since a sizable percentage of the proofs made that year were eventually melted as unsold. Perhaps the arrival of the Civil War reduced anticipated collector demand. Population: 21 in 63, 36 finer (9/05). (#7004)

Lovely Select Proof 1864 Seated Dollar

21555 **1864 PR63 NGC.** A lightly toned beauty with a penetrating strike and attractive eye appeal. Frosty devices appear to merit a Cameo designation, however, NGC was not so inclined. A tiny spot is noted near star 12, and a few faint brown freckles are encountered on the field above the eagle's head. A small mintage of 470 proofs is not satisfactory to fulfill the demand from collectors of the impressive series. (#7007)

Lightly Toned Cameo Select 1865 Silver Dollar

21556 **1865 PR63 Cameo NGC.** A fully struck and undisturbed proof representative, the last collectible date of the No Motto run. Light freckles of walnut-brown color overlay the flashy fields and frosty devices. A curious raised line on the obverse rim at 7 o'clock is as made, caused by a scratch on the die. An even 500 proofs were distributed during this famous year in American history. Population: 10 in 63 Cameo, 19 finer (9/05). (#87008)

Scarce Uncirculated Details 1866 Motto Seated Dollar

21557 **1866 Motto—Improperly Cleaned—NCS. Unc Details.** The introductory Motto issue is scarce but not rare by the difficult standards of Seated Dollars. This well struck example is moderately prooflike and has light chestnut toning on the obverse. The reverse is nearly untoned. Rotation beneath a light and a loupe reveals a few faint hairlines in the fields, but these are not distracting. The 1 in the date is nicely repunched, the 8 and second 6 show minor recutting, and the reverse is die tripled, most noticeable on TRUST. (#6959)

Peripherally Toned Choice Proof 1867 Seated Dollar

21558 **1867 PR64 NGC.** Orange color embraces the rims, more prominently on the obverse. Clean fields and modestly glowing devices ensure the eye appeal. The strike is exacting, even on trouble spots for the type, such as the eagle's left (facing) ankle and Liberty's hair. The mintage of 625 pieces guarantees the scarcity. 1867 is the last year of truly low Philadelphia Mint business strikes. Later issues were struck in greater number, intended for export to the Far East. Population: 63 in 64, 14 finer (9/05). (#7015)

Elusive AU 1868 Seated Dollar

21559 **1868 AU50 NGC.** Typically worn, for the grade, with a coating of drab brown-gray patina over both sides, along with a few minor surface blemishes and dark toning streaks. Even though 162,100 dollars were struck bearing this date, the 1868 is an elusive item in AU condition or better. Most of the dollars of this date were exported to China and used there for trade purposes—permanently lost to collectors in this country.. (#6961)

Beautifully Toned 1868 Dollar PR62 NGC

21560 **1868 PR62 NGC.** Spectacular deep mirrors lie beneath deep, smoky charcoal-gray and dark-violet toning. The reverse also displays a palette of rich, original patina, with a slight degree of milky color in the fields. Both sides are minimally hairlined, and free of bothersome handling marks. Only 600 proofs were struck. (#7016)

See the Online Session listings in the back of this volume for additional Reiver selections.

Elusive 1869 Seated Dollar XF45 NGC

21561 **1869 XF45 NGC.** A dusky violet-gray, golden-brown and sea-green example that has abundant subdued luster across the legends and devices. Sharply detailed, and free from any obtrusive heavy abrasions. Despite a sizeable mintage, survivors are very elusive at all grade levels. (#6962)

Impressive 1870 Seated Dollar PR64 Cameo NGC

21562 **1870 PR64 Cameo NGC.** Blushes of golden-tan hues enliven the fields of this attractive near-Gem. Wisps of cream-gray color also make occasional appearances, but do not diminish the radiance of the major devices. The design is well struck, if not completely brought up on Liberty's knee and on the lower feathers of the eagle's left (facing) leg. A proof mintage of 1,000 pieces is generous for the type, however, far fewer than that quantity are reported by the third party grading services, despite nearly twenty years of operation and resubmissions. (#87018)

Attractively Toned AU 1870-CC Dollar

21563 **1870-CC AU53 NGC.** Breen-5485, "Rare." Variety 3-A. The CC mintmark is closely spaced. Attractive golden-brown and slate-gray toning embraces the lightly marked surfaces. The fields have a few wispy hairlines, and an area of mint-made roughness is noted left of the pole beneath the shoulder. The "A" reverse is generally regarded as the rarest of the five reverse dies for the 1870-CC, however, Heritage auction appearances suggest that the "B" reverse is even more elusive. The 1870-CC is the most available of the four CC-mint issues of the Seated type, but it is nonetheless of considerably greater rarity than any CC-mint Morgan Dollar, especially in Mint State. The 1870-CC is also famous as the first issue struck by the Carson City Mint. (#6964)

Collectible AU Definition 1871 Seated Dollar

21564 **1871—Improperly Cleaned—NCS. AU Details.** A lightly polished example with glossy and faintly hairlined surfaces. A natural planchet streak is noted between the ST in STATES, and an interesting mint-made roller mark descends through the eagle's neck and shield. A couple of unimportant rim marks are noted before 12 o'clock. The 1871 is an available issue with the series, however, Seated Dollars are scarce as a type in better circulated grades. (#6966)

Desirable XF Details 1871-CC Dollar

21565 **1871-CC—Harshly Cleaned—NCS. XF Details.** Only briefly circulated, but this pearl-gray example has thickly hairlined fields. The reverse rim has a few tiny pits, but these are not important. The 1871-CC is the lowest mintage Silver Dollar from the Carson City Mint, and is second in rarity behind only the 1873-CC. Q. David Bowers, in his 1993 Silver Dollar Encyclopedia, estimated between 80 and 130 survivors throughout all grades. The reverse is variety B from 1870-CC, with the mintmark widely spaced and each letter on opposite sides of the feather tip. (#6967)

Important Penultimate Proof 1872 Seated Dollar

21566 **1872 PR64 Cameo NGC.** Light mauve and gold toning enriches this pleasing proof Dollar. The frost on the major devices is not diminished by the delicate patina. Assertively struck, and splendidly preserved. Many if not most Motto Seated Dollars are die doubled, noticeable on the left (facing) wing plumage. The present piece, however, also exhibits nice die doubling on the Motto, perhaps broadest on the O in GOD. A scant 950 proofs were struck. Population: 11 in 64 Cameo, 10 finer (9/05). (#87020)

Noteworthy Choice VF 1872-CC Seated Dollar

21567 **1872-CC VF35 NGC.** The four Carson City issues in the Seated Dollar series are each more rare than any Morgan Dollar CC-mint issue, including the 1889-CC. The 1872-CC is much scarcer than the 1870-CC, although it is not quite as unobtainable as the 1871-CC and 1873-CC. Nonetheless, the 1872-CC, given its scant production of 3,150 pieces and the absence of contemporary Nevada collectors, is a formidable Silver Dollar rarity. Noticeable luster emerges from the plumage and stars of this bold example, and the rich apricot-gray toning does not conceal any singularly relevant marks. Minor granularity on the center of Liberty's shield is mentioned for pedigree purposes. (#6969)

Difficult AU 1872-S Dollar

21568 **1872-S AU53 NGC.** S-mint Morgan Dollars are quite common, but their Seated Dollar counterparts are rarities. The 1870-S is a prohibitive rarity, the 1873-S has no known survivors, the 1859-S is rare, and the only obtainable Motto issue, the 1873-S, is even more difficult to find than the 1859-S. 9,000 pieces were struck, but Bowers (1992) states, "The 1872-S is rarer than the mintage indicates, a situation that can be laid at the doorstep of melting and exportation." In his 1988 Encyclopedia, Breen notes, "Many probably melted after April 1873," when the 'Crime of 1873' abolished the denomination. This briefly circulated example has dappled sea-green, battleship-gray, and golden-brown toning, and has no unpleasant marks. Population: 3 in 53, 23 finer (9/05). (#6970)

See the Online Session listings in the back of this volume for additional Reiver selections.

Final Year of Issue 1873 Seated Dollar PR62 NGC

21569 **1873 PR62 NGC.** Final year of issue and always a popular coin as such. The glassy mirrored fields show only faint hairlines and overall the piece is covered with a smoky gray-green patina that has little effect on the pleasing reflectivity in the fields. A pair of wispy pinscratches, in the left obverse field, limit the grade. Fully struck, even on the eagle's plumage. (#7021)

Desirable AU Details 1873-CC Seated Dollar

21570 **1873-CC—Whizzed—NCS. AU Details.** The 1873-CC is considered to be the rarest Silver Dollar issue from the Carson City Mint, even though the mintage is nearly double that of the 1871-CC. The difference is that a number of the 2,300 pieces struck were likely melted by the mint after the "Crime of 1873" abolished the Silver Dollar in favor of the newly introduced Trade Dollar, also struck at Carson City later the same year. An even worse fate befell the 1873-S, since all 700 pieces struck were apparently returned to bullion. Among all Seated Dollars, only the extremely rare 1866 No Motto and 1870-S are more coveted by collectors than the 1873-CC. The present piece shows little evidence of circulation wear, but the cream-gray surfaces display an unnatural sheen from a consistently applied whizzing. Like all 1873-CC Seated Dollars, it utilizes the 1870-CC 'D' reverse die, with the second C in mintmark virtually touching the branch. (#6972)

TRADE DOLLARS

First Year 1873 Trade Dollar PR62 Cameo NGC

21571 **1873 PR62 Cameo NGC.** First year of issue for the enigmatic and beautifully designed Trade Dollar. Each side is brilliant with deeply reflective fields that show minimal hairlines, for the grade. The devices are nicely frosted and provide a pronounced cameo contrast. (#87053)

Low Mintage 1873-CC Trade Dollar AU58 NGC

21572 **1873-CC AU58 NGC.** This Carson City issue has one of the lowest mintages of any business strike Trade dollar (124,500 pieces). The devices are sharply defined and there are few noticeable marks on either side. The surfaces overall have an untoned silver-gray appearance, with a pleasing, softly frosted finish. Population: 24 in 58, 31 finer (8/05). (#7032)

Elusive 1873-S Near-Gem Trade Dollar

21573 **1873-S MS64 NGC.** The San Francisco Mint began Trade Dollar production in July 1873, and a respectable total of 703,000 coins were produced by the end of that year. As one would expect for an S-mint issue in this series, the 1873-S was widely exported, many of the coins being subsequently melted in China or India. Uncirculated examples are quite rare, and this issue may very well be the most difficult S-mint Trade Dollar to locate in Mint State. This lightly toned near-Gem is among the finest coins known to both NGC and PCGS, who have certified 32 specimens in MS64 and just 7 pieces finer (10/05). Its surfaces radiant bright luster and display sharply struck design features. A few minor abrasions on Liberty's cheek and neck and in the obverse fields define the grade. Census: 13 in 64, 4 finer (10/05). (#7033)

Conditionally Elusive 1874 Trade Dollar PR63 Cameo

21574 **1874 PR63 Cameo Uncertified.** This early proof striking is impressively cameoed with a brilliant obverse center that is outlined in rings of golden, rose, and blue iridescent toning. The reverse shows golden-tan color on the devices. Hairlines are noticeable on each side, limiting the numerical grade, but the fields are beautifully reflective. Population: 8 in 63 Cameo, 16 finer in Cameo condition (8/05). (#87054)

Scarce Uncirculated 1874-CC Trade Dollar

21575 **1874-CC MS61 NGC.** Bowers-3, Minute CC mintmark. The reverse die is distinguished by a bold die scratch through the upper portion of the D in DOLLAR. A sharply struck example, the obverse lightly toned in peripheral gold and lilac colors. The luster is good, with detectable penetration of the open fields. Minor marks are distributed but inoffensive. A less common issue in Mint State, and demand from Carson City collectors is substantial. (#7035)

Collectible 1874-S Trade Dollar

21576 **1874-S—Improperly Cleaned—NCS. AU Details.** Breen-5784, Medium S mintmark. Close to Mint State in terms of sharpness, this glossy Trade Dollar is perhaps unnaturally prooflike and has a number of tiny marks across the obverse field. A lightly toned example that, unlike most of its brethren, probably never made it to the Far East. (#7036)

Choice Cameo Proof 1875 Trade Dollar

21577 **1875 PR64 Cameo NGC.** Type Two Reverse. Tawny-gold color visits the margins, while the icy devices are close to fully brilliant. This carefully preserved specimen is well struck save for slight weakness on the hair, and the eye appeal is worthy of bidder attention. A few trivial obverse hairlines limit the grade. Just 700 proofs were struck. (#87055)

See the Online Session listings in the back of this volume for additional Reiver selections.

AU Definition 1875-CC Trade Dollar

21578 **1875-CC—Obverse Planchet Flaw—NCS. AU Details.** Type One Reverse. A lightly toned CC-mint Trade Dollar that has nearly full mint luster. The strike on the eagle's left (facing) leg is indifferent, but the devices are otherwise crisp. A toned planchet flaw behind Liberty's head and a smaller flaw between the 75 in the date affirm the NCS notation, however, it must be emphasized that these flaws were on the planchet prior to the strike and do not reflect the preservation of the coin. Miniscule granularity is also noted along the lower right obverse border. Envelope Included. (#7038)

Elusive Mint State 1875-CC Trade Dollar

21579 **1875-CC MS61 NGC.** Type Two Reverse. Gentle russet toned throughout the obverse border augment the attraction of this suitably struck and lightly marked Carson City Trade Dollar. An interesting, broad die scratch (as produced) connects the bases of the letters in UNUM. Apparently struck through a short piece of wire, which passes through the top of the left (facing) wing and the scroll end above, and leaves a delicate impression on the nearby field. Scarce in Mint State, although surprisingly collectible in such condition. (#7038)

Type One Reverse 1875-S Trade Dollar

21580 **1875-S AU53 NGC.** Type One Reverse. Large S. Luster individually illuminates the stars, and shimmers throughout the devices. Contact marks are unusually few in number or severity. This pearl-gray type coin will not be featured on the catalog cover, but is an untroubled piece that any collector would be pleased to show. Envelope Included. (#7039)

1875-S Trade Dollar, Unc Details

21581 **1875-S—Improperly Cleaned—NCS. Unc Details.** Type One Reverse, Large S mintmark. What appears to be a small die break is located on the lower part of the ribbon midway between the N of IN and G of God. This specimen displays semi-bright silver-gray surfaces with wisps of peripheral light tan, and fine hairlines in the fields. The design features are well impressed, and there are no significant abrasions to report. (#7039)

Bold AU Details 1875-S Trade Dollar

21582 **1875-S—Improperly Cleaned—NCS. AU Details.** Type One Reverse, Large S mintmark. The luster is diminished by a mild cleaning, but remains evident throughout the devices and other protected areas. A few dark flecks on the central reverse, otherwise an untoned Trade Dollar with faint roller marks on the lower right reverse and a couple of ticks on the 5 in the date. Envelope Included. (#7039)

Famous 1875-S/CC Trade Dollar

21583 **1875-S/CC—Improperly Cleaned—NCS. AU Details.** FS-012.5. Type One Reverse. The more obvious of the two 1875-S/CC varieties, the presence of the C mintmark to the right of the S is irrefutable. Since the Carson City Mint was in full production in 1875, the overmintmark of a CC reverse die at the Philadelphia Mint was probably performed to provide a die quickly for San Francisco, which made the bulk of export-destined Trade Dollars. This sharp slate-gray example is moderately hairlined, but has noticeable glimpses of luster and is otherwise unimpaired. Envelope Included. (#7040)

Charming Select Proof 1876 Trade Dollar

21584 **1876 PR63 NGC.** Type One Obverse, Type Two Reverse. Luminous honey, plum, and blue-green colors enrich the obverse border, and are seen to a lesser extent on the reverse periphery. Generally razor-sharp, with a hint of incompleteness of detail on Liberty's hair. A beautiful Select proof, and not far from a Cameo designation since the devices demonstrate consistent and substantial frost. Minor die doubling in a southern direction is noted on the lower tips of Liberty's banner, and on nearby drapery folds. (#7056)

Important 1876-CC Micro CC Trade Dollar

21585 **1876-CC AU50 NGC.** Breen-5804. Type One Obverse and Reverse. Widely spaced 'micro-CC' mintmark, the distant between the Cs is nearly equal to their combined height. Breen listed the variety as "Ex. rare," while Bowers (1993) in his Silver Dollar Encyclopedia called the variety "Quite scarce." Light tan toning enriches this moderately circulated Carson City Trade Dollar, which possesses noticeable luster throughout the recesses of the devices and legends. There are no relevant marks. Envelope Included. (#7042)

Sharp 1876-CC Trade Dollar, MS62 NGC

21586 **1876-CC MS62 NGC.** Type One Obverse, Type Two Reverse. Even though the mintage for the 1876-CC was 509,000 pieces, there are very few Uncirculated pieces known. Coins with any degree of eye appeal are even more difficult. Of the chopmarked 1876-CC dollars that have been examined, Bowers reports that more are known of this obverse / reverse die combination than the Type One Obverse / Type One Reverse. This specimen displays peripheral cobalt-blue, gold-brown, and lavender toning, and sharply struck design features. A few minute, inoffensive contact marks are noted in the left (facing) obverse field, and wispy slide marks are noted in the fields over each side. (#7042)

Elusive Type Two Obverse 1876-S Trade Dollar

21587 **1876-S AU Details, Improperly Cleaned, NCS.** Breen-5803. Type Two Obverse and Reverse. Minute S mintmark. Breen believed that this subtype combination was very rare. A survey undertaken by Mark Borckardt in 1992 suggested that about 20% of the issue has the Type Two obverse and reverse dies. Certainly, the Type One obverse is more often encountered. The present example of this Centennial S-mint issue has subdued silver-gray color and an unmarked reverse. The obverse has a contact mark in the field left of the waist, and hints of granularity are noted near star 10, the northwest corner of the bale, and near the CA in AMERICA. Envelope Included. (#7043)

See the Online Session listings in the back of this volume for additional Reiver selections.

Near Mint 1876-S Trade Dollar Scarce Type One/Type Two Combo

21588 **1876-S AU58 NGC.** Breen-5802. Type One Obverse, Type Two Reverse, Minute S. Light golden-brown and olive-blue color makes occasional visits the margins, but this sharp and mostly lustrous Trade Dollar is generally lightly toned. A bagmark beneath star 7 provides the only contact worthy of mention. Envelope Included. (#7043)

Near Mint 1876-S Trade Dollar Scarce Type One/Type Two Pairing

21589 **1876-S AU58 NGC.** Breen-5802. Type One Obverse, Type Two Reverse, Minute S mintmark. The Type One/Type Two combination is scarce, relative to the Type One Obverse and Reverse pairing. This bold example has impressive cartwheel luster on the reverse, and no indication of wear is immediately evident. The obverse field is moderately abraded and has a curious prooflike gloss. (#7043)

Pleasingly Toned 1877 Trade Dollar AU58 NGC

21590 **1877 AU58 NGC.** Light orange-terra cotta toning covers both sides of this near-Mint example. Typically weak on most of the obverse stars, on Liberty's head, and on parts of the reverse design, but pleasing overall by virtue of the unique toning scheme and surprisingly smooth preservation, for a lightly circulated piece, whose stay in the channels of commerce must have been mercifully brief. Envelope Included. (#7044)

Select Proof 1877 Trade Dollar

21591 **1877 PR63 NGC.** A splendid strike with virtually all design features defined about as sharply as one could desire. Toned in a pleasing blend of gold, gray, pink, and blue. Both surfaces show considerable cameo contrast, but no such designation is mentioned on the NGC label. From a tiny proof mintage of just 510 pieces, by far the smallest production figure for any proof trade dollar issue minted prior to 1884. (#87057)

Important 1877-CC Trade Dollar, MS62 NGC

21592 **1877-CC MS62 NGC.** CC-mint Trade Dollar production remained low through 1877—just 534,000 pieces were delivered with this date and mintmark combination. Furthermore, upward of 10,000 examples may have been melted as part of the 44,148 undistributed Trade Dollars destroyed under federal authority on July 19, 1878. The majority of extant Mint State '77-CC Trade Dollars grade no finer than MS62. One should not, however, assume that this issue is common in BU. An Uncirculated 1877-CC Trade Dollar of any quality is a significant find in today's market, and one that should not be allowed to slip past the specialist. The surfaces of this specimen display soft luster, and whispers of peripheral light toning on the obverse. The design elements are sharply struck throughout. Just a few unobtrusive contact marks are noted over each side, and some wispy slide marks are visible in the fields. (#7045)

Lightly Toned 1877-S Trade Dollar MS62

21593 **1877-S MS62 NGC.** Pleasing pale golden toning complements both surfaces. The devices are frosty and the fields are satiny. Nearly all design features are boldly and deeply struck. Excellent eye appeal for the grade. (#7046)

Borderline Uncirculated 1877-S Trade Dollar

21594 **1877-S AU58 NGC.** Appealing golden toning. Nearly all of the original mint luster still survives in the fields. Envelope Included. (#7046)

Cameo Proof 1878 Trade Dollar

21595 **1878 PR62 Cameo NGC.** The central areas are brilliant; warm golden-brown and navy blue iridescence complements the rims. Virtually all design features show bold definition, and as can be inferred from the "Cameo" designation on the NGC label, the frosty devices contrast nicely against the mirror fields. Some faint hairlines on both surfaces account for the assigned grade. A desirable proof-only variety with a scant mintage of just 900 pieces, making the 1878 the third lowest-mintage trade dollar issue after the 1885 and 1884 respectively. (#87058)

Key Date 1878-CC Trade Dollar, MS62 NGC

21596 **1878-CC MS62 NGC.** The 1878-CC is the key issue in the Trade Dollar series. Although Mint records indicate that 97,000 1878-CC examples were produced, many of these coins may have been destroyed as part of the 44,148 Trade dollars melted on July 19 of this year. This specimen possesses bright silvery surfaces with nice luster, and light gold-brown patina around the peripheries. The design elements are sharply impressed, and there are no significant abrasions. Some wispy hairlines are noted in the fields of both sides. Overall, a very attractive coin. (#7047)

Borderline Uncirculated 1878-S Trade Dollar

21597 **1878-S AU58 NGC.** Mostly brilliant surfaces with wisps and blushes of mottled golden-gray toning, especially around the letters, numerals, stars, and motifs. Notable as the final trade dollar issue coined at the San Francisco Mint. (#7048)

Cameo Proof Only 1879 Trade Dollar

21598 **1879 PR62 Cameo NGC.** A splendid strike with virtually all design features sharply and deeply delineated. The obverse has pale champagne iridescence in the central area, with vivid orange-gold, pink, and blue at the rim. The reverse has pinkish-gold toning. The cameo contrast is especially bold on the reverse. The assigned grade is due to the presence of some faint hairlines on the obverse. (#87059)

See the Online Session listings in the back of this volume for additional Reiver selections.

Popular Proof Only 1879 Trade Dollar

21599 **1879 PR63 Cameo NGC.** Mostly pale champagne iridescence in the central areas and ice blue at the borders. The cameo contrast on this piece is particularly pronounced on the reverse. Liberty's hair and some of the obverse stars show striking softness as made, but the great majority of design features are boldly defined including the eagle's plumage. The 1879 ranks as a scarce and desirable proof-only issue; a scant 1,541 examples were coined during the year. (#87059)

Delicately Toned 1880 Trade Dollar PR62 Cameo

21600 **1880 PR62 Cameo NGC.** The obverse is brilliant at the center with pale gold at the border. The reverse exhibits delicate uniform champagne iridescence. Virtually all design elements are boldly and deeply delineated, and the frosty devices contrast beautifully with the mirror fields. The presence of faint hairlines in the fields accounts for the assigned grade. Struck in proof format only. A mere 1,987 examples were minted. (#87060)

Scarce Proof-Only 1881 Trade Dollar

21601 **1881 PR61 Cameo NGC.** The central areas are brilliant; wisps and tinges of pink, blue, gold, and peach iridescence ornament the borders. All design elements are sharp. Careless handling in the past has resulted in the piece being conspicuously hairlined, a feature that accounts for the assigned NGC grade designation. A mere 960 trade dollars were minted during the year, all in proof format. The 1881 ranks as a perennially popular issue with collectors due to its rarity. (#87061)

Peripherally Toned 1882 Trade Dollar

21602 **1882 PR62 Cameo NGC.** Mostly brilliant with vivid orange-gold, pink and blue iridescence visible at the obverse border. Virtually all features are sharp save for some slight flatness on two or three obverse stars. The cameo contrast is especially bold on the reverse. Faint hairlines are noted on both surfaces. A mere 1,097 trade dollars were coined in 1882, all struck in proof format to accommodate the numismatic community. (#87062)

Scarce Cameo Proof 1883 Trade Dollar

21603 **1883 PR62 Cameo NGC.** Sharply struck. Pale gold iridescence on the obverse changes to vivid pink and blue at the border. The reverse exhibits a warm blend of intermingled gold, pink, and blue. The presence of faint hairlines on both surfaces is all that keeps this beauty out of the Gem category. From a mintage of just 979 pieces, all proofs made for coin collectors. (#87063)

"BOX" DOLLARS

21604 **1873-S VF20 Uncertified.** NGC did not holder this example, describing it as a "Hollowed Portrait Dollar." The more common and recognizable term is a "Box Dollar." Remarkable well made with the hinge located at the top of the reverse. The interior is bright and fresh, with an exceptional portrait of a dapper young man in contemporary dress.

21605 **1877 VF30 Uncertified.** A box dollar as in the previous lot, and again termed a "Hollow Portrait Dollar" by NGC although not holdered. Again, the hinge is located at the top of the reverse, but on this example the hinge is broken. Inside is a sepia photograph of a mustachioed gentleman in an unidentified uniform.

MORGAN DOLLARS

Choice 1878 Doubled Tailfeathers Dollar VAM-33

21606 **1878 7/8 TF MS64 NGC.** Listed as "VAM-33 7/4 TF" per the NGC label. Sharply struck in virtually all areas except just above Liberty's ear. The devices are frosty and the fields are satiny. Essentially brilliant surfaces with just a whisper of gold at the obverse border. Walter Breen claims that dozens of different reverses were produced having the "7 Over 8 Tailfeathers" feature, also referred to as "Doubled Tailfeathers," in the *Guide Book*. Some collectors have made a specialty of assembling a set containing as many different varieties as possible. Numismatists who desire to pursue this objective may find it useful to a acquire a copy of *The Comprehensive Catalogue and Encyclopedia of U.S. Morgan and Peace Silver Dollars* by Leroy Van Allen and A. George Mallis. (#7070)

21607 **1878 7TF Reverse of 1878 MS64 NGC.** Frosty luster. Mostly brilliant, with some splashes of gold. The obverse is remarkably sharp; even the hair above Liberty's ear exhibits a degree of sharpness seldom encountered. (#7074)

Popular 1878-CC Morgan Dollar

21608 **1878-CC MS63 NGC.** Brilliant in the central areas with wisps of gold at the borders. The devices are frosty and the fields have a texture intermediate between satiny and prooflike. Virtually all design features show bold definition. A small spot is noted in front of Liberty's nose. (#7080)

Desirable Uncirculated 1879-CC Capped Die Dollar

21609 **1879-CC Capped Die MS61 Deep Mirror Prooflike NGC.** VAM-3. A Top 100 Variety. Brilliant surfaces. The devices are frosty and the fields are nicely reflective. A touch of softness is noted above Liberty's ear and at the eagle's claws, but virtually all other design features are boldly defined. The so-called "Capped CC" variety is now listed in the *Guide Book* as the "CC Over CC." The 1879-CC is one of just a comparatively small number of issues with mintages under one million pieces, and is eagerly sought in all grades or preservation. (#97089)

Choice XF 1880/79-CC Second Reverse Dollar

21610 **1880/79-CC Reverse of 1878 XF45 NGC.** VAM-4. A Top 100 Variety. The VAM-4 and VAM-7 1880-CC Dollars represent the last stand of the Second Reverse, identified by the flat eagle's breast and parallel upper arrow feather. Sky-blue and pearl-gray colors blanket this partly lustrous Silver Dollar, which has a trace of granularity on the field near the chin. (#7108)

Choice 1880-CC 8 Over High 7 Dollar

21611 **1880-CC 8 Over High 7 MS64 NGC.** VAM-5. A Top 100 Variety. This beautiful better variety Carson City Dollar has potent luster, and the reverse in particular has a semi-prooflike look. A hint of chestnut color denies full brilliance. A couple of light marks on the left obverse, but the eye appeal is unmistakable. (#7102)

Deep Mirror Prooflike 1881-CC Silver Dollar

21612 **1881-CC MS64 Deep Mirror Prooflike NGC.** Pale champagne iridescence complements both surfaces. As can be inferred from NGC's "DPL" label designation, the frosty devices contrast beautifully with the mirror fields. Very pleasing from the aesthetic perspective. A scarce and desirable date eagerly sought because of its low mintage (by Morgan dollar standards) of just 296,000 pieces. (#97127)

Lustrous 1881-O Silver Dollar

21613 **1881-O MS64 NGC.** Brilliant and lustrous. A touch of striking softness is noted above Liberty's ear, but virtually all other design features are sharp. Some tiny mint-caused planchet inclusions are noted in the fields. (#7128)

Mint State 1882-CC Morgan Dollar

21614 **1882-CC MS62 NGC.** Lustrous and mostly brilliant with some faint blushes of gold. (#7134)

Moderately Toned 1883-CC Morgan Dollar

21615 **1883-CC MS63 NGC.** Frosty luster. Mostly brilliant at the centers with orange-gold and blue peripherally. Boldly struck with just a touch of softness above Liberty's ear, a feature typical on most examples encountered. (#7144)

Condition Scarcity 1883-S Silver Dollar

21616 **1883-S MS61 NGC.** Sharply struck with brilliant surfaces. The devices are frosty, and the obverse field, in particular, shows pronounced prooflike character. The reverse field has a texture intermediate between satiny and prooflike. (#7148)

21617 **1884 MS64 NGC.** Frosty luster. Partially brilliant with wisps and blushes of gold, pink, and blue at the peripheries. Excellent eye appeal. (#7150)

Choice AU 1884-S Morgan Dollar

21618 **1884-S AU55 NGC.** Mostly brilliant surfaces. The obverse was prooflike at the time of issue, and much mirror quality survives in the field around the stars, letters, numerals, and central motif. Although readily available in the VF to XF grade range, the 1884-S ranks an important scarcity at the AU55 level. (#7156)

21619 **1885 MS63 Deep Mirror Prooflike NGC.** Almost fully brilliant save for some wisps of gold at the rims. The devices are sharp, and the frosty cameo motifs contrast beautifully with the mirror fields. (#97159)

Mint State 1885-CC Morgan Dollar

21620 **1885-CC MS62 NGC.** Mostly brilliant surfaces with very slight peripheral iridescence. Most design features are nearly fully defined. This brilliant coin has the typical combination frosty and satiny appearance of these Carson City products. The devices have decidedly frosty luster with a satiny texture in the fields. (#7160)

Lustrous Select 1886-S Morgan Dollar

21623 **1886-S MS63 NGC.** Fully lustrous and essentially brilliant with same blushes and splashes of faint gold and gray. Virtually all design features are sharp save for a few tresses of hair above Liberty's ear. (#7170)

Popular 1885-S Silver Dollar

21621 **1885-S MS63 NGC.** The devices are frosty and the fields are satiny. A hint of pale champagne iridescence complements both the obverse and reverse. Although a touch of striking softness is noted above Liberty's ear, virtually all other design features are sharp. (#7164)

Lightly Toned 1887-S Silver Dollar

21624 **1887-S MS63 NGC.** Sharply struck and almost fully brilliant save for some tinges of golden-brown at the obverse rim. The devices are frosty and the fields are satiny. (#7180)

Difficult Uncirculated 1886-O Morgan Dollar

21622 **1886-O MS61 NGC.** Brilliant surfaces. The devices are frosty and the fields are reflective, in our opinion, although there is no "PL" designation on the NGC label. Virtually all design features are sharp save for a few strands of hair above Liberty's ear. Scarce in Uncirculated condition despite an enormous original mintage of 10,710,000 pieces. Presumably all but a small percentage of the Uncirculated population ended up in the melting pot. (#7168)

Intricately Struck Proof 1888 Morgan Dollar

21625 **1888 PR62 NGC.** Pearl gray toning complements both surfaces. Sharply struck with virtually all design features defined to full advantage save for a few hair strands above Liberty's ear. A tiny spot is noted on Liberty's cheek, and some reverse streaks, caused by the presence of planchet inclusions, are mentioned for accuracy's sake. Only 832 proof silver dollars were minted during the year. Envelope Included. (#7323)

See the Online Session listings in the back of this volume for additional Reiver selections.

Scarce Mint State 1888-S Dollar

21626 **1888-S MS62 NGC.** Sharply struck with satiny luster. Both surfaces are essentially brilliant with some splashes of gray on the obverse. (#7186)

Significant Choice AU 1889-CC Dollar

21627 **1889-CC AU55 NGC.** Long regarded as the key to the Carson City Morgan Dollar series, the 1889-CC does not have the lowest mintage, but unlike the 1881-CC and 1885-CC issues, did not emerge in Uncirculated quantity within the GSA hoard. The obverse is originally toned in sky-gray and pastel apricot hues, the reverse features a nearly untoned center and has an attractive golden-russet border. Slight friction in the centers is characteristic of the grade. Luster is extensive but does not dominate the exposed fields. No marks remotely merit cataloger discussion. An excellent opportunity to add a key date Morgan Dollar with a desirable pedigree to the advanced collection. (#7190)

Brilliant Near Gem 1889-O Morgan Dollar

21628 **1889-O MS64 NGC.** Brilliant and frosty. A few scattered spots and flecks are about all that keep this lustrous beauty out of the Gem category. A touch of striking softness is noted above Liberty's ear and at the eagle's chest. (#7192)

21629 **1889-S—Altered Surface—NCS. Unc. Details.** The obverse is brilliant with pronounced prooflike character. The reverse exhibits delicate golden-gray toning. Close examination reveals some mint-caused die polish lines in the reverse field; this is a feature likely to be misidentified as hairlines by some inexperienced collectors. (#7194)

Lovely Prooflike 1890 Morgan Dollar

21630 **1890 MS63 Prooflike NGC.** Pale champagne iridescence in the central areas deepens to rich gold at the borders. Wisps of electric blue ornament the rims. The frosty devices beautifully complement the mirror fields. Here's an aesthetic treat certain to delight the numismatist who seeks pieces that exhibit outstanding eye appeal. (#7197)

Better Date 1890-CC Silver Dollar

21631 **1890-CC MS64 NGC.** Brilliant, frosty, and sharply struck. Nice in every way. One of the finest we can recall having seen at this grade level. A tiny splash of blue toning above the E in UNITED will serve to identify this specimen in the future. (#7198)

21632 **1891 MS63 NGC.** Brilliant, frosty, and sharply struck. A handsome example for the grade. Some faint hairlines on Liberty's cheek were probably all that kept this beauty out of the MS65 class. (#7204)

Satiny 1891-CC Morgan Dollar

21633 **1891-CC—Obverse Improperly Cleaned—NCS. Unc. Details.** Essentially brilliant with some tiny wisps of golden brown at the obverse rims. The devices are frosty and the fields are satiny. The great majority of design features show bold definition. A tiny obverse planchet inclusion is noted at Liberty's forehead and is mentioned for accuracy's sake. Faint obverse hairlines account for the NCS label designation. (#7206)

Impressive 1891-O Silver Dollar MS64

21634 **1891-O MS64 NGC.** Fully brilliant. The devices are frosty and the fields are satiny. Virtually all design features are sharp save for a few tresses above Liberty's ear. Magnification reveals a scattering of tiny flecks. Not an easy issue to find this nicely preserved. (#7208)

Lustrous Mint State 1892 Morgan Dollar

21635 **1892 MS63 NGC.** Sharply struck and fully brilliant with frosty silver surfaces There is no indication of toning on either side of this lovely Mint State example. (#7212)

Tough Date 1892-CC Dollar

21636 **1892-CC MS63 NGC.** Brilliant and frosty. A touch of striking softness is noted in the tresses above Liberty's ear, but virtually all other design features are sharp. A tiny rim bump is noted on the reverse at 7 o'clock. (#7214)

Semi-Key Date 1892-S Morgan Dollar AU53 NGC

21637 **1892-S AU53 NGC.** More than a million '92-S dollars were originally struck, but those that escaped melting in most cases saw extensive circulation. Today, pieces grading VG to VF can be found without excessive difficulty, and at little cost. Things begin to change rather dramatically as the condition exceeds those levels, making this issue one of the most conditionally elusive of all Morgan dollars. A well balanced silvery-gray example with some golden peripheral toning, this piece retains a generous amount of mint luster. The devices are nearly free from distractions, but the strike is a bit soft on the highpoints, and wispy hairlines are noted in the obverse and reverse fields. (#7218)

Low Mintage Select 1893 Dollar

21638 **1893 MS63 NGC.** Fully lustrous and essentially brilliant with tinges of orange-gold at the borders. Virtually all design features are sharp save for a few tresses of hair directly above Liberty's ear. A mere 378,792 1893 dollars were coined, a production figure well under par for the design type, since the great majority of mintages in the Morgan dollar series are recorded as being well over a million pieces. (#7220)

Challenging Choice AU 1893-CC Morgan Dollar

21639 **1893-CC AU55 NGC.** A nearly brilliant example of this desired CC-mint key, the only toning apparent is delicate olive color on the highpoints of the devices. Pleasing luster illuminates the borders and devices, and the absence of detrimental marks only adds to the quality. The two best CC-mint dates, 1889-CC and 1893-CC are from years of partial production, the mint resumed coining after a four year slumber in mid-1889, and the presses permanently ceased in mid-1893. The 1885-CC is also from a partial production year and does have the lowest mintage in the series, but unlike the series keys was held back in quantity. (#7222)

Desirable Choice XF 1893-S Dollar

21640 **1893-S XF45 NGC.** Every dedicated Morgan Dollar collector has committed the mintage of 1893-S Dollars to memory. An even 100,000 pieces were struck, the lowest among all business strikes in the series, since the alleged quantity of commercially produced 1895 Dollars (12,000 pieces) is now believed to be a mere accounting entry. The 1893-S is eagerly chased throughout all grades, and although every major auction seems to have a few examples, the demand for pieces is formidable, due to the enormous popularity of the Morgan Dollar series. Substantial price increases have occurred in recent years, which suggests that knowledgeable numismatists are setting aside multiple pieces.

The present example is nearly untoned, and wear visible to the naked eye is only evident on the eagle's breast and on the hair directly above the ear. Bright luster glints from the legends, star, and wreath, and illuminates recesses of Liberty's hair and the eagle's wings. Consistent with other key date Morgan Dollars in the Jules Reiver Collection, there are no distracting marks. A prize to be cherished by the advanced Silver Dollar enthusiast. (#7226)

Uncirculated Sharpness 1894 Dollar

21641 **1894—Improperly Cleaned—NCS. Unc. Details.** Cleaned long ago and since retoned in a pewter gray shade. The cleaning was probably accomplished by acid or cyanide which has imparted a rather unnatural appearance to the luster. Softness is noted above Liberty's ear and at the eagle's claws, but virtually all the other design features are sharp. A scant 110,972 1894 were minted, one of the smallest production figures in the entire Morgan series; only the celebrated 1893-S and 1895 were produced in smaller quantities. (#7228)

Borderline Uncirculated 1894-O Dollar

21642 **1894-O AU58 NGC.** Brilliant surfaces. Faint indications of circulation are noted on the highpoints, but almost all of the original mint luster still survives in the fields. The strike is about average with softness noted above Liberty's ear, and at the eagle's claws and legs. A fine line is noted in Liberty's cheek. (#7230)

Scarce Mint State Sharpness 1894-S Dollar

21643 **1894-S—Altered Surface—NCS. Unc. Details.** The central areas are brilliant with wisps and tinges of golden-brown and violet visible at the borders. Both surfaces exhibit pronounced prooflike character although there is no such designation on the NCS label. Magnification reveals faint mint-caused die polish lines in the reverse field. Most design features are sharp save for a few strands of hair above Liberty's ear. (#7232)

Key Date 1895 Dollar, PR62 NGC

21644 **1895 PR62 NGC.** With the circulation strikes seemingly lost forever to the mass meltings of 1918-20, the Proof 1895 Silver Dollar has become one of the keys to completing the enormously popular Morgan Dollar series. Sadly, many of the surviving pieces are impaired through careless handling and/or crude attempts at cleaning. The lightly toned PR62 offered in this lot is exquisitely struck, with virtually all of Liberty's hair strands delineated, including those over the ear. Likewise, the eagle's breast feathers are sharp. There are no significant abrasions, just some wispy hairlines, that define the grade. (#7330)

Lustrous Borderline Mint State 1895-O Dollar

21645 **1895-O AU58 NGC.** The key New Orleans issue within the Morgan Dollar series, the 1895-O has the second smallest production from the southern mint, surpassing only the 1893-O. The 1895-O is significantly scarcer than the 1893-O, which suggests a different pattern of distribution. Bowers (1992) states, "Apparently, no 1895-O dollars were represented in the Treasury release of 1962-1964." He also adds, "The rarity and importance of the 1895-O in Mint State cannot be overemphasized." While the present lustrous example is not quite Mint State, it comes exceedingly close, since even the cheek of Liberty has noticeable sheen. A moderate mark to the chin and another in the field in front of the nose may have helped deny an Uncirculated designation. Delicate golden toning further confirms its originality. A significant offering of this notable O-mint rarity. (#7236)

See the Online Session listings in the back of this volume for additional Reiver selections.

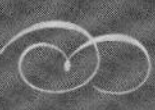

Difficult Near Mint 1895-S Dollar

21646 **1895-S AU58 NGC.** Medium blushes of olive toning grace this lustrous and momentarily circulated rare date Dollar. Only a hint of friction is detected on the central highpoints, and marks are surprisingly few, limited to a few ticks near the chin and neck. The low mintage 1895-S is invariably among the final holes filled in a collector's album of the series, and such pieces are rarely so close to Mint State. (#7238)

Lustrous Select 1899 Silver Dollar

21649 **1899 MS63 NGC.** Fully lustrous and essentially brilliant with just a whisper of pewter gray. All but a few of the highest-relief design details are boldly and deeply defined. Notable as the last issue in the Morgan series with a mintage beneath a million pieces; only 330,846 examples were coined. (#7258)

Borderline Uncirculated 1896-O Dollar

21647 **1896-O AU58 NGC.** Brilliant surfaces with almost all or the original mint luster still surviving. Close examination reveals a tiny obverse rim bump at 6 o'clock. The strike is about average with softness noted above Liberty's ear and at the eagle's claws, legs, and chest. (#7242)

Better Date 1899-S Morgan Dollar

21650 **1899-S MS63 NGC.** The devices are frosty and the fields are satiny. Both surfaces exhibit a faint blush of pale gold. Although a few strands of hair above Liberty's ear show striking softness, virtually all other design features are as sharp as could be desired. (#7262)

Prooflike Mint State 1896-S Dollar

21648 **1896-S MS62 Prooflike NGC.** Fully brilliant. The frosty devices beautifully complement the mirror fields. Most design features are sharp. Exceptional eye appeal for the grade. Scarce in all grades despite a generous mintage of 5,000,000 pieces. The only reasonable inference is that all but a small portion of the issue ended up being reclaimed into bullion pursuant to the provisions of the Pittman Act of 1918. (#7245)

Near Gem 1900-S Morgan Dollar

21651 **1900-S MS64 NGC.** The devices are frosty and the fields are nicely reflective, with the obverse showing pronounced prooflike character, a feature not designated on the NGC label. The surfaces exhibit a pleasing blend of pale orange-gold and blue-gray toning. Here's an aesthetic treat which will occupy an honored place in the cabinet of its next owner. (#7270)

Where noted, the original Reiver storage envelope is included with each lot.

Conditionally Rare 1901 Morgan Dollar MS62 NGC

21652 **1901 MS62 NGC.** New collectors to the Morgan Dollar series at first unimpressed by the 1901 Morgan Dollar, which records a plentiful production of nearly 7 million pieces. Not especially rare in VF and lower grades, the issue emerges as a surprising scarcity in AU, and is quite rare in Mint State. In fact, Bowers (1992) writes, "Of all Philadelphia Mint business strike dollars, excepting the spectral 1895, the 1901 is the rarest in Mint State." It is even more difficult in Uncirculated grades than the 1894, which had a scant mintage of 110,000 pieces. Perhaps the issue went directly into circulation, and the majority of any Uncirculated Treasury holdovers became part of the great 1918 Pittman Act melt. Regardless of the reason for its rarity, an Uncirculated 1901 Morgan Dollar is highly desirable, particularly when it is as fully lustrous as the present piece. This nearly brilliant piece has a remarkably unabraded obverse, and the reverse is also clean aside from a minor bagmark on the eagle's belly and a minor mint-made strike-thru beneath the first T in TRUST. (#7272)

Dazzling Gem 1901-S Dollar

21653 **1901-S MS65 NGC.** Gentle rose and apricot hues visit this lustrous, exactingly struck, and gorgeously preserved Morgan Dollar. Like all S-mint Dollar issues of its era, the 1901-S is very scarce in Uncirculated grades, and unblemished survivors of the present quality are undeniably rare. In fact, NGC has certified a mere three pieces finer, and only the most competitive and liquid Registry Set owner can hope to acquire a higher graded example. For the rest of us humble mortals, this 1901-S Dollar will more than suffice. (#7276)

Significant Gem 1902-S Silver Dollar

21654 **1902-S MS65 NGC.** The obverse exhibits pale champagne iridescence with wisps of golden-brown at the border. The reverse is essentially brilliant with some tinges of peach toning at the rim. The devices are satiny and the fields have a texture intermediate between satiny and prooflike. Although a touch of striking softness is noted at the tresses of hair above Liberty's ear and at the eagle's abdomen, virtually all other features are sharp. Not an easy issue to find so nicely preserved. (#7282)

Proof Near Gem 1903 Morgan Dollar

21655 **1903 PR64 NGC.** A lovely example of the issue having satiny devices, as is typical for the era, and glittering mirror fields. Almost all design features are boldly and deeply defined. The obverse exhibits pleasing bull's eye pattern toning, with golden brown at the center, violet-pink peripherally, and electric blue at the rim. The reverse displays a pleasing blend of golden-brown and pink-violet. Only 755 Proof Morgan dollars were coined in 1903. Envelope Included. (#7338)

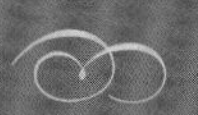

Formerly Rare 1903-O Morgan Dollar

21656 **1903-O MS63 NGC.** Brilliant and satiny. Most design features are sharp. An attractive example of this scarce and popular New Orleans Mint issue. The 1903-O was once regarded as a great rarity in the Morgan dollar series and commanded premiums that placed it in the lofty pantheon on American numismatic delicacies. The discovery of several bags of Uncirculated 1903-O dollars in the famous U.S. Treasury hoard distributed in the 1950s and 1960s, resulted in the reassessment of the rarity of the issue, and although the 1903-O is still regarded as scarce, virtually any numismatist can now afford to acquire an attractive example. (#7286)

Borderline Uncirculated 1903-S Dollar

21657 **1903-S AU53 NGC.** Essentially brilliant with a hint of pewter gray. Although faint traces of wear can be seen on the highpoints, virtually all of the original mint luster still remains intact in the fields. A faint line on the reverse is noted within the wreath, just above the tip of the olive branch. Scarce in all grades despite a mintage of more than a million pieces. Presumably the great majority of examples were never issued, but rather were simply reclaimed into bullion pursuant to the provisions of the Pittman Act of 1918. (#7288)

21658 **1904 MS63 NGC.** Brilliant, lustrous, and sharply struck. (#7290)

Challenging Mint State 1904-S Silver Dollar

21659 **1904-S MS62 NGC.** Lustrous and attractive. The obverse is brilliant at the center with tinges of orange-gold and navy blue at the rim. The reverse exhibits delicate uniform champagne iridescence. Virtually all design features are sharp save for a few tresses above Liberty's ear. Scarce in all grades and especially elusive in Uncirculated condition. (#7294)

PEACE DOLLARS

1921 Peace Dollar, MS63 NGC

21660 **1921 MS63 NGC.** Wisps of light tan and sky-blue patina adhere to lustrous surfaces that exhibit just a couple of miniscule grade-defining marks on Liberty's cheek and the eagle. The center areas are somewhat soft, as is typical of this issue. (#7356)

Near Gem 1924-S Dollar

21661 **1924-S MS64 NGC.** The 1924-S mintage of 1.728 million pieces was a tiny fraction of the quantity of 1922-S and 1923-S dollars made earlier at the San Francisco Mint. The present specimen displays light golden-gray patina which assumes slightly deeper hues around portions of the peripheries. Lustrous surfaces are nicely preserved, exhibiting just a couple of grade-defining marks on the Liberty and eagle motifs. The design elements are a little better defined than average for the issue. NGC has certified 57 coins finer (9/05). (#7364)

Attractive Premium Gem 1925 Dollar

21662 **1925 MS66 NGC.** The 1925 is one of the most plentiful Philadelphia Mint Peace dollars, though it becomes more challenging in the higher Mint State grades. Bright silver-gray surfaces display radiant luster and sharply struck design elements. A moderate milling mark in the left (facing) reverse field is mentioned for accuracy. NGC has certified a mere 22 pieces in higher grades (9/05). (#7365)

Mint State 1925-S Doubled Die Reverse Peace Dollar

21663 **1925-S MS63 NGC.** VAM-3. A Top 50 Variety. The reverse die is doubled, and this is most easily seen along the leading edge of the eagle's wing. A frosty example with brilliant silver luster. (#7366)

21664 **1926 MS61 NGC.** VAM-2. A Top 50 Variety. Struck from a doubled reverse die with the doubled clearest within the leaves by the eagle's claw. A pleasing example with satiny silver luster and pale champagne toning on the obverse. The reverse has swirling haze. (#7367)

Near Gem 1926-D Dollar

21665 **1926-D MS64 NGC.** This issue is typically well struck with nice luster. The present example is no exception, displaying excellent definition and highly lustrous surfaces that exhibit a few grade-limiting marks on the Liberty and eagle motifs. A few splashes of light gold-tan color are noted over each side. (#7368)

Near Gem 1926-S Dollar

21666 **1926-S MS64 NGC.** The '26-S is one of the more available San Francisco Mint Peace dollars of its era, with large numbers being released from this facility in 1941. The Near Gem in this lot displays bright luster and silver-gray surfaces. The obverse devices are very well struck, while the reverse center is somewhat soft, all of this being characteristic of the issue. A few minute marks on Liberty's cheek and on the eagle define the grade. (#7369)

1927-D Dollar, MS63 NGC

21667 **1927-D MS63 NGC.** Highly lustrous surfaces display wisps of light tan color, and the design features are well impressed throughout. Some small marks occurring on the central devices preclude a higher grade. (#7371)

Challenging 1927-S Dollar, MS64 NGC

21668 **1927-S MS64 NGC.** The '27-S is readily available in the lower Mint State grades, but becomes somewhat scarce at the MS64 level. On the present coin, reddish-gold and cobalt-blue patina hugs the rims, and the bright lustrous surfaces reveal just a few grade-defining marks on each side. All of the design elements are well brought up. NGC has certified 60 specimens grading higher (9/05). (#7372)

See the Online Session listings in the back of this volume for additional Reiver selections.

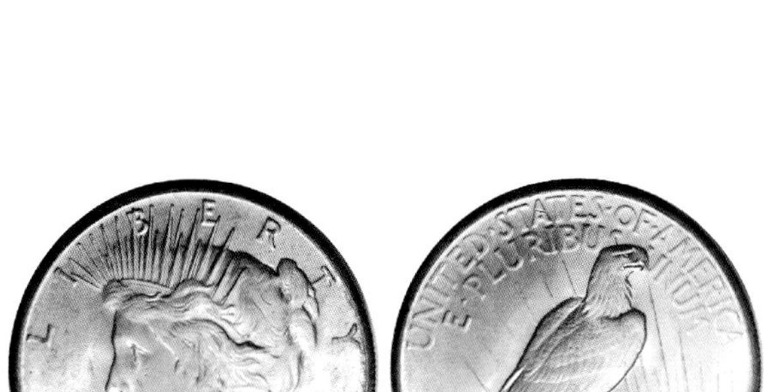

Low Mintage 1928 Near Gem Dollar

21669 **1928 MS64 NGC.** The low mintage of only 360,649 coins is the lowest production figure in the Peace dollar series, except for the 1922 High Relief (most of which were melted). Mint State 1928s are common, but because of the low mintage they are always in demand. The present near Gem is sharply struck, except for the reverse center, which is typical of the issue. The bright surfaces have a somewhat satiny appearance, again characteristic of the date, and display a light mottled gray patina. A few minute marks on Liberty and on the eagle account for the grade. NGC has seen just 71 pieces grading higher (9/05). (#7373)

Pleasing Near Gem 1934-D Dollar

21670 **1934-D MS64 NGC.** David Bowers, in his *Silver Dollars and Trade Dollars of the United States*, indicates that the '34-D is the second rarest Denver Mint Peace dollar in all Mint State grades (1927-D is the rarest). The specimen offered in this lot displays limited touches of tan-gold patination visiting lustrous surfaces. The design elements exhibit nice definition, especially those on the obverse. Some light scuffs on Liberty's cheek and neck, and a few minor contact marks on the eagle, limit the grade. (#7376)

Key MS65 1934-S Peace Dollar

21671 **1934-S MS65 NGC.** A lovely example of this important key issue. The surfaces are frosty and attractively toned in a delicate golden-gray hue. A faint hairline on Liberty's cheek, noted under magnification, is mentioned for accuracy's sake. The S-mintmark is bold. The 1934-S ranks as the scarcest issue in the Peace dollar series in Uncirculated grade, and because of the popularity of the series with collectors, the 1934-S undoubtedly is high on the numismatic wish lists of thousands of specialists. The scarcity of the 1934-S in grades higher than VF isn't due so much to its low mintage, just 1,011,000 pieces, but rather because few coin dealers thought to set aside supplies for the numismatic community. Perhaps the pressing circumstances of the Great Depression was a factor that prevented Uncirculated examples from being stockpiled in coin dealer inventories. It appears that all but a tiny portion went from the coinage presses directly into the channels of commerce and stayed there; accordingly, in grades of VG to Fine, examples can be picked up for only a small premium above the price for a common date, but at the VF level the scarcity of the issue sets it apart from most other Peace dollar issues, and at the MS60 level, the 1934-S ranks head and shoulders above the rest. (#7377)

Near Gem 1935 Dollar

21672 **1935 MS64 NGC.** The design elements are nicely struck, save for minor softness on the eagle's right leg. The surfaces display a satiny-like luster and faint hints of ran color, especially around the margins. A shallow scratch on Liberty's lower neck is mentioned for accuracy. (#7378)

1935-S Dollar, MS63 NGC

21673 **1935-S MS63 NGC.** The '35-S is readily available through MS64, and even MS65s are not that difficult to obtain. The MS63 coin we offer in this lot displays attractive satin-like luster and light golden-gray patina. A few scuffs and light contact marks on Liberty's cheek and neck account for the grade. (#7379)

GOLD DOLLARS

1849 Closed Wreath Dollar, MS62 NGC

21674 **1849 Closed Wreath MS62 NGC.** Large head, With L. An attentively struck and radiant peach-gold representative with light green accents. Scarce in Mint State, and a good value at the MS62 level. A few light handling marks are noted over each side, especially on the obverse. Die striations are visible in the obverse fields. Envelope Included. (#7503)

Unc Details 1853 Gold Dollar

21675 **1853—Improperly Cleaned—NCS. Unc Details.** Bright brassy-gold surfaces exhibit some light wispy hairlines. The design elements are sharply impressed, though the 1 and 8 of the date are a trifle soft. A few minute contact marks are visible on Liberty's cheek and neck, and slightly more extensive abrasions appear in the central reverse field. Overall, a decent looking coin, despite the "Improperly Cleaned" designation. Envelope Included. (#7521)

Collectible Type Two 1854 Gold Dollar

21676 **1854 Type Two—Obverse Scratched—NCS. AU Details.** Bright yellow-gold surfaces retain considerable luster, and the design elements are generally well impressed, though Liberty's hair and some of the leaf ribbing is soft. A shallow scratch extends from the last A in AMERICA to the lower part of the bonnet. A few hardly noticeable pinscratches also appear on the cheek and neck. Envelope Included. (#7531)

Type Two 1854 Gold Dollar, AU58 NGC

21677 **1854 Type Two AU58 NGC.** One of the goals of modifying the design of the gold dollar in 1854 was to increase the striking definition and wearability. However, this proved not to be the case. The new coins were generally softly struck and they quickly wore down. By 1861, some eight million of the original 11 million pieces that had been produced had been returned, melted, and recoined into Type Three gold dollars, quarter eagles, and double eagles. This piece shows the characteristic softness on the obverse highpoints, but on the reverse the central digits in the date (the usual soft spots) are fully brought up. The peach-gold surfaces display faint traces of mint luster around the devices, and show just a few small marks on the obverse. Envelope Included. (#7531)

1855 Gold Dollar, Unc Details

21678 **1855—Damaged—NCS. Unc Details.** Bright brass-gold surfaces display considerable luster and adequately struck design elements. A few small abrasions are noted on Liberty's cheek and neck and in the central reverse field, and a shallow scrape occurs on the cheek between the nose and mouth. (#7532)

Frosty MS62 1855 Gold Dollar

21679 **1855 MS62 NGC.** Brilliant and frosty. Outstanding eye appeal for the grade. Struck from lightly clashed dies as is typical of many Type Two gold dollars seen. The letters LL in DOLLAR are softly defined, but most other design features are crisp. Type Two gold dollars were struck at the Philadelphia Mint only in the years 1854 and 1855, and accordingly, Uncirculated examples rank high in popularity with collectors. (#7532)

See the Online Session listings in the back of this volume for additional Reiver selections.

AU Details 1855-O Dollar

21680 **1855-O—Obverse Scratched, Improperly Cleaned—NCS. AU Details.** Very fine hairlines are noted on the brassy-gold surfaces, and a squiggly shallow scratch occurs in the lower left (facing) obverse quadrant. Liberty's hair is somewhat weak, as is typical for the issue. About 200 or so specimens are known out of an original mintage of 55,000 pieces. Envelope Included. (#7535)

Pleasing 1858 Gold Dollar, MS62 NGC

21681 **1858 MS62 NGC.** The 1858 is quite elusive in the Mint State grades. NCS and PCGS have each certified about 100 Uncirculated pieces (9/05). Of course, many of these are undoubtedly resubmissions. The present specimen displays soft luster and peach-gold patina with light green and orange-gold accents, and sharply struck design elements. A few unobtrusive handling marks are visible over each side. Overall, a nice looking coin for the grade level. Population: 43 in 62, 27 finer (9/05). Envelope Included. (#7548)

Attractive MS64 1859 Gold Dollar

21682 **1859 MS64 NGC.** Frosty and attractive. Most design features are sharp, save for a two or three letters and numerals. Magnification reveals two tiny spots on the upper portion of the wreath. Here's an excellent candidate for inclusion in a high-grade 19th-century gold type set. Envelope Included. (#7551)

Uncirculated 1862 Gold Dollar

21683 **1862 MS62 NGC.** Minimally marked for the assigned grade, but the luster is too subdued for a finer rating. Envelope Included. (#7560)

Attractive Mint State 1873 Open 3 Gold Dollar

21684 **1873 Open 3 MS62 NGC.** A boldly struck and unblemished piece that has original tan-gold color and good eye appeal. The mintages of 1873 and 1874 Gold Dollars, while still far below the level of the 1862, were significant larger than any other post-1862 issue. Most likely, the Treasury intended to return gold coins to circulation, where they had been absent (except in the far west) since early in the Civil War. Envelope Included. (#7573)

Appealing Premium Gem 1874 Gold Dollar

21685 **1874 MS66 ★ NGC.** A common date in the gold dollar series that is bright and possesses full, softly frosted luster. Winner of the "Star" designation, from NGC, designating exceptional eye appeal. Sharply struck and essentially mark-free, an excellent type coin. (#7575)

Low Mintage 1883 Gold Dollar

21686 **1883 MS62 NGC.** This sharply impressed and lustrous representative has a pair of faint pinscratches near the nose, but is generally undisturbed. Except for a short-lived increase in production in 1873 and 1874, Gold Dollars had low mintages from 1863 until the end of the series. Fortunately for collectors, a number of Mint State examples were set aside as souvenirs, presumably by knowledgeable East Coast numismatists. Envelope Included. (#7584)

CLASSIC QUARTER EAGLES

Impressive 1834 Quarter Eagle MS62 NGC

21687 **1834 Classic MS62 NGC.** Breen-6138, Small Head, R.2. A beautiful straw-gold first year Classic Quarter Eagle. The mildly prooflike fields are refreshingly unmarked, and the strike is needle-sharp on the eagle and the obverse stars. Liberty's curves on the top of her head are less prominent than on the Large Head subtype. The Classic Head design was produced through 1839, but the Small Head portrait was only struck from one 1834-dated die pair. Envelope Included. (#7692)

Bold 1836 Block 8 Quarter Eagle

21688 **1836 Block 8—Reverse Damage—NCS. AU Details.** McCloskey-B Head of 1834, Breen-6142, R.3. Three inconspicuous pinscratches are noted near the denomination, but the group of pinscratches beneath OF are not readily dismissed. This intricately struck Quarter Eagle is golden-brown in color, and the obverse by itself appears to merit an AU58 grade. Envelope Included. (#97694)

LIBERTY QUARTER EAGLES

Mint State 1853 Quarter Eagle

21689 **1853 MS61 NGC.** A nicely struck and carefully preserved example. The luster is good, and no marks are detected with the naked eye. Several vertical shield lines are weak, particularly the second stripe, caused by the die preparation rather than the strike. 1853 was a plentiful year for gold coinage, since old tenor silver denominations were hoarded while gold remained in circulation. Envelope Included. (#7767)

Charming 1856 Quarter Eagle MS62 NGC

21690 **1856 MS62 NGC.** An assertive strike and abundant luster combine with an unmarked cheek and a clean obverse field to provide good eye appeal. An inconspicuous mark on the chin is evident only upon close evaluation. Not common in Mint State, despite a plentiful mintage for the era. Envelope Included. (#7777)

1873 Open 3 Quarter Eagle, MS61

21691 **1873 Open 3 MS61 NGC.** The more common of the two varieties of this year, this piece is exceptionally well struck with just a few minor surface marks. The luster is too subdued for a finer grade. Envelope Included. (#7817)

Uncirculated Details 1877-S Quarter Eagle

21692 **1877-S—Improperly Cleaned—NCS. Unc. Details.** Incorrectly designated by NCS as a rare 1877 Quarter Eagle. A thickly hairlined but sharply struck golden-brown example from the final years of S-mint production of this design; only the Philadelphia Mint produced the denomination between 1880 and 1910. Envelope Included. (#7827)

Choice AU 1878 Quarter Eagle

21693 **1878 AU58 NGC.** Light wear, the deep, coppery-pink-golden appearance is quite attractive. Some dark encrustation is visible on the reverse. Envelope Included. (#7828)

1878 Quarter Eagle, MS60

21694 **1878 MS60 NGC.** Dull and quite subdued with a typical mark count for the assigned grade. An affordable type coin. Envelope Included. (#7828)

Difficult Choice 1895 Quarter Eagle

21695 **1895 MS64 NGC.** Intricately struck, and without unpleasant contact. Just 6,000 pieces were struck, and Mint State examples are scarce. Among such pieces, not many possess the clean surfaces of the present near-Gem. Better date Quarter Eagles provide good value relative to their peers in higher gold denominations. Envelope Included. (#7847)

Sharp Gem MS66 1898 Quarter Eagle

21696 **1898 MS66 NGC.** Sharply struck and lustrous. Essentially brilliant with just a hint of olive iridescence which attests to the originality of this lovely Gem. Although 1898 quarter eagles aren't particularly difficult to find in Uncirculated condition, only a tiny portion of them could match the quality offered here. The presently offered piece, in terms of technical quality, certainly ranks among the finest quarter eagles to emerge from the Jules Reiver Collection. Envelope Included. (#7850)

21697 **1902 AU58 NGC.** Well struck with a few noticeable blemishes on each side. Both sides exhibit subdued luster, the grade limiting factor. Envelope Included. (#7854)

Uncirculated 1903 Quarter Eagle

21698 **1903 MS62 NGC.** With deep yellow-gold surfaces, a razor sharp strike, and few distracting bagmarks, this is a pleasing type coin for the grade. Envelope Included. (#7855)

Select 1904 Quarter Eagle

21699 **1904 MS63 NGC.** Quite lustrous and well struck with a pleasing appearance for the MS63 assigned grade. A small "x" is scratched under the eagle's left (facing) wing. Envelope Included. (#7856)

Original Gem 1905 Quarter Eagle

21702 **1905 MS65 NGC.** An original golden-brown Gem with a needle-sharp strike and vibrant cartwheel sheen. Well preserved, only a vertical, solitary slide mark beneath the hair bun merits mention. Minor obverse alloy spots near the nose and at 11:30 could likely be removed without effect through proper conservation. Envelope Included. (#7857)

Charming Choice 1904 Quarter Eagle

21700 **1904 MS64 NGC.** This lustrous and intricately struck near-Gem is splendidly unabraded, and is a worthy addition to a high quality twentieth century gold type set. A solitary fleck of green debris beneath the L in LIBERTY is of little consequence. 1904 marked the 25th consecutive year of Philadelphia-only production, although its Half Eagle counterpart had been struck at San Francisco for most dates within that span. Envelope Included. (#7856)

Lovely Gem 1906 Quarter Eagle

21703 **1906 MS65 NGC.** An inordinately preserved honey-gold Gem, fully lustrous and exceptionally attractive from a technical perspective. Not fully struck on LIBERTY or the top of the curl beneath the ear, and a small wine-colored spot is noted beneath the D in the denomination. Envelope Included. (#7858)

Choice Uncirculated 1905 Quarter Eagle

21701 **1905 MS64 NGC.** This well struck example has appealing, satiny luster and a few copper colored toning spots, with very few detracting surface marks. (#7857)

Bold Gem 1907 Quarter Eagle

21704 **1907 MS65 NGC.** This luminous olive-gold Gem has a crisp strike and no mentionable marks. The base of the 7 in the date is recut, a situation that could not occur in future years, since the Indian Quarter Eagle series exclusively used hubbed dates. Desirable but not especially rare as a Gem, since the smaller diameter Quarter Eagle tended to survive loose bag storage better than its larger denomination counterparts. Envelope Included. (#7859)

See the Online Session listings in the back of this volume for additional Reiver selections.

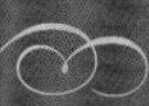

INDIAN QUARTER EAGLES

21705 **1909 AU58 NGC.** Attractive and sharply struck throughout with nearly complete mint luster. Minimally marked for the grade. Envelope Included. (#7940)

Lustrous, Select 1911 Quarter Eagle

21706 **1911 MS63 NGC.** The bright, lustrous surfaces exude a warm rosy glow. A couple of minuscule contact marks limit the grade. Envelope Included. (#7942)

Uncirculated 1912 Indian Quarter Eagle

21707 **1912 MS61 NGC.** Bright golden color, some minor weakness of strike and several abrasions on the reverse limit the grade. Envelope Included. (#7944)

1912 Quarter Eagle, MS62

21708 **1912 MS62 NGC.** Well struck with rich color and full luster. There are a few grade-limiting pinscratches on the reverse of the piece. Envelope Included. (#7944)

Uncirculated 1913 Quarter Eagle

21709 **1913 MS62 NGC.** Nicely struck with apricot toning. Just a few hardly-noticeable marks are seen on the obverse field. Envelope Included. (#7945)

21710 **1914—Improperly Cleaned—NCS. AU Details.** This nicely struck type coin features blended olive and apricot colors. Thick hairlines occupy the upper reverse and left obverse fields. Envelope Included. (#7946)

Mint State Sharpness 1915 Quarter Eagle

21711 **1915—Obverse Improperly Cleaned—NCS. Unc. Details.** NCS has incorrectly recorded the date as 1913 on the insert. Thorough inspection is required to locate the hairlines on the reverse field. A sharply struck piece, more pleasing than the NCS designation implies. The final Philadelphia Mint issue until 1926, since World War I interrupted international specie payments. After the World War ended, Double Eagles were the denomination of convenience for foreign trade. Struck from moderately rotated dies. (#7948)

Uncirculated 1915 Quarter Eagle

21712 **1915 MS61 NGC.** An orange-golden beauty displaying muted mint luster, but with excellent detail on the cheek, bonnet, and highpoint of the eagle's wing. (#7948)

Well Detailed, Near-Gem 1926 Quarter Eagle

21713 **1926 MS64 NGC.** Intricately detailed and only a lengthy, but shallow mark above the eagle from consideration as a Gem. (#7950)

Popular Near Gem 1927 Quarter Eagle

21714 **1927 MS64 NGC.** Well struck save for the usual incompleteness on the lowest two headdress feathers, this apricot-gold type coin has no unpleasant marks, and radiant luster dominates. Envelope Included. (#7951)

Attractive 1928 Indian Quarter Eagle

21715 **1928 MS63 NGC.** A beautiful and crisply struck representative of this popular and collectible series. Even the Indian's cheekbone shows little indication of contact. Envelope Included. (#7952)

Select 1929 Quarter Eagle

21716 **1929 MS63 NGC.** This final year Quarter Eagle exhibits a reasonable strike and is only lightly marked for the assigned grade. The mintage is less than the Half Eagle of the same date, also from the final date of its series. The Half Eagle is a great rarity, since most examples never left the Treasury and were melted after the 1933 gold recall. The 1929 Quarter Eagle, on the other hand, is available, perhaps because its lesser face value made it more affordable for gifts, collecting, or hoarding. Envelope Included. (#7953)

THREE DOLLAR GOLD PIECES

Near Mint 1854 Three Dollars

21717 **1854 AU58 NGC.** Faint wear on the corn husks and on Liberty's hair confirms momentary circulation in commerce. Light marks include a wispy blemish behind Liberty's head and a tiny obverse rim ding near 9 o'clock. The introductory 1854 issues include two important mintmark varieties, the 1854-D and 1854-O, the only date that a southern branch mint struck the denomination. (#7969)

Undisturbed Uncirculated 1854 Three Dollar

21718 **1854 MS61 NGC.** A golden-brown representative without obtrusive marks. Extensive luster and a crisp strike further the eye appeal. The 1854-dated issues are an important subtype within the series, since DOLLARS is formed with much smaller letters than in subsequent years. Envelope Included. (#7969)

See the Online Session listings in the back of this volume for additional Reiver selections.

Popular 1856 Three Dollars

21719 **1856—Improperly Cleaned—NCS. AU Details.** A wipe from a jeweler's cloth has given this bold example a bright and glossy appearance. Considerable luster beckons from the legends and devices. Minor contact marks are generally limited to the left obverse field. A scarce denomination, never struck in large numbers since the similar valued Quarter Eagle sufficed in commerce. Envelope Included. (#7974)

Popular Near Mint 1874 Three Dollars

21720 **1874 AU58 NGC.** Liberty's forehead has a hint of wear, and luster does not deeply penetrate the open obverse field, but this problem-free Princess otherwise approaches a Mint State designation. By the standards of Three Dollar Gold Pieces, a relatively plentiful date, but always in demand from type collectors because of the scarcity of the denomination. Envelope Included. (#7998)

Lustrous Premium Gem 1878 Three Dollar Gold

21721 **1878 MS66 NGC.** This Premium Gem represents one of the two most common dates within the series of three-dollar gold pieces, and it is an excellent candidate for the type collector. This is especially so as it could be argued that these coins have the best overall eye appeal of any date in the series. Fully brilliant with intense and frosty yellow-gold luster. The surfaces are nearly perfect, with only a few insignificant blemishes on either side. (#8000)

EARLY HALF EAGLES

Near Mint 1804 Small 8 Half Eagle Dramatic Late Obverse Die State

21722 **1804 Small 8 AU58 NGC.** Breen-6443, B. 3-E, Miller-66, R.5. This well struck Borderline Uncirculated Early Half Eagle displays substantial olive-gold luster, diminished but not broken in the exposed fields. A few minor handling marks on the obverse field and on Liberty's cap do not distract. The rare Breen 3-E variety features a high, recut 4 in the date, and the lowest right leaf on the olive branch is unfinished. The bases of AME in AMERICA are connected.

The present piece exhibits a dramatic late die state. A network of at least eight die cracks converge upon the portrait, and a relatively large rectangular die break is located on the back of Liberty's jaw. The cataloger is unaware of another example with such advanced cracks, and it is unlikely that many further pieces could have been coined from the shattered obverse die. In contrast, the reverse has two lengthy but slender cracks from the rim to the eagle's shield. Both dies are boldly clashed. Envelope Included. (#8085)

Splendid Select 1807 Bust Left Half Eagle

21723 **1807 Bust Left MS63 NGC.** Breen-6453, B. 5-D, Miller-101, R.3. A lovely representative of this scarce and popular early gold type. Luster dominates the open fields, and the strike is precise throughout. The reverse, on its own, appears to merit a Gem designation, while the obverse grade is limited only by three faint grazes that converge near Liberty's chin. Light clash marks (as made) from the eagle's shield are noted near Liberty's covered ear. Struck from moderately rotated dies. The 1807 Half Eagle is significant as the introduction of John Reich's eagle motif, which persisted in modified form on the denomination for a full century, finally replaced in 1908. Envelope Included. (#8101)

CLASSIC HALF EAGLES

Original AU 1836 Half Eagle

21724 **1836 AU50 NGC.** Breen-6509, Second Head, Large Date, McCloskey 4-C, R.3. Honey-gold luster bathes protected areas of this nicely struck and lightly marked Classic Half Eagle. Breen distinguishes between three different portrait styles of 1836 Half Eagles, but the differences are by no means obvious. A reduction in tenor of gold coins in 1834 led to their increased use in circulation, although privately issued bank notes were also commonplace. Envelope Included. (#8174)

Elusive 1837 Five Dollars AU53 NGC

21725 **1837 AU53 NGC.** Breen-6512, Large Date, Large 5, McCloskey 2-B, R.3. A straw-gold representative of this scarcer Classic Five issue. Luster is subtle but extensive, and no handling marks are readily located. The centers are well struck for the type, with any softness of detail limited to the left borders. Envelope Included. (#8175)

LIBERTY HALF EAGLES

Scarce 1846 Large Date Half Eagle

21726 **1846 Large Date—Improperly Cleaned—NCS. AU Details.** A reasonably struck and somewhat bright honey-gold example. A circular defect on the upper portion of the second vertical shield stripe is from the die and is seen on various denominations from this era. The scarcer of the two date logotypes used on 1846 Half Eagles. The rule to distinguish Large Dates from their more available Small Date counterparts is the spacing between the digits. The Large Date is spaced 1 846, the Small Date is spaced 18 4 6. The challenge is greater for Large Cent collectors, who have three different 1846 date logotypes to choose from. Envelope Included. (#8226)

Important AU55 1852-D Half Eagle

21727 **1852-D AU55 NGC.** Olive-gold toning complements both surfaces. Traces of original mint luster can be seen around the stars, letter, and numerals. Both surfaces appear to be entirely devoid of the planchet flaws that plague a large portion of Dahlonega's surviving output. Scarce this nicely preserved. The great majority of 1852-D half eagles encountered are in the VF to XF grade range. Worth a generous bid from the alert specialist. Envelope Included. (#8252)

Select 1881 Five Dollars

21728 **1881 MS63 NGC.** A lustrous and attentively struck Half Eagle that has a clean reverse and a couple of moderate marks on the face. The 1881 is the highest mintage Half Eagle, but is a target for cherrypickers, who seek the elusive 1881/0 overdate. Envelope Included. (#8354)

Attractive Near Mint 1882-S Half Eagle

21729 **1882-S AU58 NGC.** An original and lustrous Half Eagle with the look of an Uncirculated grade, although the purist will note the whisper of friction on the nostril, eyebrow, and bust truncation. Peach and lime hues only supplement the eye appeal of this lightly marked piece. Envelope Included. (#8360)

Uncirculated 1882-S Half Eagle

21730 **1882-S MS61 NGC.** Peach hues invigorate this crisply struck and suitably lustrous Mint State Half Eagle. Unlike most examples at the MS61 level, there are no individually noticeable marks. The 1881-S and 1882-S Half Eagles have identical reported mintages of 969,000. Envelope Included. (#8360)

Lustrous 1882-S Liberty Five MS62 NGC

21731 **1882-S MS62 NGC.** A sharply struck and highly lustrous Half Eagle, perhaps kept from the Select level by a few wispy horizontal slide marks in the field southwest of Liberty's chin. Envelope Included. (#8360)

Nice Uncirculated 1887-S Half Eagle

21732 **1887-S MS61 NGC.** This available date Liberty Half Eagle provides ample mint luster and a good strike. No handling marks are of individual relevance. The Liberty Half Eagle is the largest gold series in terms of date and mintmark combinations, since all five contemporary mints participated. Envelope Included. (#8371)

Uncirculated 1894 Half Eagle

21733 **1894 MS61 NGC.** A hint of peach color affirms the originality of this shimmering Five Dollar gold piece, which has a moderately abraded obverse and a clean reverse. Philadelphia Mint Liberty Half Eagles dated between 1892 and the end of the series are readily available in Mint State. Envelope Included. (#8387)

Select 1900 Half Eagle

21734 **1900 MS63 NGC.** This boldly struck Half Eagle provides pleasing luster, and is quite clean aside from a single handling mark above the eagle's head. The banner border is absent beneath the W in WE, the outcome of die polishing at the mint. McKinley was re-elected in 1900, which confirmed the commitment of the United States to the gold standard. Envelope Included. (#8400)

1901 Five Dollars MS62 NGC

21735 **1901 MS62 NGC.** Light recutting is noted west of the bases of the 19 in the date. This lustrous and intricately struck Half Eagle possesses vibrant luster and is not offensively abraded. Minor alloy spots are above the hair bun and the I in UNITED. Envelope Included. (#8402)

Mint State 1901-S Half Eagle

21736 **1901-S MS61 NGC.** Bright luster and clean surfaces provide good eye appeal for the grade. A well struck type coin with one small contact mark near the mouth. Although Christian Gobrecht died in 1844, his designs for the Quarter Eagle, Half Eagle, and Eagle continued for more than sixty years. Envelope Included. (#8404)

See the Online Session listings in the back of this volume for additional Reiver selections.

Charming 1906 Half Eagle MS63 NGC

21737 **1906 MS63 NGC.** Booming luster and unmarked surfaces provide pleasing eye appeal. This crisply struck apricot-gold late date Liberty Five Dollars has only a few wispy slide marks that deny the Choice designation. By 1906, gold coins were generally replaced in circulation with paper money on the Eastern half of the nation, and Philadelphia Mint issues were struck primarily for export. (#8413)

Vivacious Mint Details 1907 Half Eagle

21738 **1907—Obverse Improperly Cleaned—NCS. Unc. Details.** Patient rotation of this penultimate date Liberty Half Eagle finally reveals a patch of faint hairlines on the upper left obverse field. A few specks of possible PVC residue are at 9 o'clock, and on the reverse near the left (facing) wingtip. Some closely spaced marks are found above the eagle's head. A well struck and fully lustrous example. Envelope Included. (#8416)

INDIAN HALF EAGLES

Uncirculated 1908 Half Eagle

21739 **1908 MS62 NGC.** A sharply struck and minimally abraded (for the grade) example of this popular first year of issue gold coin. Bright golden color overall. Envelope Included. (#8510)

Borderline Uncirculated 1909-D Five Dollars

21740 **1909-D AU58 NGC.** Substantial luster glimmers throughout the pale gold devices, but faint friction on the cheekbone and headdress prevents an Uncirculated designation. In terms of eye appeal, however, the present piece is superior to many abraded Mint State examples. Envelope Included. (#8514)

Eye Appealing 1910 Half Eagle

21741 **1910 MS62 NGC.** A sharply struck and thoroughly lustrous Half Eagle, refreshingly void of contact and perhaps held back in grade by only a couple of areas of subtle gray color on the upper obverse field and the Indian's headband. (#8517)

Uncirculated 1913 Half Eagle

21742 **1913 MS62 NGC.** An olive-gold representative, notable for its shimmering luster and its absence of singularly detrimental marks. In 1913, the Buffalo Nickel was introduced, the third contemporary denomination to feature a Native American on the obverse. Envelope Included. (#8525)

LIBERTY EAGLES

Scarce Choice XF 1884-CC Eagle

21743 **1884-CC XF45 NGC.** A richly detailed and slightly glossy medium gold CC-mint Eagle with faint slide marks from moderate circulation. There are no mentionable abrasions, aside from a pinscratch above TEN. Heavy die lines beneath Liberty's ear and near the I and T in LIBERTY are diagnostic for the issue, and perhaps represent damage to the obverse die during its journey from Philadelphia to Carson City. Less than 10,000 pieces were struck. Envelope Included. (#8704)

Low Mintage 1888-O Eagle

21744 **1888-O MS62 NGC.** A low mintage New Orleans issue that can be obtained in near-Mint and basal Mint State condition, but NGC has only certified two pieces in finer grades, both at the MS63 level. This crisply impressed example has good luster and no more marks than is customary for the grade. A curious rim defect at 9 o'clock on the reverse would require inspection of the edge to determine its origin. Envelope Included. (#8713)

Lustrous Select 1893 Liberty Eagle

21745 **1893 MS63 NGC.** Well struck except for the final obverse star, and the cartwheel luster dazzles the eye. A small mark on the cheek and a few wispy grazes stand in the way of near-Gem assignment. A good candidate for a 19th century gold type set. Envelope Included. (#8725)

Low Mintage 1896 Eagle MS62 NGC

21746 **1896 MS62 NGC.** This well struck low mintage Ten Dollar gold piece has unbroken cartwheel luster, and the fields are clean for the grade. Faint scrapes behind the eye and on the lower cheek determine the grade. A small spot is noted near the M in AMERICA. Envelope Included. (#8735)

Near Mint 1897 Ten Dollars

21747 **1897 AU58 NGC.** Light wear on the wingtips and Liberty's chin preclude a Mint State designation, but this bold example has a clean obverse and only a few inconspicuous marks beneath the left (facing) wing. Envelope Included. (#8737)

Affordable Near Gem 1899 Eagle

21748 **1899 MS64 NGC.** This lustrous Choice Liberty Eagle has undiminished luster and relatively clean surfaces. Assertively struck and attractive. The upper loops of the 899 in the date exhibit recutting. A few flecks of olive-russet color are noted on the right obverse. (#8742)

See the Online Session listings in the back of this volume for additional Reiver selections.

Uncirculated Details 1905 Ten Dollars

21749 **1905—Improperly Cleaned—NCS. Unc Details.** The strike is needle-sharp, but noticeable hairlines diminish the luster. Considered a scarce issue at one time due to its relatively low mintage, but hoards from European vaults have made the 1905 available in typical Mint State grades. Envelope Included. (#8757)

INDIAN EAGLES

Vibrant Mint State 1910-D Eagle

21750 **1910-D MS62 NGC.** Peach-gold in color, this lustrous Indian Eagle possesses a decent strike and a few moderate marks. The largest mintage of the denomination at Denver. Local demand there must have been sated, since the 1911-D had a vastly reduced production of 30,100 pieces. Envelope Included. (#8866)

Collectible Uncirculated Sharpness 1912 Eagle

21751 **1912—Improperly Cleaned—NCS. Unc. Details.** This canary-gold type coin possesses vibrant cartwheel luster and a penetrating strike. Liberty's cheek is somewhat bright, and light hairlines appear when the piece is rotated beneath a light. (#8871)

Near Mint 1912 Indian Eagle

21752 **1912 MS64 NGC.** Impressive luster and an attentive strike combine with undisturbed fields for exemplary eye appeal. A few tiny marks near the cheekbone do not allow classification as a full Gem. A trace of struck-in grease, as made, reaches the 2 in the date and the reverse rim at 9 o'clock. (#8871)

Select 1913 Indian Ten

21753 **1913 MS63 NGC.** Very lustrous with a good strike, and with fields that lack the numerous small abrasions that are usually seen at the MS63 level. However, there are a couple of abrasions on the lower eagle that limit the grade. Some brick-red color has accumulated near the top of the obverse and reverse. Envelope Included. (#8873)

Pleasing Near Gem 1926 Eagle

21754 **1926 MS64 NGC.** Potent cartwheel luster fails to reveal any relevant marks. This suitably struck Choice Indian Eagle has a couple of pinpoint alloy spots on the reverse, but these do not affect the eye appeal. While Double Eagles were struck annually at Philadelphia during the 1920s, Eagles were only struck at the mother mint in 1926, their only production at the facility between 1916 and 1931. The Double Eagle was more convenient for foreign trade and bank reserve purposes, as a result, coinage of Eagles was infrequent after 1916. Envelope Included. (#8882)

LIBERTY DOUBLE EAGLES

Obtainable Near Mint 1875-S Double Eagle

21755 **1875-S AU58 NGC.** Peach and greenish-gold colors drape this dusky and partly lustrous Type Two Twenty. Moderate abrasions are noted near the final obverse star and beneath the ICA in AMERICA. The mintmark is affected by a vertical mark. Envelope Included. (#8975)

Uncirculated 1896 Twenty Dollars Dramatic Repunched Date

21756 **1896 MS61 NGC.** Breen-7322, which he considered "very rare." The date is widely and clearly repunched north. The obverse field and the reverse are clean for the grade, but a few moderate marks are concealed on the portrait. Small spots are noted on the bun and the E in AMERICA. (#9029)

Uncirculated Sharpness 1897 Double Eagle

21757 **1897—Improperly Cleaned—NCS. Unc. Details.** When tilted at a certain angle beneath a lens and a light, a few wispy hairlines appear, but this fully lustrous and crisply struck Double Eagle is otherwise nearly unblemished, and should provide good value for the alert bidder. Envelope Included. (#9031)

Collectible 1897-S Double Eagle

21758 **1897-S—Improperly Cleaned—NCS. AU Details.** A lightly circulated golden-brown Double Eagle with ample luster and generally bagmark-free surfaces. Glossy from a mild cleaning, but not offensively hairlined. Envelope Included. (#9032)

Borderline Uncirculated 1898-S Twenty

21759 **1898-S AU58 NGC.** Vibrant luster has a slight break over Liberty's cheek, but many observers would regard the present coin as Mint State. As is the case with most San Francisco Mint issues from the later half of the Liberty Double Eagle series, the 1897-S is not a rarity at the near-Mint level, since these pieces were struck in quantity and used as bank reserves, in the United States and abroad. (#9034)

See the Online Session listings in the back of this volume for additional Reiver selections.

Smooth Mint State 1899 Double Eagle

21760 **1899 MS61 NGC.** An undisturbed and shimmering representative, quite attractive despite a small dark spot near the lower hair bun. Like most years in the series, fewer pieces were struck in Philadelphia than San Francisco, but the race was close in 1899, 1.67 million versus 2.01 million coins. Envelope Included. (#9035)

Lustrous Uncirculated 1899-S Double Eagle

21763 **1899-S MS61 NGC.** A radiant honey-gold turn of the century Double Eagle, lustrous and not unduly abraded. A small russet spot is encountered on Liberty's forehead. Like most S-mint Liberty Twenties, the 1899-S is common enough in basal Mint State, but is very rare in Gem condition. Envelope Included. (#9036)

Borderline Uncirculated 1899 Twenty Dollars

21761 **1899 AU58 NGC.** A small depression on the rim near star 13 is noted, but this Double Eagle is otherwise refreshingly unmarked, and is only kept from Mint State by a whisper of friction on Liberty's cheek. The eye appeal is superior to many abraded Mint State examples. Envelope Included. (#9035)

Lovely Near Gem 1900 Double Eagle

21764 **1900 MS64 NGC.** A beautiful sunrise-gold Liberty Double Eagle, sharply struck and shimmering. The eye appeal is such that is worthy of selection as a representative of the type, with greater numismatic interest than the typically encountered 1904. A trace of lacquer is noted above the IT in UNITED. (#9037)

Uncirculated 1899 Liberty Twenty

21762 **1899 MS62 NGC.** Peach and lime tints grace this lustrous Double Eagle, which has a few moderate marks on the left obverse and a couple of tiny charcoal spots on each side. The denomination celebrated its fiftieth anniversary in 1899, unlike the Gold Dollar, also introduced in 1849 but limited to Commemorative issues after 1889. Envelope Included. (#9035)

Borderline Uncirculated 1900-S Twenty

21765 **1900-S AU58 NGC.** Faint slide marks above the date suggest momentary circulation, but the cartwheel luster is essentially complete. Recutting is noted within the upper inner loop of the final 0 in the date, a remnant of an earlier and largely effaced impression of the date into the working obverse die. Envelope Included. (#9038)

Uncirculated 1903-S Liberty Twenty

21766 **1903-S MS61 NGC.** Satin luster sweeps across this pale peach-gold Double Eagle. Delicate luster grazes preclude a higher Mint State grade, but the eye appeal is reasonable since there are no heavy marks. Most surviving Mint State pre-1933 gold coins avoided government melting through years of storage as bullion reserves in foreign bank holdings. Envelope Included. (#9044)

1904 Twenty Dollars MS63 NGC

21767 **1904 MS63 NGC.** This lightly marked type coin features rich apricot color and undiminished cartwheel luster. Crisply struck, although some incompleteness of detail is found in the hair, as always for business strikes of the type. Double Eagles have long been the preferred denomination of bullion holders, since the premium above melt is comparatively small. Envelope Included. (#9045)

Ubiquitous Select 1904 Double Eagle

21768 **1904 MS63 NGC.** A lustrous and beautiful type coin with the occasional modest mark to limit the grade. The 1904 is the most common date in the series in Uncirculated grades, and has the largest mintage of the type, more than 6 million pieces. The 1904 does not have the highest mintage of the denomination, however. That honor belongs to the 1928, which had a production of more than 8.8 million pieces. (#9045)

Promising Mint State 1906 Double Eagle

21769 **1906 MS62 NGC.** Assertively struck and fully lustrous with the only occasional minor mark. A high end example of this popular low mintage issue, which had a production of less than 70,000 pieces. While the San Francisco Mint delivered large mintages of the denomination on an annual basis, Philadelphia Mint production varied widely from year to year, presumably dependent upon export demand and bullion availability. Envelope Included. (#9049)

1907 Liberty Twenty Dollars MS62 NGC

21770 **1907 MS62 NGC.** This honey-gold Double Eagle has impressive luster and a precise strike. Minor marks are distributed but none distract. The final year of the Liberty Head design. A diverse collection can be comprised from Double Eagles of this year, although the proofs and Roman Numerals issues range from costly to non-collectible. Envelope Included. (#9052)

See the Online Session listings in the back of this volume for additional Reiver selections.

SAINT-GAUDENS DOUBLE EAGLES

Popular 1908 No Motto Saint-Gaudens

21771 **1908 No Motto—Improperly Cleaned—NCS. Unc. Details.** A satiny is somewhat subdued olive-gold Double Eagle. Careful study under a loupe locates nearly imperceptible obverse hairlines. Glimpses of russet patina accompany portions of the obverse border. The eagle's beak shows the strike doubling typical of this short-lived type. Envelope Included. (#9142)

Popular 1908 No Motto Twenty Dollars

21772 **1908 No Motto MS63 NGC.** A nicely struck and satiny representative of this popular two-year type. President Theodore Roosevelt opposed the Motto on coinage, and believed it to be blasphemous, since money could be used for immoral or illicit purposes. Congress disagreed, however, since no one seeking re-election wanted to be labeled an atheist. Envelope Included. (#9142)

Choice AU 1908 Motto Saint-Gaudens

21773 **1908 Motto AU55 NGC.** The 1908 No Motto is among the most common dates in the series, especially in high grades, but the 1908 Motto is many times more scarce, and has a reported mintage of just 156,258 pieces. Although not rare, its low production makes it a target for hoarders. Light friction on the eagle's breast and Liberty's chest and raised knee deny a Mint State grade, but satiny luster is noted throughout the fields. Envelope Included. (#9147)

1908-D Motto Double Eagle MS63 NGC

21774 **1908-D Motto MS63 NGC.** Lustrous and radiant with clean honey-gold surfaces. A better date because of a relatively low mintage of just under 350,000 pieces. Not as coveted, though, as the 1908-S, which had a scant production of 22,000 pieces, the lowest in the series aside from the desirable Roman Numerals varieties. Envelope Included. (#9148)

Choice Uncirculated 1914-S Twenty

21775 **1914-S MS64 NGC.** Both obverse and reverse are awash in attractive reddish patina, but numerous moderate abrasions on the reverse limit the grade. Envelope Included. (#9166)

Brilliant, Lustrous MS64 1915 Double Eagle

21776 **1915 MS64 NGC.** Brilliant, lustrous, and sharply struck. Nice in every way. Although the 1915 is not particularly elusive at the MS60 level, it is certainly scarce in MS63 condition in comparison with most other Philadelphia Mint issues, and rises to the status of a rarity at the MS64 level. We doubt that another example this nice could be located without a long and diligent search. Envelope Included. (#9167)

Collectible 1920 Double Eagle

21777 **1920 MS62 NGC.** Luster sweeps across the moderately marked fields and devices of this boldly struck example. Numismatists have often pondered the 1920 and 1921 issues, and their relative mintages and rarity. The 1920 has less than half the production of the 1921, yet the 1920 is available, while the 1921 is a great rarity. Presumably, a few bags of the 1920 were shipped to Europe, where they waited out the belligerent U.S. policy toward bullion gold. 1921 Double Eagles apparently went into the backs of Treasury vaults, and only escaped in small numbers. The 1920 does offer good value relative to the more plentiful 1922 to 1928 P-mint dates. Envelope Included. (#9170)

Vibrant 1922 Double Eagle

21778 **1922 MS63 NGC.** Well struck save for the central portions of AMERICA, this lustrous Twenty Dollars has the first glance appearance of a finer grade, although a few inconspicuously placed contact marks are apparent upon thorough evaluation. Philadelphia Mint issues between 1922 and 1928 often represent this imposing and popular design within type sets. Envelope Included. (#9173)

Select 1923 Twenty

21779 **1923 MS63 NGC.** Boldly struck and fully lustrous, with lovely green-gold and pink-gold colors, and a moderate number of surface blemishes. Some red toning spots are seen mostly on the reverse. Envelope Included. (#9175)

Choice 1924 Double Eagle

21780 **1924 MS64 NGC.** Booming luster and an absence of detrimental marks confirms status as a near-Gem. Although the 1924 is of course a common date, the present piece is distinguished by subtle die doubling on the eagle's feathers, most apparent on the leg. Envelope Included. (#9177)

Choice 1924 Saint-Gaudens Twenty

21781 **1924 MS64 NGC.** Sharply struck except for the Capitol building, this lustrous sunrise-gold Double Eagle exhibits generally clean surfaces. The 1924 is the quintessential United States gold type coin, common but under demand from gold hoarders seeking numismatic value. Envelope Included. (#9177)

Select 1925 Twenty Dollars

21782 **1925 MS63 NGC.** A shimmering and sharply struck type coin with distributed tiny marks but no offensive abrasions. Part of a run of available Philadelphia Mint issues (1921 to 1928) bookended by significant rarities (the 1920 and 1929). Envelope Included. (#9180)

See the Online Session listings in the back of this volume for additional Reiver selections.

Handsome Choice 1925 Saint-Gaudens

21783 **1925 MS64 NGC.** This lustrous and pleasing near-Gem has a couple of tiny rose-colored alloy spots on the reverse, which could likely be removed harmlessly through proper conservation. The greenish-gold surfaces are only faintly marked and exhibit prominent eye appeal. Envelope Included. (#9180)

Splendid Near Gem 1925 Double Eagle

21784 **1925 MS64 NGC.** A lustrous and beautiful apricot-gold near-Gem that has a refreshingly unmarked obverse field. A common date, but often hoarded for its gold content, since the handsome Saint-Gaudens designs make it preferable among numismatic alternatives. (#9180)

1927 Twenty Dollar, MS64

21785 **1927 MS64 NGC.** Good color and luster, a hallmark of this issue, with several reverse contact marks visible over the eagle upon close inspection. Envelope Included. (#9186)

Uncirculated 1928 Twenty Dollar

21786 **1928 MS62 NGC.** Bright yellow-gold patina overlays lustrous surfaces that reveal light contact marks on Liberty's midriff and legs, and on the eagle's wings. Envelope Included. (#9189)

COMMEMORATIVE SILVER

1893 Isabella Quarter, Unc. Details

21787 **1893 Isabella Quarter—Improperly Cleaned—NCS. Unc. Details.** Wispy, sparse hairlines are somewhat more prominent on the obverse. This lustrous and boldly defined example exhibits golden-brown toning in protected areas. The only Commemorative Quarter in the classic Commemorative series, with the possible exception of the 1932 Washington Quarter. (#9220)

Mint State Sharpness 1900 Lafayette Dollar

21788 **1900 Lafayette Dollar—Improperly Cleaned—NCS. Unc. Details.** DuVall 2-C. A hairlined but well struck representative with attractive honey-brown patination across the obverse border. The verbose legends for this issue were not present on the hub, and were instead entered by hand on the working die, perhaps because the mint was in a hurry to strike the entire issue on the exact Centennial of Washington's death; December 14, 1899. A better type, and the sole Commemorative Dollar prior to 1983. (#9222)

Conditionally Scarce Gem 1921 Alabama

21789 **1921 Alabama MS65 NGC.** The 1921 Alabama followed the example of the recent Missouri issue, which had varieties with and without the union admission order. The Alabama used the St. Andrew's cross to separate the 22, while the Missouri used a star to separate the 21. Although the No 2X2 variety has a higher production and is more available in typical Mint State, prices for the 2X2 and No 2X2 are close at the Gem level. The reason for this is that the No 2X2 issue was not as well made, and typically comes with a soft strike on the eagle's leg and back claw. The strike on the present piece is not razor-sharp, but is certainly above average, and minor handling marks are generally relegated to the portrait of Governor Kilby. (#9224)

Satiny Albany Commemorative

21790 **1936 Albany—Improperly Cleaned—NCS. Unc Details.** A lovely cream-gray Commemorative with satin luster and a meticulous strike. No contact marks are observed, and evidence of past cleaning is extremely slight. (#9227)

Brilliant 1937 Antietam Half Dollar

21791 **1937 Antietam—Improperly Cleaned—NCS. Unc. Details.** This brilliant and lightly toned example shows little indication of a prior cleaning, but close inspection does locate several wispy pinscratches amid STATES. A popular Commemorative type that has a noble portrait of Confederate General Robert E. Lee. (#9229)

21792 **1937-D Arkansas MS66 NGC.** A satiny, nearly flawless example that stands up to the most stringent inspection. Both sides are lightly toned in speckled russet, green, and apricot coloration, which appears chiefly near the peripheries. Census: 69 in 66, 5 finer (12/05). Envelope Included. (#9242)

Attractive Choice 1939 Arkansas Half Dollar

21793 **1939 Arkansas MS64 NGC.** Gentle tan toning encroaches upon the centers of this exactingly struck and shimmering Choice Commemorative. A solitary tick on Liberty's cheekbone denies Gem assignment. The five year Arkansas program suffered from dwindling mintages during its final three years, and those alert numismatists who purchased the 1939 PDS set received one of the scarcest in the entire commemorative series. (#9249)

Elusive Gem 1939-S Arkansas Half

21794 **1939-S Arkansas MS65 NGC.** This meticulously struck pearl-gray Gem features smooth, shimmering surfaces and obvious eye appeal. The 1939 PDS set is the key to the Arkansas series, since just 2,100 sets were produced, plus a few strays for assay. 1939 was the last year of commemorative production during Roosevelt's administration; the 1946-dated Iowa and Booker T. Washington types were signed into law by Truman. (#9251)

See the Online Session listings in the back of this volume for additional Reiver selections.

Original Gem 1936-S Bay Bridge

21795 **1936-S Bay Bridge MS65 NGC.** Chestnut, dove-gray, and russet colors ensure the originality of this lustrous Gem. Attentively struck, and minor contact is only detected on the bear's flank. The Bay Bridge type was unusual in that it commemorated a contemporary event. It also the marked the third appearance of a grizzly bear on a California-themed Half Dollar type. (#9254)

Gem 1935-D, 1934 in Field Boone Half Dollar

21796 **1935/34-D Boone MS65 NGC.** Lightly toned in tan and cream-gray colors, this satiny Gem is virtually unabraded and has a good strike, with only slight incompleteness found on WE and the TR in TRUST. Noteworthy as the lowest mintage Silver Commemorative, although the difference in mintage between the Denver and San Francisco issues of the 1935, 1934 in field Boone Half Dollars consists of a single assay-destined piece. Six different varieties of 1935 Boone Half Dollars were struck that year. (#9263)

Low Mintage 1935-S, 1934 in Field Boone Half MS64 NGC

21797 **1935/34-S Boone MS64 NGC.** Apricot and slate-gray colors blend throughout this satiny, well struck, and essentially unabraded example. The five-year Arkansas and Boone types provided the eight lowest mintage varieties in the Silver Commemorative series. Collectors who wanted more than three varieties of 1935 Boone Halves must have pleased when a new trio was offered with 1934 added to the reverse field above PIONEER YEAR. Just 2,004 1935/34-S Boone Halves were struck. Depression-era collectors were inundated with Silver Commemorative Half Dollar issues in 1935 and 1936, the peak two years of the series. (#9264)

21798 **1937-D Boone MS66 NGC.** An appealing blend of pale pewter gray and golden-brown toning complements the lustrous surfaces. Very pleasing from the aesthetic perspective. From a tiny issue of just 2,506 pieces, which were distributed in 1937 Boone PDS sets. (#9271)

Low Mintage Gem 1937-S Boone Half

21799 **1937-S Boone MS65 NGC.** Lovely satiny luster characterizes both the obverse and reverse. Delicately toned in blended hues of pewter gray and gold. Outstanding eye appeal. Only 2,506 pieces were issued, one of the smallest net production figures in the commemorative half dollar series. (#9272)

21800 **1936 Cincinnati MS65 NGC.** A delightful Gem example. Fully lustrous and attractively toned in delicate pearl gray and gold hues; a quality that characterizes many of commemorative half dollars that Jules Reiver selected for inclusion in his celebrated cabinet. From and issue of just 5,005 pieces. The initial cost of $7.75 for a PDS set, made the issue among the most expensive in the commemorative half dollar series up to that point in time. (#9283)

Gem 1936-D Cincinnati Half

21801 **1936-D Cincinnati MS65 NGC.** Frosty and attractive. Both surfaces exhibit pearl gray toning with pleasing pink, sea green, and lemon yellow iridescent highlights. Outstanding both technically and aesthetically. From a tiny original issue of just 5,005 pieces. (#9284)

21802 **1936-S Cincinnati MS64 NGC.** Lustrous surfaces. Pearl gray toning overall, with a faint dusting of golden-brown on both the obverse and reverse. A few tiny bag marks, noted under magnification, were probably all that prevented NGC from assigning a considerable higher grade. Only 5,006 examples were issued, among the lowest net production figures in the commemorative series. (#9285)

1935 Connecticut Half Dollar MS65

21803 **1935 Connecticut MS65 NGC.** Fully lustrous and essentially brilliant with some hints of lilac-gray and gold. A handsome example of this beautifully-designed and popular commemorative classic. The famous Charter Oak, depicted on the reverse and still venerated by Connecticut residents today, is said to have been destroyed during a storm on August 21, 1856. (#9299)

Pastel Toned 1936 Delaware

21804 **1936 Delaware MS66 NGC.** A splendid Gem example, nearly as nice as the day is was struck. Beautifully toned in delicate pastel hues of pewter gray, golden-brown, and lilac. Here's a prize certain to be admired by every numismatist who lays eye on it. (#9301)

Premium Gem 1936 Elgin Half Dollar

21805 **1936 Elgin MS66 NGC.** Intense frosty luster as is typical of virtually all examples seen. Toned in delicate intermingled hues of gold and gray. What appears to be a small scuff over the head of the young pioneer on the right side of the tableau is actually due to die polish at that point; accordingly, the same feature is present on many and possibly most of the examples that a numismatist is likely to have the opportunity to view. Several decades elapsed between the issue of the half dollar in 1936 and the erection of the Elgin Pioneer Memorial, which was finally dedicated on November 11, 2001. Visitors to Elgin, Illinois will be able to view the memorial near the city's public library. An interesting article on the subject appeared in the January 2002 issue of *Chatter*, published by the Chicago Coin Club. (#9303)

Lovely Gem 1936 Gettysburg Half Dollar

21806 **1936 Gettysburg MS65 NGC.** Pale golden-gray toning complements satiny surfaces. Scarce and desirable this beautifully preserved. Issued to commemorate the 75th anniversary of the famous Civil War battle. (#9305)

See the Online Session listings in the back of this volume for additional Reiver selections.

Gem Mint State 1922 Grant With Star Half Dollar

21807 **1922 Grant with Star MS65 NGC.** Two varieties of the Grant Half Dollars and the Grant Gold Dollars were minted in 1922, either with or without a star in the obverse field over the N of GRANT. This was incuse, or punched into the field, meaning the feature was raised on the actual die. Like nearly every surviving Mint State example of this issue, the mostly brilliant surfaces have satiny luster and extensive die polishing lines in the fields. Just a trace of blue and iridescent toning is visible on both sides. Minor clash marks are seen on both sides, but they are especially visible inside the reverse border. (#9307)

Key Type 1928 Hawaiian Half

21808 **1928 Hawaiian—Improperly Cleaned—NCS. Unc. Details.** Pewter gray toning on subdued surfaces. Wisps of vivid golden-brown and lilac complement the obverse border. One of the most desirable and eagerly sought issues in the commemorative half dollar series. Only 9,958 pieces were issued, a figure that many numismatists believe would have been substantially higher if the issue price hadn't been a staggering two dollars per coin, the highest initial price for a commemorative half dollar up till that time. (#9309)

Scarce Gem 1935 Hudson Half Dollar

21809 **1935 Hudson MS65 NGC.** A satiny pearl-gray and chestnut tinged Gem, nearly undisturbed by contact, and boldly struck except for the usual incompleteness on Poseidon. The Hudson is one of the lowest mintage Silver Commemorative types. The production is nearly identical to the Hawaiian and Spanish Trail, two other keys to a type collection of the 1892 to 1954 series. (#9312)

21810 **1918 Lincoln MS64 NGC.** Fully lustrous. Pewter gray toning complements the central areas and wisps and blushes of golden-brown and blue ornament the rims. Outstanding quality for the grade. (#9320)

21811 **1936 Long Island—Improperly Cleaned—NCS. UNC Details.** Satiny luster. Toned in an appealing golden-gray shade. If the grade were based exclusively on the presence of contact marks, we are confident that many numismatists would cheerfully assign the MS65 designation. (#9322)

21812 **1936 Lynchburg MS65 NGC.** Fully lustrous and delicately toned in a pleasing blend of gold and gray. Interestingly, Senator Carter Glass of Virginia, who is portrayed on the obverse, was still alive at the time the coin was issued. (#9324)

Gem 1920 Maine Half Dollar

21813 **1920 Maine MS65 NGC.** Pleasing pewter gray toning complements the frosty surfaces. Delicate pink, golden-brown, and lilac iridescent highlights ornament both the obverse and reverse. (#9326)

21814 **1934 Maryland—Improperly Cleaned—NCS. Unc. Details.** Satiny and essentially brilliant with just a whisper of delicate golden-gray iridescence. (#9328)

Scarce 1921 Missouri Half

21815 **1921 Missouri—Improperly Cleaned—NCS. Unc. Details.** Pewter gray toning on frosty surfaces. The presently offered example is typical of many survivors of the issue, which in large measure was distributed to people who desired to celebrate Missouri's Centennial, but who lacked the training that would have benefited them regarding the care of their numismatic treasure. Accordingly, many pieces were tossed in dresser drawers, and ultimately sold to collectors, but as an AU55 to MS60 examples instead of MS65 as would have been the case had appropriate care been provided. (#9330)

Collectible 1921 Missouri 2x4 Half Dollar

21816 **1921 Missouri 2x4—Improperly Cleaned—NCS. Unc. Details.** Lustrous surfaces. Pearl gray iridescence in the central areas deepens to a pleasing gold at the borders. The overall level eye appeal is high, in our opinion, despite the NCS label designation. A scarce variety having a net mintage of just 5,000 pieces. Eagerly sought in all grades. (#9331)

21817 **1938 New Rochelle—Improperly Cleaned—NCS. Unc. Details.** Gunmetal gray toning with pale champagne highlights. Appealing satiny luster. Only 15,266 examples were issued making the New Rochelle half dollar one of the scarcest design types in the commemorative half dollar series. (#9335)

21818 **1936 Norfolk—Improperly Cleaned—NCS. Unc. Details.** Lead gray toning with pale gold highlights. We're confident that many collectors would assign the MS65 designation to this piece if they were to base their grade on the fact that the surfaces are virtually devoid of contact marks. (#9337)

21819 **1926-S Oregon MS64 NGC.** Fully lustrous and essentially brilliant with blushes of golden gray. Considered by many numismatists to be the most beautiful design type in the commemorative half dollar series. The celebrated sculptors James Earle Fraser and Laura Gardin Fraser created the designs. (#9341)

21820 **1928 Oregon—Improperly Cleaned—NCS. Unc. Details.** Warm gray toning with pale gold iridescent highlights. Subdued satiny luster. A few contact marks are noted, but not hairlines as would be consistent with the NCS label designation. (#9342)

21821 **1933-D Oregon MS65 NGC.** Warm golden-gray toning complements lustrous surfaces. Here's a lovely Gem example of one of America's favorite commemorative design types. From a net mintage of on 5,008 examples. (#9343)

21822 **1934-D Oregon—Improperly Cleaned—NCS. Unc. Details.** Pearl gray toning overall with a hint of golden-brown at the obverse rim. There don't appear to be any hairlines due to cleaning as one might expect based on the NCS label designation. (#9344)

21823 **1936-S Oregon MS64 NGC.** Mostly golden-gray toning on lustrous surfaces. Hints of lilac, sea green, and golden brown enhance the obverse border. (#9346)

21824 **1938 Oregon MS65 NGC.** Warm gray toning with faint champagne highlights. A dusting of golden-brown iridescence can be seen at the obverse border. Here's a 20th-century scarcity with a net mintage of just 6,006 pieces. (#9348)

21825 **1938-D Oregon MS66 NGC.** Pleasing golden-gray toning on satiny surfaces. Outstanding both technically and aesthetically. Only 6,005 examples of the variety were issued, and its doubtful that more than just a small percentage of the survivors could match the quality offered here. (#9349)

Outstanding 1938-S Superb Gem Oregon Commemorative

21826 **1938-S Oregon MS67 NGC.** Nearly brilliant surfaces display a few whispers of light tan peripheral patina and vibrant luster. Sharply struck with near pristine surfaces. Census: 100 in 67, 17 finer (12/05). (#9350)

21827 **1939 Oregon MS64 NGC.** Pleasing golden-gray iridescence complements satiny surfaces. Very conservatively graded, in our opinion, as there appear to be scarcely any contact marks on the Indian's torso and legs. Only 3,004 examples of the variety were issued. (#9352)

21828 **1939-D Oregon MS64 NGC.** Fully lustrous and attractively toned in a delicate golden-gray shade. Outstanding quality for the grade with a bare minimum of contact marks. From a tiny original net mintage of just 3,004 pieces. (#9353)

21829 **1939-S Oregon MS63 NGC.** Pearl-gray toning with hints of pale gold. Pleasing satiny luster complements both the obverse and reverse. Only 3,005 examples of the variety were issued. It appears that all were included in PDS sets distributed to numismatists. 1939 marks the final year in the Oregon Trail commemorative series. The Oregon Trail commemorative program had commenced in 1926, and altogether 14 different varieties were issued; those dated 1939 have by far the lowest mintages in the series. (#9354)

Quality Near Gem 1915-S Panama-Pacific Half Dollar

21830 **1915-S Panama-Pacific MS64 NGC.** Rich peripheral russet and olive-green colors bound the gunmetal-gray centers. Not pristine, but very clean for the MS64 level. A crisply struck and satiny souvenir from the 1915 Panama-Pacific Exposition, which also provided the numismatic community with the two famous $50 varieties. A scarce type in better Mint State grades. (#9357)

21831 **1921 Pilgrim—Improperly Cleaned—NCS. Unc. Details.** Sharply struck. Delicate golden-gray toning on satiny surfaces. Scarcer than the 1920 Pilgrim issue, and accordingly more desirable in all grades. (#9360)

Attractive Premium Gem 1936 Rhode Island Commemorative

21832 **1936 Rhode Island MS66 NGC.** Speckles of russet patina visit the peripheries of this lustrous Premium Gem. Well struck, and devoid of significant marks. (#9363)

21833 **1937 Roanoke MS65 NGC.** A satiny and brilliant Gem example. A splash of brown toning on Sir Walter Raleigh's collar is mentioned for accuracy's sake. (#9367)

Attractive 1936-D San Diego Half Dollar, MS67 NGC

21834 **1936-D San Diego MS67 NGC.** Congress approved the coinage of Half Dollars for the San Diego-California-Pacific Exposition on May 3, 1935. Gold and lime-green patination bathes lustrous surfaces that exhibit sharply struck design elements. The surfaces are well preserved throughout. Census: 28 in 67, 1 finer (12/05). (#9372)

21835 **1926 Sesquicentennial MS63 NGC.** Brilliant and satiny. A scattering of tiny contact marks on Washington's cheek accounts for the assigned grade. Issued to commemorate the 150th anniversary of American independence. (#9374)

Low Mintage 1935 Spanish Trail

21836 **1935 Spanish Trail MS64 NGC.** Appealing golden gray toning complements subdued satiny surfaces. Virtually all design features show bold definition. Issued to commemorate the 400th anniversary of a Spanish expedition through Florida, Alabama, Mississippi, Louisiana, and Texas. A famous numismatist of yesteryear, L.W. Hoffecker, created the designs. Only 10,008 examples were issued. (#9376)

21837 **1938 Texas MS64 NGC.** Fully lustrous and attractively toned in a pleasing golden-gray shade. Only 3,780 examples of the variety were issued, almost all of which were included in 1938 Texas PDS sets distributed to coin collectors. (#9394)

21838 **1938-D Texas MS65 NGC.** Fully brilliant with satiny silver luster. An especially attractive example. (#9395)

21839 **1938-S Texas MS65 NGC.** Satiny luster. Both surfaces exhibit pleasing pearl gray toning with pale champagne iridescent highlights. Not easy to find this beautifully preserved. From a tiny net mintage of just 3,814 pieces. (#9396)

21840 **1925 Vancouver—Obverse Improperly Cleaned—NCS. Unc. Details.** Satiny luster. Both surfaces are partially brilliant with blushes of intense golden-brown, electric blue, pewter gray, and lilac. Dr. John McLoughlin, popularly referred to a the "father of Oregon," is depicted on the obverse. Although struck at the San Francisco, the S-mintmark was omitted from the designs. (#9399)

21841 **1927 Vermont MS64 NGC.** Satiny and essentially brilliant with just a whisper of pale gold. Issued to commemorate the Battle of Bennington, one the many clashes that occurred between the Americans and British during the American War for Independence. (#9401)

21842 **1948 Booker T. Washington PDS Set MS65 NGC.** Brilliant Gem examples of each issue, the D and S Mint coins with faint champagne toning. The Denver Mint example grades MS66, the others each grade MS65. (Total: 3 coins) (#9415)

Gem 1949 Booker T. Washington PDS Set NGC-Certified

21843 **1949 Booker T. Washington PDS Set MS65 to MS66 NGC.** The set includes: **1949 MS65,** lustrous and lightly toned, seemingly pristine fields, a decent strike; **1949-D MS66,** boldly struck and lustrous with light speckled coloration; and a **1949-S MS65,** a good strike, pleasing luster, a few small marks on the face. (Total: 3 coins) (#9419)

Well Preserved 1950 B.T.W. Set MS64 to MS66

21844 **1950 Booker T. Washington PDS Set MS64 to MS66 NGC.** The set includes: **1950 MS65,** pale olive-gray and gold toning, a good strike, a few nicks on the obverse; **1950-D MS64,** well struck, lustrous, cream-gray and speckled olive-gold color; and a **1950-S MS66,** crisply struck, lustrous, light alabaster-gray patina. (Total: 3 coins) (#9423)

21845 **1951 Booker T. Washington PDS Set MS65 to MS66 NGC.** The set includes: **1951 MS65,** bright full luster illuminates the lightly toned, carefully preserved surfaces; **1951-D MS66,** creamy color blankets each side, the design features are crisply struck; and a **1951-S MS66,** well struck with creamy-beige toning and nearly immaculate surfaces. The 1951-D and 1951-S have mintages of just 7,000 pieces. (Total: 3 coins) (#9427)

21846 **1951 Washington-Carver PDS Set MS64 to MS65 NGC.** The set includes: **1951 MS65,** well struck, with light pastel toning near the edges, faint die clashing also occurs near the border areas on each side; **1951-D MS65,** satiny and lightly toned, with essentially unmarked surfaces; and a **1951-S MS64,** splendid bright luster, speckled light coloration, a few minor contact marks on the upper reverse and near the obverse center. (Total: 3 coins) (#9433)

21847 **1952 Washington-Carver PDS Set MS64 to MS65 NGC.** The set includes: **1952 MS65,** lightly toned, lustrous, and well preserved, save for a few small marks on the face of G.W. Carver; **1952-D MS64,** a very light degree of pale gold color visits the obverse borders, and a faint layer of speckled olive-gray toning is noted on the reverse; and **1952-S MS64,** whispers of russet color visit lustrous surfaces. All three pieces are well struck and devoid of severe contact marks. (Total: 3 coins) (#9437)

Near-Gem 1953 Washington-Carver PDS Set NGC-Certified

21848 **1953 Washington-Carver PDS Set MS64 NGC.** The set includes: **1953 MS64,** well struck and lustrous, with creamy coloration and a faint pinscratch near the center of the obverse; **1953-D MS64,** boldly struck and lightly toned, with a few small blemishes; and a **1953-S MS64,** lustrous and essentially untoned. (Total: 3 coins) (#9441)

21849 **1954 Washington-Carver PDS Set MS64 NGC.** A nicely matched set of this issue. The Philadelphia issue grades MS64 NGC while the Denver and San Francisco coins each grade MS65 NGC. Brilliant surfaces with frosty luster and pale champagne toning on each of these coins. (Total: 3 coins) (#9445)

COMMEMORATIVE GOLD

Impressive 1903 Jefferson Gold Dollar

21850 **1903 Louisiana Purchase/Jefferson MS65 NGC.** Brilliant and lustrous, with virtually all design features showing bold definition save for the letters HAS in PURCHASE which show striking softness as made. A splash of coppery orange toning is noted at the rim beneath Jefferson's bust. Scarce this beautifully preserved. It appears that most of the mintage ended up in the hands of casual buyers, many of whom had no idea as to the proper way to care for coins. Accordingly, only a small proportion of the original mintage has survived at the MS65 grade level. Envelope Included. (#7443)

Gem 1903 Louisiana Purchase/Jefferson Gold Dollar

21851 **1903 Louisiana Purchase/Jefferson MS65 NGC.** Brilliant, lustrous, and sharply struck. Nice in every way. A splendid Gem example suitable for inclusion in the finest of cabinets. One of the most desirable and eagerly sought issues in the commemorative series at the MS65 level. Envelope Included. (#7443)

Lustrous Gem 1903 Louisiana Purchase/McKinley Gold Dollar

21852 **1903 Louisiana Purchase/McKinley MS65 NGC.** Dazzling cartwheel luster, unmarked surfaces, and a penetrating strike confirm the quality of this impressive Gem. Straw-gold in color with occasional deeper peach-gold tints. The 1903 Louisiana Purchase Gold Dollars were the first Gold Commemoratives, and marked the first use of the Gold Dollar denomination since its retirement in 1889. Surprisingly, the Gold Dollar was the most called upon denomination within the commemorative series until 1918, when the Illinois Centennial set a precedent for the silver Half Dollar. Envelope Included. (#7444)

Gem MS66 Louisiana Purchase Gold Dollar

21853 **1903 Louisiana Purchase/McKinley MS66 NGC.** Sharply struck and essentially brilliant with just a hint of olive iridescence which attests to the originality of this outstanding Gem. The devices are frosty, while the fields are satiny at the centers and frosty at the peripheries. Examples of the variety were sold to visitors at the Louisiana Purchase Exposition in 1904. The famous numismatic dealer and showman Farran Zerbe handled the distribution. Although 17,500 examples of the variety were issued, it's doubtful that more than just a small percentage of the survivors could match the quality offered here. Envelope Included. (#7444)

Scarce Near Gem 1915-S Pan-Pac Gold Dollar

21854 **1915-S Panama-Pacific Gold Dollar MS64 NGC.** A handsome example. Brilliant, frosty, and sharply struck. Nice in every way. Issued to commemorate the completion of the Panama Canal, one of the great engineering marvels of the era, and still of great economic value to the entire world. Envelope Included. (#7449)

Choice 1916 McKinley Gold Dollar

21855 **1916 McKinley MS64 NGC.** A pleasing honey-gold piece that has an especially undisturbed reverse. A solitary mint-made roller mark through McKinley's earlobe denies a higher grade. Although martyred President McKinley had previously been honored on a 1903 Louisiana Purchase Gold Dollar, he was again the subject of remembrance in 1916, with proceeds destined for a birthplace memorial in Niles, Ohio. Envelope Included. (#7454)

Handsome Gem 1922 Grant With Star Dollar

21856 **1922 Grant with Star MS65 NGC.** A satiny and splendidly preserved mustard-yellow Gem, essentially perfect aside from the customary indifference of strike on the tree trunk left of the window. The 1922 Grant Commemorative program was unique in that identical designs were used for two different denominations, the Half Dollar and the Gold Dollar. Both denominations also had two similar varieties, with and without a star above GRANT. The star signified nothing other than to create a further scarce variety to collect, thus increase revenues for the distributors. The issue did continue the recent numismatic practice of the 1921 Alabama and Missouri Commemoratives, both released with low mintage star varieties. Envelope Included. (#7459)

Near-Mint Sesqui Quarter Eagle

21857 **1926 Sesquicentennial AU58 NGC.** Deep, rich color with just a slight amount of cabinet friction. Lustrous with good eye appeal. Envelope Included. (#7466)

Gem Quality 1926 Sesquicentennial Quarter Eagle

21858 **1926 Sesquicentennial MS65 NGC.** This is a delightful Gem with amazing eye appeal and brilliant yellow-gold surfaces and only a few of the slightest abrasions. (#7466)

See the Online Session listings in the back of this volume for additional Reiver selections.

Brilliant, Near-Gem Sesqui Quarter Eagle

21859 **1926 Sesquicentennial MS64 NGC.** The luster is outstanding and much brighter than usually seen for this popular commemorative Quarter Eagle issue. Pleasing shades of rose patina serve to heighten the aesthetic appeal, making this a sure-fire top-of-the-line MS64 coin. (#7466)

CALIFORNIA FRACTIONAL GOLD

21860 **1856 Liberty Octagonal 50 Cents, BG-310, High R.6, MS62 NGC.** Greenish-gold surfaces display well struck design elements. (#10435)

21861 **1852 Liberty Round 50 Cents—Mount Removed—NCS. AU Details. BG-401, R.3, AU50.** Bright yellow-gold surfaces do not appear to be adversely affected by the mount removal. Sharply defined throughout. (#10437)

21862 **1853 Liberty Round 50 Cents—Holed—NCS AU Details. BG-428, R.3.** Multicolored surfaces display two neatly drilled holes in the center. (#10464)

21863 **1854 Liberty Octagonal 1 Dollar—Mount Removed—NCS. AU Details. BG-510, Low R.5.** Mount removed at 12 o'clock. The surfaces are a medium yellow-gold. (#10487)

21864 **1853 Liberty Octagonal 1 Dollar—Reverse Improperly Cleaned—NCS. AU Details. BG-530, R.2.** Orange-gold surfaces display fine reverse hairlines. The design elements are sharply struck throughout. (#10507)

1870 Liberty Head Octagonal Quarter, BG-713

21865 **1870 Liberty Octagonal 25 Cents, BG-713, R.4, MS65 NGC.** Sharply struck, with greenish-gold surfaces that are virtually mark free. (#10540)

21866 **1871 Liberty Octagonal 25 Cents, BG-765, R.3, MS63 NGC.** Bright yellow-gold surfaces are devoid of significant marks, The design elements are adequately struck. (#10592)

21867 **1871 Liberty Octagonal 25 Cents, BG-767, R.3, MS61 NGC.** Orange-gold surfaces display no significant contact marks, but are lightly hairlined. (#10594)

21868 **1876 Indian Octagonal 25 Cents, BG-799, At least High R.6, MS65 NGC.** Sharply defined, with lustrous yellow-gold surfaces. (#10626)

21869 **1880 Indian Octagonal 25 Cents—Edge Damage—NCS Unc Details. BG-799X, R.30.** Yellow-gold surfaces display well struck devices and nice luster. The edge damage is not readily apparent in the holder. (#10650)

21870 **1871 Liberty Round 25 Cents—Mount Removed—NCS. AU Details. BG-813, R.3.** Yellow-gold surfaces reveal evidence of mount removal at 11 o'clock. The coin also appears wavy, or slightly bent. (#10674)

21871 **1871 Liberty Round 25 Cents, BG-813, R.3, MS63 NGC.** Yellow-gold patina bathes lustrous surfaces. The design elements are sharply defined. (#10674)

21872 **1869 Liberty Round 25 Cents—Obverse Planchet Flaw—NCS. AU Details. BG-826.** Yellow-gold surfaces reveal several obverse planchet flakes. The design elements are somewhat weakly struck. (#10687)

21873 **1881 Indian Round 25 Cents, BG-887, R.3, MS64 NGC.** Bright yellow-gold surfaces display sharply defined motifs. Both sides are well preserved. (#10748)

21874 **1873 Liberty Octagonal 50 Cents, BG-915, Low R.4, MS64 NGC.** Reddish-gold surfaces exhibit sharply defined motifs. Both sides are well preserved. Sharp looking coin. (#10773)

21875 **1870 Goofy Head Octagonal 50 Cents—Mount Removed—NCS. AU Details. BG-936, Low R.5.** Yellow-gold surfaces reveal several fissures, voids, and scratches. (#10794)

PATTERNS

Near-Gem 1858 Flying Eagle Cent, Judd-191

21876 **1858 Flying Eagle Cent, Judd-191, Pollock-233-234, R.5, PR64 NGC.** A transitional pattern that combines the regular dies, Small Letters obverse from 1858 with the laurel wreath reverse of 1859. The leaves on the reverse are arranged in clusters of five. Struck in copper-nickel with a plain edge. Deeply mirrored with somewhat streaky reddish-tan surfaces. (#11840)

Small Letters 1858 Flying Eagle Cent Pattern, Judd-192

21877 **1858 Flying Eagle Cent, Judd-192, Pollock-235, R.5, PR64 NGC.** The obverse is the familiar Small Letters 1858 Cent. The pattern reverse generally resembles the 1860 regular issue reverse, but there is no shield at the top and the wreath is closed. On this piece, the obverse lettering is small. This is the more commonly encountered of the two variants. Struck in copper-nickel with a plain edge. Nicely mirrored, the honey-tan surfaces show just the slightest speckling of underlying reddish color. (#11842)

Judd-193 Flying Eagle Cent Pattern With Small Letters, PR62 NGC

21878 **1858 Flying Eagle Cent, Judd-193, Pollock-236, R.5, PR62 NGC.** The obverse is identical to the regular issue 1858 Small Letters cent. The reverse, while similar to that adopted for the Indian cent in 1860, displays a broad, ornamented shield at the top. Again, like the Judd-192 above, this piece was struck from the Small Letters obverse, the more frequently seen variant of this pattern. Struck in copper-nickel with a plain edge. Speckled honey-tan coloration with several larger carbon spots on the obverse. (#11844)

1858 Flying Eagle Cent Pattern Judd-202 Rare Six Leaf Clusters Variety

21879 **1858 Flying Eagle Cent, Judd-202, Pollock-246, PR64 NGC.** Snow-PT20, R.7. Snow states, "A very rare pattern, probably no more than 10 struck in all. These were probably struck after the 6 leaf laurel wreath reverse was adopted in 1859." In other words, PT20 is likely a restrike from muled dies. The variety with six leaf clusters within the laurel wreath, which is much scarcer than the Pollock-245, Snow-PT19 five leaf clusters variety. Struck in copper-nickel with a plain edge. A lovely and well struck golden-brown piece with no relevant post-strike imperfections. (#11867)

Scarce Select 1858 Flying Eagle Cent Pattern Judd-203

21880 **1858 Flying Eagle Cent, Judd-203, Pollock-247, R.5, PR63 NGC.** Snow-PT18. The flying eagle is smaller in scale and differently styled. The reverse features a broad oak wreath without a shield. The layout of legends is similar to the contemporary Flying Eagle Cent. Struck in copper-nickel with a plain edge. This well struck light tan and orange-gold example is pleasing aside from a few carbon flecks. A small spot resides within the C in CENT. Struck from rotated dies. (#11869)

Judd-204 1858 Hook-Neck Eagle Small Cent Pattern, PR64 NGC

21881 **1858 Flying Eagle Cent, Judd-204, Pollock-248, R.5, PR64 NGC.** Flying Eagle pattern with a hook-necked eagle in flight on the obverse. The reverse has an oak wreath with a broad, ornamented shield at the top. Struck in copper-nickel with a plain edge. Rich reddish-brown surfaces with slight blue undertones and no obvious or distracting marks. (#11871)

Beautiful 1858 Flying Eagle Cent Pattern Judd-206

21882 **1858 Flying Eagle Cent, Judd-206, Pollock-242, R.5, PR64 NGC.** Snow-PT16, Die pair 1. The regular issue Low Leaves, Open E (in ONE) reverse is paired with Paquet's smaller (and perhaps more ungainly) flying eagle design. Struck in copper-nickel with a plain edge. Originally sold to select collectors as part of a 12 coin pattern cent set. This lovely piece has subtle orange and steel-blue colors, and the appearance is exemplary to the unaided eye. A couple of wispy obverse hairlines are detected with a loupe. (#11877)

Transitional 1858 Indian Cent Pattern Rare Pollock-254, Snow-PT35 Subvariety

21883 **1858 Indian Cent, Judd-208, Pollock-254, PR63 NGC.** Snow-PT35, R.7. There are four notable subvarieties of Judd-208; these include each combination of narrow or broad bust point obverses paired with either five or six leaf cluster laurel wreath reverses. The present piece pairs the narrow bust point obverse with a six leaf clusters wreath reverse. Struck in copper-nickel with a plain edge. Snow states, "Rare and popular as the true transitional - The exact style of 1859." This well struck light golden-brown specimen is pleasing despite a few faint slide marks on the neck and cheekbone and a tiny spot within the C in CENT. (#11884)

1858 Indian Cent Pattern Judd-211 Pollock-262 Subvariety With Unlisted Obverse Die

21884 **1858 Indian Cent, Judd-211, Pollock-262, PR64 Brown NGC.** Snow-PT26, R.5. The Broad Bust Point subvariety of Judd-211. The Indian Cent obverse of 1859, except dated 1858 and with a broad bust point instead of the issued narrow bust point. The reverse features a broad oak wreath sans shield, the denomination as usual centered within the wreath. Struck in copper-nickel with a plain edge. Snow's Reverse A with a die doubled O in ONE, but the obverse die differs, and it features a slender cud on the rim beneath the date, and a bold die line from the dentils above the left upright of the N in UNITED. A well struck and beautiful golden-brown specimen, nearly perfect aside from the occasional minute carbon spot. (#11892)

1858 Indian Cent Pattern Judd-213 Rare Narrow Bust, Low Leaves Subvariety

21886 **1858 Indian Cent, Judd-213, Pollock-252, PR62 NGC.** Snow-PT30, R.7. Snow writes, "The adopted head used in 1859 and 1860 (Type 1). Much scarcer than the broad bust point combinations. Probably no more than 10 examples struck." The Narrow bust point, low leaves subvariety of Judd-213. The denomination appears to be misaligned, with ONE a little too far to the left above CENT. Struck in copper-nickel with a plain edge. A tall wire rim is present across most of the reverse and on the obverse between 12 and 3 o'clock, and the reverse rim is sharply beveled, as made, between 6 and 9 o'clock, features for study by the specialist. This golden-brown piece is sharply struck but ONE CENT appears lightly hubbed. Several wispy pinscratches across the central reverse limit the grade. (#11897)

Popular 1858 Indian Cent Shield Reverse Judd-212

21885 **1858 Indian Cent, Judd-212, Pollock-263, R.4, PR63 NGC.** Snow-PT25, Die Pair 1. Minute die doubling on the bases of RICA in AMERICA identifies this Broad Bust Point subvariety. The Indian Cent obverse, nearly as issued in 1859. The reverse features an oak wreath and an ornamented shield; ONE CENT as always arranged at the center. Struck in copper-nickel with a plain edge. Light golden-brown in color, this intricately struck example has flashy fields, and is impressive for the grade despite inconspicuous spots on the feather beneath the E in AMERICA and on the middle arrow head. (#11895)

Choice 1865 Three Cent Nickel Prototype Judd-410

21887 **1865 Three Cent Nickel, Judd-410, Pollock-481, Low R.6, PR64 NGC.** Very similar to the adopted design, the most obvious difference being in the width of the ribbon ends, which reach the dentils. Struck in nickel with a plain edge. 1865 is the scarcest date in the proof Three Cent Nickel series, but its lesser known pattern predecessor is even more elusive. This mildly reflective pearl-gray near-Gem has a needle-sharp strike and clean surfaces. (#60591)

Rarely Seen 1942 Cent Pattern, Pollock-2075

21888 **1942 "One Cent" Pattern, Judd-2056, Pollock-2075, R.8 (?), MS61 NGC.** An experimental piece that was struck in various metals at the mint and in various plastics by private firms as a possible replacement for copper, tin, and nickel which were needed in World War II. The obverse design was apparently copied from the Columbian two centavo and the reverse from a Washington medalet (Baker-155). Struck in white metal, possibly the piece reported by Pollock as manganese. Struck with a plain edge. Deep gray patina overall with golden accents scattered about. Again, lightly hairlined.

Rare 1942 Cent Pattern, Pollock-2075

21889 **1942 "One Cent" Pattern, Judd-2056, Pollock-2075, R.8 (?), MS61 NGC.** Same design, composition, and plain edge as the piece above. Dull gray surfaces and lightly hairlined.

Interesting 1942 Cent Pattern

21890 **1942 "One Cent" Pattern, Judd-2065, Pollock-4005, Low R.7, MS60 Uncertified—Broken in Two Pieces.** Same design and plain edge as the pieces above. Seen here struck in transparent amber plastic.

Bakelite Composition Cent Pattern, Judd-2067

21891 **1942 "One Cent" Pattern, Judd-2067, unlisted in Pollock, Low R.7, MS63 NGC.** Same design and plain edge as the pieces above. Seen here struck in bakelite. Deep cobalt-charcoal coloration with a few surface imperfections noted with magnification.

Brown Plastic 1942 Cent Pattern, Judd-2060

21892 **1942 "One Cent" Pattern, Judd-2060, unlisted in Pollock, Low R.7, MS66 NGC.** Same design and plain edge as the piece(s) above, but seen here struck in brown plastic. The surfaces have the appearance of milk chocolate and there are no obvious surface impairments.

Interesting General Motors Pattern Cent

21893 **Undated (ca. 1967) General Motors Pattern Cent, Pollock-4060, R.5. MS64 Brown NGC.** An experimental striking on the General Motors roller press with the head of Liberty facing left on the obverse, a wreath on the reverse, and nonsensical devices on each side. Control code 7-M. Struck in copper with a plain edge. Smooth, glossy brown surfaces with some darker color around the devices. Envelope Included.

1964 INCO Quarter Dollar, Pollock-5365

21896 **1964 International Nickel Company Quarter Dollar, Pollock-5365, R.6 (?), MS63 NGC.** An apparent second example of this INCO pattern quarter that appears to be struck in copper-nickel on a copper core. However, the insert has the enigmatic attribution of P-F721. A few specks of color are seen on each side of this otherwise dazzling, brilliant private pattern. Envelope Included.

Gem GM Pattern Cent, Pollock-4060

21894 **Undated (ca. 1967) General Motors Pattern Cent, Pollock-4060, R.5. MS65 Red and Brown NGC.** A second example of these interesting experimental pieces. This one has control code 34-M. A splendid Gem example with rich cherry-red and deep blue coloration. Envelope Included.

Silicon Alloy 1964 Quarter Dollar Pattern, Pollock-5380

21897 **1964 International Nickel Company Quarter Dollar, Pollock-5380, R.8 (?), MS64 NGC.** Same design and also struck with a reeded edge. However, this piece is a nickel-silicon composition. Bright and semi-reflective with a small spot on Merica's temple. Envelope Included.

Inco Quarter Dollar Pattern, Pollock-5365

21895 **1964 International Nickel Company Quarter Dollar, Pollock-5365, R.6 (?), MS63 NGC.** Designed by Gilroy Roberts, the obverse has a likeness of Paul D. Merica in the center with his name above and LABORATORY below. The reverse shows a view of the INCO laboratory as photographed by Kenn Henderson around 1964. Immediately above is DEDICATED and below 1964. The peripheral legends read: INTERNATIONAL NICKEL COMPANY INC. Struck in copper-nickel over a copper core with a reeded edge. Very bright with just a trace of haziness.d Envelope Included.

Important Dupont Indian Chief Test Piece, P-5389

21898 **(1964) Pattern Quarter Dollar. Pollock-5389, R.7. MS63 NGC.** Indian Chief design, above, OHI—YESA. The reverse has a ship in full sail with the legend TREASURE ISLAND DOUBLOON. Apparently part of the DuPont testing for a suitable alloy, in this case silver bonded to a copper core and certainly similar to the "clad" Kennedy half dollars issued from 1965 to 1970. Reflective bright silver surfaces. Envelope Included.

See the Online Session listings in the back of this volume for additional Reiver selections.

Rare DuPont Silver-Clad Test Piece

21899 **(1964) Pattern Quarter Dollar. P-5389, R.7. MS64 NGC.** Indian Chief design. Another example of the DuPont test piece in silver-clad alloy, prepared for the Government's consideration. Attractive with reflective surfaces and hints of light gold toning. Envelope Included.

Probably Unique DuPont Explosion Bonded Detaclad Ingot

21900 **Undated (ca. 1964) DuPont Detaclad Ingot.** An ingot of DuPont's "Explosion Bonded Detaclad" that was used to produce that company's experimental alloy trial pieces. The ingot measures 54 x 30 x 12 mm and has three layers. The layers appear to be brass, nickel, and bronze, but frankly, this is just a guess. The wording EXPLOSION BONDED DETACLAD is also seen on the few pattern coins produced by DuPont. Most likely a unique item. Accompanied by an envelope from Jules with the enigmatic notes: D-1 / group 2 / 5. Jules is cited as one of two persons, the other being Kenn Henderson, on page 447 of Pollock's reference who had information about these pieces.

Circa 1964 DuPont Quarter Pattern

21901 **Undated (ca. 1964) DuPont Pattern Quarter Dollar, Pollock-5391, R.2-3, MS64 NGC.** Head of Benjamin Franklin facing left on the obverse, surrounded by 1706 BENJAMIN FRANKLIN 1790. The reverse has the DuPont logo in the center and is surrounded by THIS TOKEN MADE FROM EXPLOSION BONDED "DETACLAD". Struck with a 25% nickel alloy bonded to a copper core with a plain edge. Untoned with a light haziness. Envelope Included. (#661000)

Scarce DuPont Quarter Pattern

21902 **Undated (ca. 1964) DuPont Pattern Quarter Dollar, Pollock-5391, R.2-3, MS65 NGC.** A second example of this seldom-offered modern pattern. Lightly toned with the same haziness as the MS64 piece above. Envelope Included.

Gem DuPont Pattern, Pollock-5391

21903 **Undated (ca. 1964) DuPont Pattern Quarter Dollar, Pollock-5391, R.2-3, MS65 NGC.** A hazy, lightly toned example that shows a bit of semi-prooflikeness in the fields. Envelope Included.

Semi-Reflective DuPont Pattern Pollock-5391

21904 **Undated (ca. 1964) DuPont Pattern Quarter Dollar, Pollock-5391, R.2-3, MS64 NGC.** Same composition and plain edge as the pieces above. This is a lovely, high grade example with flashy semi-reflective fields. Envelope Included.

Copper Alloy Dupont Test Piece, J-5393

21905 **(1964) Pattern Quarter Dollar. P-5393, R.7. MS62 Red and Brown NGC.** Plain edge. This is similar to the other DuPont pieces, but in a composition of 4% nickel and 96% copper, according to notes provided to Andrew Pollock by Jules Reiver. Essentially full red in color with some mellowing on the devices, and with a number of tiny spots on each side. The actual rarity of this issue is not known, but Jules Reiver had two of these in his collection, both being offered in this sale. Envelope Included.

Rare Copper Alloy Dupont Test Piece

21906 **(1964) Pattern Quarter Dollar. P-5393, R.7. MS62 Red and Brown NGC.** Struck by medalist August Frank of Philadelphia for the DuPont Corporation. DuPont was clearly interested in being a supplier of new alloy for the non-silver coinage under consideration, but was not a coining facility of and by itself. Light brown toning over considerable original red color. Heavy corrosion is visible, especially on the reverse. Envelope Included.

Superb Gould Inc. Washington Dollar Pattern

21907 **Undated (ca.1977) George Washington Dollar, Pollock-5445, R.7. MS67 NGC.** A Gould Incorporated privately minted pattern dollar. The obverse is attractively designed with a bust of Washington and the Washington Monument and above is GOULD INCORPORATED / TITANIUM. The reverse has the Great Seal of the United States. Struck in titanium with a plain edge. Brilliant throughout with exceptionally well-preserved surfaces. Envelope Included.

CONFEDERATE STATES OF AMERICA

Popular 1861 C.S.A. Haseltine Restrike Cent

21908 **1861 Confederate States of America Restrike PR62 Brown NGC.** Breen-8008. Restrike C.S.A. Cents were offered by Capt. John W. Haseltine in early 1874. According to Haseltine, the dies were authorized by the Confederacy and made by noted engraver Robert Lovett, Jr. in 1861. Fearful of having committed treason, Lovett kept his involvement with the project a secret until he accidentally spent one of the few struck cents at a bar in late 1873. The Confederate Cent found its way to Haseltine, who procured the original dies from Lovett and produced restrikes. Nearly a century later, Robert Bashlow obtained the dies, which were by then defaced, and struck further pieces. The present piece is a Haseltine and not a Bashlow striking, since the dies are perfect. This crisply struck example has faded orange-red borders and milky olive-brown and steel-blue centers. Four small spots on the obverse field decide the grade. Listed on page 375 of the 2006 *Guide Book*. Envelope Included. (#340405)

MISCELLANEOUS

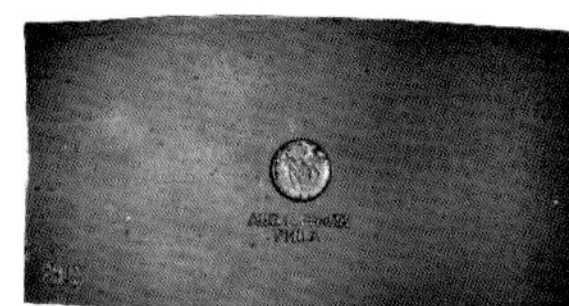

Bashlow Restrike Impressions Set in a Block of Copper

21909 **1861 Confederate States of America Obverse and Reverse Restrikes. Restruck by Robert Bashlow. Bronze.** Breen-8013. Obverse and reverse die impressions are set in a large bronze or copper block. Produced by August C. Frank, a Philadelphia medallist, whose imprint, name, and location are located on the back of the block. Undoubtedly a unique numismatic item.

End of Session Six

VOLUME II ONLINE SESSION

Internet and Mail Bid Auction Only #391 • No Floor Session
Online bidding closes Monday, January 30, 2006 • 6 PM – 10 PM CT • Lots 28698-29366

SPECIAL INTERNET BIDDING FEATURE

Lots in our Online Sessions close at different times. Since each lot closes individually over a continuous period of time, from 6 PM until 10 PM CT, you can bid on each lot as you can in a live auction.

Visit **HeritageGalleries.com/Coins** to view full-color images and bid.

A 15% Buyer's Premium ($9 minimum) Will Be Added To All Lots.

FLYING EAGLE CENTS

28698 1857—Improperly Cleaned—NCS. Unc. Details.

28699 1858 Small Letters—Improperly Cleaned—NCS. Unc. Details.

28700 1858 Small Letters AU58 NGC.

INDIAN CENTS

28701 1860—Improperly Cleaned—NCS. Unc. Details.

28702 1860 MS62 NGC.

28703 1862 MS61 NGC.

28704 1863—Improperly Cleaned—NCS. Unc. Details.

28705 1864 Bronze No L—Improperly Cleaned—NCS. Unc. Details.

28706 1864 Bronze No L—Improperly Cleaned—NCS. Unc. Details.

28707 1864 L On Ribbon—Improperly Cleaned—NCS. AU Details.

28708 1865 Plain 5 MS64 Brown NGC.

28709 1866—Improperly Cleaned—NCS. Unc. Details.

28710 1868—Improperly Cleaned—NCS. Unc. Details.

28711 1871—Improperly Cleaned—NCS. AU Details.

28712 1874—Altered Color—NCS. Proof.

28713 1875—Improperly Cleaned—NCS. Unc. Details.

28714 1876—Altered Color—NCS. Unc. Details.

28715 1878—Improperly Cleaned—NCS. Unc. Details.

28716 1879—Improperly Cleaned—NCS. Unc. Details.

28717 1880—Improperly Cleaned—NCS. Unc. Details.

28718 1881—Improperly Cleaned—NCS. Unc. Details.

28719 1883—Improperly Cleaned—NCS. Unc. Details.

28720 1883 MS62 Brown NGC.

28721 1884—Improperly Cleaned—NCS. Unc. Details.

28722 1885—Improperly Cleaned—NCS. Impaired Proof.

28723 1887—Altered Color—NCS. Unc. Details.

28724 1888—Altered Color—NCS. AU Details.

28725 1889—Altered Color—NCS. Unc. Details.

28726 1891—Altered Color—NCS. Unc. Details.

28727 1892—Altered Color—NCS. Unc. Details.

28728 1893—Altered Color—NCS. Unc. Details.

28729 1894—Altered Color—NCS. Unc. Details.

28730 1896—Altered Color—NCS. Unc. Details.

28731 1898—Altered Color—NCS. Unc. Details.

28732 1899—Altered Color—NCS. Unc. Details.

28733 1900—Altered Color—NCS. Impaired Proof.

28734 1901—Altered Color—NCS. Unc. Details.

28735 1901—Improperly Cleaned—NCS. Unc. Details.

28736 1902—Altered Color—NCS. Unc. Details.

28737 1905—Altered Color—NCS. Unc. Details.

28738 1907—Altered Color—NCS. Unc. Details.

28739 1908—Altered Color—NCS. Unc. Details.

28740 1909—Altered Color—NCS. Unc. Details.

28741 1909-S—Altered Color—Brown NCS. Unc. Details.

Please visit HeritageGalleries.com to view other collectibles auctions.
See the Online Auction listings in the backs of Volumes I and III for additional Reiver selections.

LINCOLN CENTS

28742 1909 VDB—Altered Color—NCS. Unc. Details.

28743 1909 MS64 Red and Brown NGC.

28744 1910 MS64 Red and Brown NGC.

28745 1911-D—Reverse Corroded—NCS. Unc. Details.

28746 1912-D MS63 Red and Brown NGC.

28747 1912-S MS63 Brown NGC.

28748 1913 MS63 Red and Brown NGC.

28749 1914—Altered Color—NCS. Unc. Details.

28750 1915-D MS63 Red and Brown NGC.

28751 1916—Altered Color—NCS. Unc. Details.

28752 1916-D—Improperly Cleaned—NCS. Unc. Details.

28753 1918 MS64 Brown NGC.

28754 1918-D—Altered Color—NCS. Unc. Details.

28755 1918-S MS63 Brown NGC.

28756 1919 MS64 Red NGC.

28757 1919-S MS63 Brown NGC.

28758 1920 MS63 Red and Brown NGC.

28759 1921—Altered Color—NCS. Unc. Details.

28760 1922-D—Altered Color—NCS. Unc. Details.

28761 1923 MS63 Red and Brown NGC.

28762 1923-S—Improperly Cleaned—NCS. AU Details.

28763 1924 MS65 Red and Brown NGC.

28764 1925-D MS62 Red and Brown NGC.

28765 1926 MS63 Red and Brown NGC.

28766 1927 MS63 Red and Brown NGC.

28767 1928-D—Altered Color—NCS. Unc. Details.

28768 1928-S—Altered Color—NCS. Unc. Details.

28769 1929-D MS64 Red and Brown NGC.

28770 1929-S MS63 Red and Brown NGC.

28771 1933 MS65 Red and Brown NGC.

28772 1937 PR63 Red and Brown NGC.

28773 1938 PR63 Red and Brown NGC.

28774 1939 PR64 Red and Brown NGC.

THREE CENT SILVER

28775 1851—Improperly Cleaned—NCS. Unc. Details.

28776 1853—Damaged—NCS. Good Details.

28777 1853—Bent—NCS. AU Details.

28778 1853 MS62 NGC.

28779 1854—Bent—NCS. Unc. Details.

28780 1854 AU50 NGC.

28781 1854 AU58 NGC.

28782 1859—Improperly Cleaned—NCS. VF Details.

28783 1859—Improperly Cleaned—NCS. AU Details.

28784 1859 AU55 NGC.

28785 1860—Bent—NCS. Unc. Details.

28786 1861—Bent—NCS. Unc. Details.

28787 1861—Bent—NCS. VF Details.

28788 1861 AU55 NGC.

28789 1862—Damaged, Improperly Cleaned—NCS. XF Details.

THREE CENT NICKELS

28790 1865—Improperly Cleaned—NCS. VF Details.

28791 1865 AU58 NGC.

28792 1867 AU58 NGC.

28793 1870—Reverse Corroded—NCS. Unc. Details.

28794 1872—Improperly Cleaned—NCS. AU Details.

28795 1872 MS63 NGC.

28796 1875—Corroded—NCS. Unc. Details.

28797 1881—Improperly Cleaned—NCS. AU Details.

PROOF LIBERTY NICKELS

28798 1904 PR64 NGC.

28799 1905 PR63 NGC.

28800 1906 PR62 NGC.

28801 1907 PR63 NGC.

28802 1908 PR64 NGC.

28803 1912 PR64 NGC.

BUFFALO NICKELS

28804 1913-D Type One AU58 NGC.

28805 1915-D—Improperly Cleaned—NCS. AU Details.

28806 1923—Improperly Cleaned—NCS. AU Details.

28807 1930 MS64 NGC.

28808 1934 MS62 NGC.

28809 1936-D MS65 NGC.

SEATED HALF DIMES

28810 1837 Small Date (Flat Top 1)—Improperly Cleaned—NCS. VF Details.

28811 1837 Small Date (Flat Top 1) AU53 NGC.

28812 1838 Large Stars—Damaged—NCS. AU Details.

28813 1838 Large Stars—Damaged—NCS.XF Details.

28814 1838 Large Stars—Environmental Damage—NCS. Unc. Details.

28815 1838 Large Stars VF35 NGC.

28816 1838 Large Stars XF45 NGC.

28817 1839 No Drapery—Environmental Damage—NCS. AU Details.

28818 1839 No Drapery—Environmental Damage—NCS. AU Details.

28819 1839 No Drapery XF40 NGC.

28820 1840 No Drapery—Improperly Cleaned—NCS. AU Details.

28821 1840 No Drapery XF45 NGC.

28822 1840-O No Drapery AU50 NGC.

28823 1840-O No Drapery XF45 NGC.

28824 1840 Drapery XF45 NGC.

28825 1840 Drapery—Bent—NCS. VF Details.

28826 1840-O Drapery VF25 NGC.

28827 1841—Improperly Cleaned—NCS. Fine Details.

28828 1841-O—Damaged—NCS. VF Details.

28829 1841-O XF40 NGC.

28830 1842-O—Improperly Cleaned—NCS. VF Details.

28831 1842-O—Corroded—NCS. XF Details.

28832 1843 F15 NGC.

28833 1843 VF35 NGC.

28834 1843 AU58 NGC.

28835 1843 AU58 NGC.

28836 1844 AU55 NGC.

28837 1845—Damaged—NCS. VF Details.

28838 1845 VF20 NGC.

28839 1845 XF40 NGC.

28840 1845 AU55 NGC.

28841 1845 AU55 NGC.

28842 1845 AU55 NGC.

28843 1847 —Improperly Cleaned—NCS. VG Details.

28844 1847 VF30 NGC.

28845 1848 Medium Date XF45 NGC.

28846 1848 Medium Date AU55 NGC.

28847 1848-O—Environmental Damage, Damaged—NCS. VF Details.

28848 1849—Environmental Damage—NCS. XF Details.

28849 1849—Damaged—NCS. XF Details.

28850 1849—Obverse Improperly Cleaned—NCS. AU Details.

28851 1849/8/6 VF35 NGC.

28852 1849/8 VF25 NGC.

28853 1850—Whizzed—NCS. XF Details.

28854 1850 XF40 NGC.

28855 1850 AU55 NGC.

28856 1850 MS62 NGC.

28857 1851 F12 NGC.

28858 1851 XF40 NGC.

28859 1851 AU55 NGC.

28860 1851-O F12 NGC.

28861 1851-O—Scratched—NCS. XF Details.

28862 1852—Damaged—NCS. VF Details.

28863 1852—Obverse Damaged—NCS. XF Details.

28864 1852—Bent—NCS. Unc. Details.

28865 1853-O Arrows AU58 NGC.

28866 1854 Arrows MS61 NGC.

28867 1855 Arrows MS61 NGC.

28868 1857—Scratched Obverse—NCS. AU Details.

28869 1859—Improperly Cleaned—NCS. XF Details.

28870 1861 AU58 NGC.

28871 1862—Environmental Damage—NCS. AU Detaill.

28872 1868-S—Scratched Reverse—NCS. XF Details.

28873 1869-S—Improperly Cleaned—NCS. AU Details.

28874 1870—Improperly Cleaned—NCS. Unc. Details.

28875 1871—Improperly Cleaned—NCS. AU Details.

28876 1872-S Mintmark Below Bow—Improperly Cleaned—NCS. AU Details.

SEATED DIMES

28877 1840 No Drapery AU53 NGC.

28878 1840 Drapery VF20 NGC.

28879 1845 XF45 NGC.

28880 1850—Reverse Scratched—NCS. AU Details.

28881 1852 XF45 NGC.

28882 1855 Arrows AU55 NGC.

28883 1858-O—Polished—NCS. XF Details.

28884 1859-S—Improperly Cleaned, Bent—NCS. VG Details.

28885 1861-S VF20 NGC.

28886 1862-S—Damaged—NCS. F Details.

28887 1867-S F12 NGC.

28888 1873 Arrows—Obverse Improperly Cleaned—NCS. XF Details.

28889 1873-S Arrows—Improperly Cleaned—NCS. AU Details.

28890 1874-S Arrows—Improperly Cleaned—NCS. F Details.

28891 1875—Obverse Improperly Cleaned—NCS. AU Details.

28892 1875-S Mintmark Above Bow AU58 NGC.

28893 1876—Improperly Cleaned—NCS. AU Details.

28894 1876-CC—Improperly Cleaned—NCS. AU Details.

28895 1876-S AU55 NGC.

28896 1877—Improperly Cleaned—NCS. AU Details.

28897 1877-CC—Improperly Cleaned—NCS. AU Details.

28898 1877-S—Damaged—NCS. XF Details.

28899 1883 AU58 NGC.

28900 1886—Improperly Cleaned—NCS. AU Details.

28901 1887—Environmental Damage—NCS. XF Details.

28902 1888 AU58 NGC.

28903 1888-S—Improperly Cleaned—NCS. XF Details.

28904 1889 AU58 NGC.

28905 1889-S VF35 NGC.

BARBER DIMES

28906 1894-O VG8 NGC.

28907 1895-O G6 NGC.

28908 1895-S VF20 NGC.

28909 1896 XF45 NGC.

28910 1896-O G4 NGC.

28911 1896-S G4 NGC.

28912 1897-S F15 NGC.

28913 1898 MS63 NGC.

28914 1898-O VF25 NGC.

28915 1898-S AU55 NGC.

28916 1899 AU55 NGC.

28917 1899-O—Improperly Cleaned—NCS. Unc. Details.

28918 1899-S AU58 NGC.

28919 1900-O—Improperly Cleaned—NCS. XF Details.

28920 1901 AU58 NGC.

28921 1901-S G6 NGC.

28922 1902 AU58 NGC.

28923 1902-O MS61 NGC.

28924 1902-S AU58 NGC.

28925 1903 AU58 NGC.

28926 1903-S—Reverse Improperly Cleaned—NCS. Good Details.

28927 1905—Improperly Cleaned—NCS. AU Details.

28928 1905-S MS62 NGC.

28929 1907 MS62 NGC.

28930 1907-S—Improperly Cleaned—NCS. AU Details.

28931 1911-S—Improperly Cleaned—NCS. AU Details.

28932 1912 MS63 NGC.

28933 1913-S F15 NGC.

28934 1914—Environmental Damage—NCS. Unc. Details.

28935 1914-D MS65 NGC.

28936 1915 MS62 NGC.

28937 1916 MS63 NGC.

MERCURY DIMES

28938 1916 MS64 Full Bands NGC.

28939 1917—Improperly Cleaned—NCS. Unc. Details.

28940 1917-S MS61 NGC.

28941 1918 MS64 Full Bands NGC.

28942 1918-D—Improperly Cleaned—NCS. Unc. Details.

28943 1918-S MS62 NGC.

28944 1919-S—Damaged—NCS. AU Details.

28945 1920 MS65 NGC.

28946 1921-D—Improperly Cleaned—NCS. VG Details.

28947 1923 MS62 Full Bands NGC.

28948 1924 MS63 NGC.

28949 1925 MS64 Full Bands NGC.

28950 1926 MS64 Full Bands NGC.

28951 1927-D XF45 NGC.

28952 1929-D—Improperly Cleaned—NCS. Unc. Details.

28953 1929-S MS65 NGC.

28954 1930 MS65 NGC.

28955 1930-S MS64 NGC.

28956 1931 MS64 NGC.

28957 1931-D MS64 NGC.

28958 1931-S MS64 NGC.

28959 1935-D MS65 NGC.

28960 1937-S MS65 Full Bands NGC.

28961 1938 MS65 Full Bands NGC.

28962 1938-D MS65 NGC.

28963 1943-S MS65 Full Bands NGC.

TWENTY CENT PIECES

28964 1875—Damaged—NCS. AU Details.

28965 1875—Polished—NCS. Proof.

28966 1875-CC VG10 NGC.

28967 1875-CC VF25 NGC.

28968 1875-S—Improperly Cleaned—NCS. XF Details.

28969 1875-S VG10 NGC.

28970 1875-S—Improperly Cleaned—NCS. VG Details.

28971 1875-S—Obverse Damaged—NCS. AU Details.

28972 1875-S—Improperly Cleaned—NCS. VF Details.

28973 1875-S—Environmental Damage—NCS. Fine Details.

28974 1875-S—Improperly Cleaned—NCS. Fine Details.

28975 1875-S—Obverse Improperly Cleaned—NCS. Fine Details.

28976 1875-S—Damaged—NCS. Fine Details.

28977 1875-S/S MPD F12 NGC.

28978 1875-S/S MPD F15 NGC.

28979 1875-S/S MPD VF20 NGC.

28980 1875-S/S MPD VF20 NGC.

SEATED QUARTERS

28981 1841—Obverse Improperly Cleaned—NCS. XF Details.

28982 1843—Improperly Cleaned—NCS. XF Details.

28983 1845 AU50 NGC.

28984 1849—Improperly Cleaned—NCS. VF Details.

28985 1851—Improperly Cleaned—NCS. VF Details.

28986 1853 Arrows and Rays XF45 NGC.

28987 1854 Arrows—Improperly Cleaned—NCS. AU Details.

28988 1855-O Arrows—Improperly Cleaned—NCS. VF Details.

28989 1856-O—Improperly Cleaned—NCS. XF Details.

28990 1857—Improperly Cleaned—NCS. Unc. Details.

28991 1857—Damaged—NCS. AU Details.

28992 1857-O—Reverse Damage—NCS. XF Details.

28993 1857-S—Damaged—NCS. Fine Details.

28994 1859—Damaged—NCS. AU Details.

28995 1859-S—Damaged—NCS. Good Details.

28996 1861 XF45 NGC.

28997 1865-S—Obverse Damaged—NCS. Fine Details.

28998 1868-S—Improperly Cleaned—NCS. Fine Details.

28999 1869 AG3 NGC.

29000 1870 VF25 NGC.

29001 1872 XF45 NGC.

29002 1873 Open 3 VG8 NGC.

29003 1873-S Arrows VF35 NGC.

29004 1875-S—Improperly Cleaned—NCS. VF Details.

29005 1876-S—Improperly Cleaned—NCS. Unc. Details.

29006 1877-S XF45 NGC.

29007 1891-S AU50 NGC.

BARBER QUARTERS

29008 1892—Improperly Cleaned—NCS. Unc. Details.

29009 1893—Improperly Cleaned—NCS. Unc. Details.

29010 1894-O VG8 NGC.

29011 1895-S G4 NGC.

29012 1896-O VG8 NGC.

29013 1897-O VG10 NGC.

29014 1897-S G4 NGC.

29015 1898-O VG8 NGC.

29016 1898-S VG8 NGC.

29017 1899 VF35 NGC.

29018 1899-O—Environmental Damage—NCS. VF Details.

29019 1899-S—Glue Residue—NCS. VF Details.

29020 1900-O VF35 NGC.

29021 1901 VF25 NGC.

29022 1901-O VG10 NGC.

29023 1902—Improperly Cleaned—NCS. AU Details.

29024 1902-O VF30 NGC.

29025 1902-S G6 NGC.

29026 1903-O VG8 NGC.

29027 1903-S VG10 NGC.

29028 1904-O F15 NGC.

29029 1905 AU58 NGC.

29030 1905-O VG8 NGC.

29031 1905-S VG8 NGC.

29032 1906—Obverse Damaged—NCS. XF Details.

29033 1906-D VF20 NGC.

29034 1906-O VF20 NGC.

29035 1907 AU58 NGC.

29036 1907-D—Improperly Cleaned—NCS. VG Details.

29037 1907-O VG8 NGC.

29038 1907-S VG10 NGC.

29039 1908—Obverse Improperly Cleaned—NCS. Unc. Details.

29040 1908-S F12 NGC.

29041 1909—Improperly Cleaned—NCS. Unc. Details.

29042 1909-D AU58 NGC.

29043 1909-O G6 NGC.

29044 1909-S—Environmental Damage—NCS. AU Details.

29045 1910 AU58 NGC.

29046 1910-D VG10 NGC.

29047 1911 VF25 NGC.

29048 1911-S VG8 NGC.

29049 1914 AU55 NGC.

29050 1914-S AG3 NGC.

29051 1915 AU58 NGC.

29052 1915-D—Environmental Damage—NGC. Unc. Details.

STANDING LIBERTY QUARTERS

29053 1917-D Type Two—Improperly Cleaned—NCS. AU Details.

29054 1918-S XF45 NGC.

29055 1918-S—Improperly Cleaned—NCS. AU Details.

29056 1920 MS62 NGC.

29057 1920-D—Improperly Cleaned—NCS. AU Details.

29058 1924 MS62 NGC.

29059 1924-S AU53 NGC.

29060 1926-S XF45 NGC.

When available, the original Reiver storage envelope is included with each lot.

29061 1927-D MS63 NGC.

29062 1927-S VF25 NGC.

29063 1928 MS62 NGC.

WASHINGTON QUARTERS

29064 1934 Light Motto MS63 NGC.

29065 1935-S MS64 NGC.

29066 1936-S MS63 NGC.

29067 1938 MS65 NGC.

29068 1939 PR65 NGC.

29069 1939-D MS65 NGC.

29070 1940 PR62 NGC.

29071 1940-D MS64 NGC.

29072 1940-S MS65 NGC.

29073 1941 PR64 NGC.

29074 1941-D MS65 NGC.

29075 1941-S MS65 NGC.

29076 1942 PR66 NGC.

29077 1950 PR65 NGC.

29078 1951 PR64 NGC.

29079 1952 PR67 NGC.

29080 1953 PR68 NGC.

29081 1954 PR66 Cameo NGC.

29082 1955 PR67 NGC.

29083 1956 PR66 NGC.

29084 1957 PR67 NGC.

29085 1958 PR66 NGC.

29086 1959 PR65 NGC.

29087 1960 PR68 NGC.

29088 1960 PR64 NGC.

29089 1961 PR66 NGC.

29090 1962 PR68 NGC.

29091 1963 PR66 NGC.

29092 1964—PVC Damage—NCS. Proof.

SEATED HALF DOLLARS

29093 1842-O Medium Date, Large Letters XF45 NGC.

29094 1844-O XF45 NGC.

29095 1845—Improperly Cleaned—NCS. AU Details.

29096 1846 Tall Date—Environmental Damage—NCS. Unc. Details.

29097 1846-O Medium Date—Improperly Cleaned—NCS. AU Details.

29098 1850-O—Improperly Cleaned—NCS. XF Details.

29099 1854 Arrows—Improperly Cleaned—NCS. AU Details.

29100 1856—Improperly Cleaned—NCS. AU Details.

29101 1856—Improperly Cleaned—NCS. AU Details.

29102 1856-S—Reverse Tooled—NCS. XF Details.

29103 1857 XF40 NGC.

29104 1858—Improperly Cleaned—NCS. AU Details.

29105 1858-O—Improperly Cleaned—NCS. Unc. Details.

29106 1859—Improperly Cleaned—NCS. AU Details.

29107 1859-O—Improperly Cleaned—NCS. XF Details.

29108 1860-O VF35 NGC.

29109 1861 —Improperly Cleaned—NCS. AU Details.

29110 1863—Improperly Cleaned—NCS. XF Details.

29111 1863-S—Improperly Cleaned—NCS. XF Details.

29112 1864-S VF35 NGC.

29113 1865-S VF30 NGC.

29114 1866 Motto—Polished—NCS. XF Details.

29115 1868 F15 NGC.

29116 1870 VG8 NGC.

29117 1871—Improperly Cleaned—NCS. XF Details.

29118 1872—Improperly Cleaned—NCS. VF Details.

29119 1873 Closed 3, No Arrows—Improperly Cleaned—NCS. XF Details.

29120 1873 Arrows—Obverse Damage—NCS. Good Details.

29121 1873-S Arrows F12 NGC.

29122 1875-CC—Improperly Cleaned—NCS. VF Details.

29123 1876—Improperly Cleaned, PVC Damage—NCS. AU Details.

29124 1876-S—Improperly Cleaned—NCS. XF Details.

29125 1877 XF45 NGC.

29126 1878—Improperly Cleaned—NCS. Good Details.

BARBER HALF DOLLARS

29127 1892—Improperly Cleaned—NCS. VF Details.

29128 1893-O—Improperly Cleaned—NCS. AU Details.

29129 1894 VG8 NGC.

29130 1894-O—Improperly Cleaned—NCS. VF Details.

29131 1895 VG10 NGC.

29132 1895-S VF20 NGC.

29133 1896—Improperly Cleaned—NCS. XF Details.

29134 1896-O VG8 NGC.

29135 1897—Damaged—NCS. Fine Details.

29136 1897-O VG8 NGC.

29137 1898 VF35 NGC.

29138 1899 AU50 NGC.

29139 1899-O XF45 NGC.

29140 1900 XF45 NGC.

29141 1901 F12 NGC.

29142 1901-O—Improperly Cleaned—NCS. Fine Details.

29143 1901-S—Improperly Cleaned—NCS. VF Details.

29144 1902 AU53 NGC.

29145 1902-O—Improperly Cleaned—NCS. XF Details.

29146 1902-S—Polished—NCS. XF Details.

29147 1903 VG8 NGC.

29148 1904—Reverse Damaged—NCS. AU Details.

29149 1904-O VG8 NGC.

29150 1905-O VG8 NGC.

29151 1905-S VF20 NGC.

29152 1906—Improperly Cleaned—NCS. VG Details.

29153 1906-O VG8 NGC.

29154 1906-S—Environmental Damage—NCS. AU Details.

29155 1907—Environmental Damage, Improperly Cleaned—NCS. AU Details.

29156 1908 VG8 NGC.

29157 1908-O VF25 NGC.

29158 1909 F12 NGC.

29159 1909-O VG8 NGC.

29160 1909-S—Improperly Cleaned—NCS. VF Details.

29161 1910 VG8 NGC.

29162 1912-S XF40 NGC.

29163 1913 Good 6 NGC.

29164 1914—Improperly Cleaned—NCS. Fine Details.

29165 1915 VG8 NGC.

WALKING LIBERTY HALF DOLLARS

29166 1917 MS62 NGC.

29167 1917-S Reverse—Improperly Cleaned—NCS. AU Details.

29168 1934 MS64 NGC.

29169 1935 MS64 NGC.

29170 1935 MS64 NGC.

29171 1936-S—Obverse Improperly Cleaned—NCS. Unc. Details.

29172 1937 MS64 NGC.

29173 1938 MS64 NGC.

29174 1939 MS64 NGC.

29175 1940-S MS64 NGC.

29176 1941 PR55 NGC. No "AW."

29177 1941-D MS64 NGC.

29178 1942 MS64 NGC.

29179 1942-S MS64 NGC.

29180 1943 AU58 NGC.

29181 1943-D MS66 NGC.

29182 1943-S—Obverse Improperly Cleaned—NCS. Unc. Details.

29183 1944 MS65 NGC.

29184 1944-S MS64 NGC.

29185 1945 MS65 NGC.

29186 1945-D MS65 NGC.

29187 1945-S MS63 NGC.

29188 1946 MS64 NGC.

29189 1946-S MS65 NGC.

29190 1947 MS64 NGC.

29191 1947-D MS65 NGC.

FRANKLIN HALF DOLLARS

29192 1953 PR65 NGC.

29193 1958 PR66 NGC.

29194 1959 PR64 NGC.

29195 1960 PR66 NGC.

29196 1960 PR66 NGC.

29197 1961 PR66 NGC.

29198 1962 MS66 NGC.

29199 1963 MS65 NGC.

TRADE DOLLARS

29200 1873—Improperly Cleaned—NCS. AU Details.

29201 1874—Improperly Cleaned—NCS. AU Details.

29202 1874—Improperly Cleaned—NCS. Unc. Details.

29203 1874-S AU53 NGC.

29204 1875-S—Improperly Cleaned—NCS. AU Details.

29205 1876 VF35 NGC.

29206 1876-CC—Damaged—NCS. VF Details.

29207 1876-S—Improperly Cleaned—NCS. AU Details.

29208 1876-S—Improperly Cleaned—NCS. XF Details.

29209 1876-S AU55 NGC.

29210 1877 AU50 NGC.

29211 1877 AU50 NGC.

29212 1877-S—Improperly Cleaned—NCS. XF Details.

29213 1877-S—Improperly Cleaned—NCS. XF Details.

29214 1877-S—Improperly Cleaned—NGC. Unc. Details.

29215 1877-S—Improperly Cleaned—NCS. XF Details.

29216 1877-S Fine 12 NGC.

29217 1877-S VF35 NGC.

29218 1877-S XF40 NGC.

29219 1877-S AU50 NGC.

29220 1877-S AU50 NGC.

29221 1877-S AU55 NGC.

29222 1878-S—Environmental Damage—NCS. AU Details.

29223 1878-S—Improperly Cleaned—NCS. XF Details.

29224 1878-S—Improperly Cleaned—NCS. VF Details.

29225 1878-S AU50 NGC.

29226 1878-S AU55 NGC.

MORGAN DOLLARS

29227 1878 8TF MS62 NGC.

29228 1878 7TF Reverse of 1879 MS63 NGC.

29229 1878-S MS63 NGC.

29230 1879 MS62 Deep Mirror Prooflike NGC.

29231 1879-O AU58 NGC.

29232 1879-S Reverse of 78—Dip Residue—NCS. Unc. Details.

29233 1879-S MS64 Prooflike NGC.

29234 1880 MS64 NGC.

29235 1880-O AU58 NGC.

29236 1880-S MS65 NGC.

29237 1881 MS63 NGC.

29238 1881-S MS65 NGC.

29239 1882 MS64 NGC.

29240 1882-O MS62 NGC.

29241 1882-S MS65 NGC.

29242 1883-O MS64 NGC.

29243 1883-O MS64 NGC.

29244 1884-CC MS63 NGC.

29245 1884-O MS63 NGC.

29246 1885-O MS65 NGC.

29247 1886—Improperly Cleaned—NCS. Unc. Details.

29248 1887 MS63 NGC.

29249 1887-O MS62 NGC.

29250 1888 MS65 NGC.

29251 1888-O MS64 NGC.

29252 1889 MS65 NGC.

See the Online Auction listings in the backs of Volumes I and III for additional Reiver selections.

29253 1890-O MS62 NGC.

29254 1890-S—PVC Damage—NCS. Unc. Details.

29255 1891-S AU58 NGC.

29256 1892-O AU58 NGC.

29257 1896 MS64 NGC.

29258 1897 MS65 NGC.

29259 1897-O AU58 NGC.

29260 1897-S MS63 NGC.

29261 1898 MS64 Prooflike NGC.

29262 1898-O MS64 NGC.

29263 1898-S AU58 NGC.

29264 1899-O MS63 Prooflike NGC.

29265 1900 MS64 NGC.

29266 1900-O MS65 NGC.

29267 1901-O MS64 NGC.

29268 1902 AU58 NGC.

29269 1902-O MS64 Prooflike NGC.

29270 1903 MS64 NGC.

29271 1904-O MS65 NGC.

29272 1921 MS64 NGC.

29273 1921-D MS63 NGC.

29274 1921-S MS64 NGC.

PEACE DOLLARS

29275 1922 MS63 NGC.

29276 1922-D MS62 NGC.

29277 1922-S MS63 NGC.

29278 1923—Improperly Cleaned—NCS. Unc. Details.

29279 1923-D—Improperly Cleaned—NCS. Unc. Details.

29280 1923-S MS63 NGC.

29281 1924 MS64 NGC.

29282 1926-D MS63 NGC.

29283 1927 MS64 NGC.

29284 1928-S AU58 NGC.

29285 1934 MS63 NGC.

GOLD DOLLARS

29286 1853—Improperly Cleaned—NCS. AU Details.

29287 1861 AU58 NGC.

LIBERTY QUARTER EAGLE

29288 1861 New Reverse, Type Two—Improperly Cleaned—NCS. AU Details.

INDIAN QUARTER EAGLES

29289 1908 AU53 NGC.

29290 1910 AU55 NGC.

29291 1912 AU55 NGC.

29292 1925-D—Improperly Cleaned—NCS. AU Details.

29293 1929 MS61 NGC.

LIBERTY HALF EAGLES

29294 1882 AU58 NGC.

29295 1902-S—Improperly Cleaned—NCS. AU Details.

29296 1906—Improperly Cleaned—NCS. AU Details.

INDIAN HALF EAGLES

29297 1911 AU58 NGC.

29298 1912 AU53 NGC.

29299 1912 AU55 NGC.

29300 1914-D AU55 NGC.

29301 1915 AU58 NGC.

COMMEMORATIVE SILVER

29302 1921 Alabama 2x2—Improperly Cleaned—NCS. Unc. Details.

29303 1935 Arkansas—Improperly Cleaned—NCS. Unc. Details.

29304 1935-D Arkansas MS65 NGC.

29305 1935-S Arkansas MS65 NGC.

29306 1936 Arkansas—Improperly Cleaned—NCS. Unc. Details.

29307 1936-D Arkansas—Improperly Cleaned—NCS. Unc. Details.

29308 1936-S Arkansas MS64 NGC.

29309 1937 Arkansas MS65 NGC.

29310 1937-S Arkansas MS64 NGC.

29311 1938 Arkansas MS64 NGC.

29312 1938-D Arkansas MS64 NGC.

29313 1938-S Arkansas—Improperly Cleaned—NCS. Unc. Details.

29314 1939-D Arkansas—Obverse Improperly Cleaned—NCS. Unc. Details.

29315 1934 Boone—Improperly Cleaned—NCS. Unc. Details.

29316 1935-D Boone MS64 NGC.

29317 1935-S Boone—Improperly Cleaned—NCS. Unc. Details.

29318 1935-S Boone MS65 NGC.

29319 1935/34 Boone MS65 NGC.

29320 1936 Boone—Improperly Cleaned—NCS. Unc. Details.

29321 1936-D Boone—Improperly Cleaned—NCS. Unc. Details.

29322 1936-S Boone—Improperly Cleaned—NCS. Unc. Details.

29323 1937 Boone—Improperly Cleaned—NCS. Unc. Details.

29324 1938 Boone MS65 NGC.

29325 1938-D Boone MS64 NGC.

29326 1938-S Boone MS65 NGC.

29327 1936 Bridgeport—Improperly Cleaned—NCS. Unc. Details.

29328 1925-S California—Improperly Cleaned—NCS. Unc. Details.

29329 1936 Cleveland MS64 NGC.

29330 1936 Columbia—Improperly Cleaned—NCS. Unc. Details.

29331 1936-D Columbia—Improperly Cleaned—NCS. Unc. Details.

29332 1936-S Columbia MS64 NGC.

29333 1892 Columbian—Improperly Cleaned—NCS. Unc. Details.

29334 1893 Columbian MS62 NGC.

29335 1922 Grant no Star MS64 NGC.

29336 1924 Huguenot—Improperly Cleaned—NCS. Unc. Details.

29337 1946 Iowa MS66 NGC.

29338 1925 Lexington MS65 NGC.

29339 1923-S Monroe MS64 NGC.

29340 1926 Oregon AU58 NGC.

29341 1936 Oregon—Improperly Cleaned—NCS. Unc. Details.

29342 1937-D Oregon—Improperly Cleaned—NCS. Unc. Details.

29343 1920 Pilgrim MS64 NGC.

29344 1936-D Rhode Island—Improperly Cleaned—NCS. Unc. Details.

29345 1936-S Rhode Island—Improperly Cleaned—NCS. Unc. Details.

29346 1936 Robinson MS64 NGC.

29347 1935-S San Diego—Improperly Cleaned—NCS. Unc. Details.

29348 1925 Stone Mountain MS64 NGC.

29349 1934 Texas MS65 NGC.

29350 1935 Texas—Improperly Cleaned—NCS. Unc. Details.

29351 1935-D Texas—Improperly Cleaned—NCS. Unc. Details.

29352 1935-S Texas—Improperly Cleaned—NCS. Unc. Details.

29353 1936 Texas—Improperly Cleaned—NCS. Unc. Details.

29354 1936-D Texas—Improperly Cleaned—NCS. Unc. Details.

29355 1936-S Texas—Improperly Cleaned—NCS. Unc. Details.

29356 1937 Texas—Improperly Cleaned—NCS. Unc. Details.

29357 1937-D Texas—Improperly Cleaned—NCS. Unc. Details.

29358 1937-S Texas—Improperly Cleaned—NCS. Unc. Details.

29359 1936 Wisconsin—Improperly Cleaned—NCS. Unc. Details.

29360 1936 York—Improperly Cleaned—NCS. Unc. Details.

29361 1946 Booker T. Washington MS64 NGC.

29362 1946-D Booker T. Washington MS64 NGC.

29363 1946-S Booker T. Washington MS64 NGC.

29364 1947 Booker T. Washington MS64 NGC.

29365 1947-D Booker T. Washington MS64 NGC.

29366 1947-S Booker T. Washington MS66 NGC.

End of Volume II

See the Online Auction listings in the backs of Volumes I and III for additional Reiver selections.